To Ruth - a la

Edgar D. Goodwig
Texas Ranger

Ed Gooding

Soldier, Texas Ranger

Dedicated to
the most wonderful parents in the world,
Papa John and Mama Nellie Gooding
-Ed Gooding

Dedicated to
my daughter Stacey
and my granddaughters Madison and Allie
-Robert Nieman

Ed Gooding

Soldier, Texas Ranger

by **Ed Gooding**

with

Robert Nieman

First Edition—October 2001

ISBN: 0-9673319-1-9

Jacket and book design by Pam S. Baird

Published by
Ranger Publishing
35 Circle Drive
Longview, Texas 75602-4840

Printed by
Vaughan Printing
411 Cowan Street
Nashville, Tennessee 37207

Table of Contents

Introduction

God granted me three of the greatest privileges any law enforcement officer can ever dream of. The first was being able to pin on the badge of a Texas Ranger. Words simply cannot describe such a feeling. The second was being able to be a Ranger captain. But by far, the greatest reward He bestowed upon me was being able to work with some of the best men I have ever known. No finer people can be found anywhere in the world than those who wear the badge of a Texas Ranger.

Texas Rangers are truly a rare breed. Clichés like "best of the best" do not begin to tell the half of it, but I can think of no term that better exemplifies Ed Gooding. The honor was mine to have had Ed as one of my men. He was an absolute delight to work with. He was one of those men that I knew I could count on if something needed to be done. With Ed, not only could I consider the job done, but just as importantly, I also knew it would be completed in a timely manner. For, you see, Ed Gooding is one of a rare breed of men who need no supervision: tell him what you want done, and it's done. Period.

I know of no one in the criminal justice system that does not admire and respect Ed. As the Captain of Company F, I know that his fellow Rangers loved, admired, and respected Ed to the highest degree. You will read in these pages how my good friend Captain Joe Wylie almost cried the day of Ed's retirement. Well, Joe, you weren't the only one.

Ed is a hero in the truest sense of the word. He was part of what is now fittingly described as "The Greatest Generation." The service he gave to this great country of ours during World War II was truly inspiring.

But there is another side of Ed that few in law enforcement saw. This alone would have made Ed a great man, even if he had not been a soldier or worn the badge of a Texas Ranger.

Ed cares about people and he shows it not with lip service, but by his actions. He is an elder in the First Christian Church in his hometown of

Cleburne. Members of that church will quickly point out that Ed is always generous in the extreme with not only his donations, but even more importantly, with his time.

Ed and Lena were never fortunate enough to have had children of their own, but they had many nieces and nephews that they loved. I know from personal observations that Ed and Lena were always there to help whether it was assisting in buying a car, taking care of medical aid, or helping to remodel a home. No one can ever say that Ed and Lena ever failed their family. When you read about Ed's childhood, that will come as no surprise. That was the way his parents, Papa John and Mama Nellie, raised all their kids: you take care of your family.

In our glorious history, Texas has produced many, many heroes. As far as I'm concerned, Ed Gooding takes a backseat to no one. He is one of the finest heroes the great state of Texas has ever had.

In closing, I want to say to Ed, "Thanks for all you've done as an American, a Texan, a soldier, and a Texas Ranger. But Ed, most of all, thanks for being my friend."

Captain Bob Mitchell, Retired

Texas RangersCompany F, Waco

Forward

In June 2000, I was honored when Captain Bob Mitchell approached me at the annual Texas Ranger Reunion in Waco about helping Ed Gooding write his autobiography. Captain Mitchell is one of the great Ranger captains of all time and I don't think I ever considered saying no. Besides, as anyone who knows Captain Mitchell will tell you, he is not the kind of man you say no to. I accepted.

I knew Ed Gooding fairly well. I had conducted an oral history of his Ranger career several months before. I had also visited with Ed at the Reunion before Captain Mitchell talked to me. I walked over and visited with Ed again. After only a few minutes, I knew I had made the right decision. As time went by and I got to know Ed better, I found not only a great Ranger, but a great man and a real-live hero. During World War II, Ed had fought from the Normandy invasions until the surrender in Germany eleven months later. He had seen enough death and destruction to last a hundred lifetimes.

As I worked on Chapter II (the war years), my thoughts turned time after time to my father, Robert Nieman, Sr. Like Ed, Dad had seen heavy combat in Europe: he was with the 96th Division. Hearing so many of the stories Ed shared with me was like listening to Dad, even down to returning from Europe on the *Queen Elizabeth*. The names and outfits were different, but many times as I listened to Ed, I could close my eyes and hear my dad. What a shame they never had the opportunity to meet and share some of those times; Daddy died in 1996.

Ed is typical of most Rangers. He was never involved in an "I" case; it was always a "we" case. I had been told by several of his peers that Ed never backed away from a job. Most Rangers carry a staggering workload, so I didn't think that much about it. It wasn't until Ed's successor in Temple, Johnny Aycock, sent me copies of the pending cases Ed had been working when he retired that I realized just how industrious Ed had been. It was an astonishingly long list. I showed the list to retired Ranger and self-confessed workaholic, Glenn Elliott. Looking at the list, Glenn shook his head and said, "Well, Ed was known as a working Ranger." That is the highest compliment Glenn can pay any Ranger.

No book can be written without the help of many. I want to extend a special thanks to the libraries and librarians of Southeast Texas and the Texas Hill Country. For helping research Ed's years in Bell County, I owe a debt of gratitude to Bonnie Norman and Fran Hargrove of the Temple Public Library, and no less a debt to the Killeen Public Library. Casey Edward Greene and Shelly Henley Kelly of the Rosenberg Library in Galveston were invaluable with their assistance for the years that the Rangers battled the gambling operations on their island city. Paula Rudolph of the Huntsville Public Library made possible the research of the Sam Houston Museum burglary. Betsy Anderson of Baytown's Sterling Municipal Library aided my research of Ed's Highway Patrol years in Baytown. A special thanks to Douglas Weiskopf of the Houston Public Library's Texas Room. Douglas' tolerance of me as I asked for file after file that dealt with Ed's Houston years was truly remarkable. Thank you, Byron Johnson, Christina Stopka, and Judy Shofne of the Texas Ranger Hall of Fame and Museum in Waco for helping with this book and so many other projects.

Many took the time to read the unedited manuscript and give valuable insights and thoughts. Tony Hill, retired chief of police of Stephen F. Austin State University in Nacogdoches, Texas, and retired Texas Rangers Glenn Elliott and Bob Mitchell. Special thanks goes to retired Army Sergeant Harold Spikes of Martin, Tennessee, for not only taking the time to read the manuscript, but also for converting World War II Army ranks into today's ranks.

Rick Miller of Harker Heights, Texas, is not only a friend, but also a brilliant historian whose help with the Zina Denker murder case is greatly appreciated.

Without the help of Lieutenant Nelson Zoch of the Houston

Police Department's Homicide Division and retired Houston Police Detective Tony Colca, the story of the fatal shootout at the neon sign company in Houston would not have been possible. And I owe a debt of thanks to Ed's former Highway Patrol partner, Gene Lockart, for helping with the details of two horrendous wrecks that Ed and Gene worked together near Baytown.

When Ed joined the Rangers, one of the men he served with was Hollis Sillavan. Hollis' son Randy followed his father into law enforcement, and Randy provided us with many of the pictures in this book. The help of the officers of the Bell County Sheriff's Office was of enormous importance. James Roper furnished a copy of the picture taken during the anti-war protests. Former deputy Wayne Oldham helped Ed and me recall many details of the kidnapping case involving the three young ladies in the last chapter. Very special thanks goes to the current head of the Bell County Criminal Investigation Division, Bill Miller, for help on Ed's Temple years.

We are indebted to Jodey Fleming for the graphic work he provided for this book. Thanks also to Ms. Leonie Koppers of Sonsbeck, Germany for her assistance in translating several German phrases for us.

Many current and former Texas Rangers gave me valuable assistance answering questions. They always took the time to help me in any way they could. Thanks to retired Rangers Jim Ray, Joe Davis, Joaquin Jackson, and Henry Ligon, as well as to current Rangers Carl Weathers of Lubbock, Johnny Aycock of Temple, Tom Davis of Nacogdoches, Joe Haralson of Galveston, Kyle Dean of Kerrville, and L. C. Wilson of Beaumont.

I want to give credit and very special thanks to our editors: Pam Baird and her Checkmates, Judith Corvin and Nelda Durham. I can imagine their tolerance was tested, but they were unfailingly patient and kind. Every writer should be so fortunate to have editors like these.

A special note of thanks goes to one very important person, David Stroud of Kilgore (Texas) College's history department. Over the many years that I have known David, he has become my historical mentor and inspiration. David is simply the very best there is, bar none.

An incalculable debt of gratitude goes to my wife Donna. For years, she has given so much of herself so that I could pursue my passion for history. I will never forget her support and sacrifice. I have truly been blessed.

And finally, thank you, Ed Gooding, for allowing me the privilege of sharing your life's experiences. It is truly a great honor that you bestowed upon me. Ed, you're a very, very special man and I have been fortunate indeed to work with you and to know you.

Robert Nieman

Longview, Texas

Bobby Nieman and Ed Gooding

Ed Gooding

Soldier, Texas Ranger

Mama Nellie and Papa John Gooding
These are the best parents
I could have ever wished for.

Chapter 1

The Early Years
1924-1942

Mama Nellie on my left and
Aunt Bessie on my right.

With Mama Nellie about 1956.

1953 Family Reunion: Loma, Ed, Johnnie, Bill, Wanda, Papa John,
Mama Nellie, and in front, the latecomer Edith Kay.

Photo, opposite page: I was in the 11th grade at Ingleside High in this picture.

4

My Friends Call Me Ed

I sign my name Edgar Dalton Gooding, but my friends call me Ed. I was born on a ranch near Ingleside in San Patricio County, Texas, on July 10, 1924. I am the oldest of two boys and four girls born to Papa John and Mama Nellie Winslett Gooding. I have spent the better part of my life chasing cows and outlaws or dodging bullets from Germans or some old thug.

When I was born, Papa John worked for the Texas Livestock Sanitation Commission. He helped combat the deadly Mexican tick fever that was rampaging through the Texas cattle industry, literally destroying whole herds. In those years, there was only one way to combat this deadly disease—dipping. On the surface this is a pretty simple operation. You dig a hole in the ground (called a dipping vat), fill it with creosote and water, and drive the cattle into the vat. Like I said, it sounds like a fairly easy procedure. Well, it's not.

Often the biggest obstacle the Livestock Sanitation workers faced wasn't Mexican tick fever, but the small ranchers. Most ranchers wanted no part of dipping, and I can honestly say that they had a point. To their way of thinking, the *possible* loss of all or part of their herd to the fever did not equal the losses they *knew* they would incur by dipping their cattle. These losses could easily lead to the potential danger of losing their farms and their entire herds to the neighboring ranches, especially the large ones. This would be devastating. But neither the state of Texas nor most of the large neighboring ranchers were having any part of the no-dipping attitude. The cattle herds of South Texas were going to be dipped—one way or the other.

Dipping was hard work. Vats were about twenty feet long, three feet wide, and about five feet deep. They didn't just suddenly appear. Today it

5

wouldn't take a bulldozer or backhoe anytime to dig a vat, but this was long before bulldozers and backhoes, so vats had to be dug the old-fashioned way—by hand, using picks and shovels. In a perfect world, the vats would have been dug close to the cattle, but in 1924 the world was no more perfect than it is today. One thing was essential: the vats had to be close to a large water supply so they could be kept full of the water needed to mix with the creosote. Again, today that wouldn't be a big deal: either have a large tank truck loaded with water to keep the vat filled, or hook up a pump and hose to a nearby water supply and pump the water into the vat. Either way, you have plenty of water. But in 1924, most ranchers and cowhands hadn't heard of tankers and electric- or gas-powered pumps. So, like the digging of the vat, the water had to be supplied the old-fashioned way—dipped and carried by hand.

Once the vats were ready to receive the cattle, that didn't mean the work was over; it was just getting started. Corrals at each end of the vat had to be built to hold the cattle before and after dipping. Once the vats were dug and the holding corrals built, then the cattle had to be rounded up and driven into the corrals. South Texas ranches, even the small ones, are big. It took a lot of time and effort to round up the cattle and drive them to the holding pens at the vats. When the cattle had been herded to the dipping site, as many cattle as possible would be crammed into the holding pen until another cow could not possibly be pushed in. Then the gate that led into the dipping pool was opened and the cattle were driven into the vats. Of course, some of the cows didn't think much of the idea of jumping into a hole filled with a stinking chemical. That left the cowboy with only one option: get off his horse and, one way or another, drive or push the contrary cow into the vat. Believe me when I say that cowboys just hated this. I have never met a cowboy in my life, including Papa John, who would hit a lick at a snake if he had to dismount to do it. Needless to say, once he got off his horse, that old cowboy was usually madder than a wet hornet, and that old cow was going to be dipped—more often than not, none too gently.

Once the cow climbed out of the dipping vat, the job was finally finished. Wrong. Before the cattle could be driven back to their pasture, they were forced to stand in the holding pen at the other end of the dipping vat until they dripped dry. Then the job was finally completed and the beeves were driven back to their grazing range.

All this moving of the cattle was the primary reason the small ranchers resisted dipping—weight loss. All this activity took lots of weight off their herds. Cattle are sold by the pound, so it is not hard to understand why many owners—especially the small ranchers who had to count every penny—wanted no part of anything that would take even an ounce off their herd. Many of these ranchers, of both large and small holdings, lived on the verge of bankruptcy and knew they had little to lose by taking their chances that their herds would not be infected by the deadly fever.

Papa John's job with the Texas Livestock Sanitation Commission was to help round up the cattle and run them through the dipping vats. Rounding up and dipping the beeves—not enforcing the law—was the job of the Texas Rangers who rode with Livestock Sanitation Commission officers like Papa John. Then, like now, not many men were willing to take on a Texas Ranger. I do not remember Papa John ever telling of any cattle that didn't get dipped.

By 1926, the Mexican tick fever scare had passed and so had the need for many of the Livestock Sanitation Commission officers, including Papa John. My parents and paternal grandparents had heard they could get rich quick in Kimble County in the pecan groves, so we moved to Junction, in Kimble County, to gather pecans. It didn't take long before the adults realized that they were not going to get rich quick—or get rich, period—picking pecans. Papa John had to quickly find a job just to feed his family. Luckily, Terry Jetton was looking for a cowboy to work on his ranch near Junction.

Kimble County is a long way from San Patricio County in more ways than the three hundred miles as the crow flies. Ingleside is situated on the shores of the Gulf of Mexico between Aransas Pass and Corpus Christi, deep in the heart of South Texas. It gets plenty of rain and has lots of grass. Junction is in West Texas and it has very little rain and even less grass.

I was only two years old when we moved to Kimble County and six when we left, so I have few memories of my life there. But I am very fond of the memories that I do have. I remember like it was yesterday Papa John riding up to the front of our little house on that big horse he rode. Mama Nellie would lift me up to him and we would ride over to a nearby spring and let the horse drink. I felt about ten feet tall sitting on that horse with Papa John. It was right then that I started my lifelong love affair with horses. I am a little too old to ride anymore, but I still love horses.

My sister, Loma Laverne, was born at the Jetton Ranch. She is two years younger than me. The ranch owner's wife served as Mother's midwife. Midwives were common in those days. Except for Laverne and Edith

7

This was made in 1928.
I was 4 & my sister Loma was 2.

Kay, who was born in a hospital in 1944 while I was in combat in Europe, midwives brought all of us kids into the world. My grandmother Theodosia Upchurch Gooding midwifed my brother, two sisters, and me into this world. Billy Joe followed Laverne; then came Wanda Joyce, Johnnie Jean, and my baby sister Edith Kay. Sadly, Wanda Joyce died several years ago.

Papa John and Mama Nellie taught us children by example, and they showed us that nothing was greater than the responsibility to family. My maternal grandparents, Arthur and Viola Holdon Winslett, lived nearby. Grandpa Winslett loved all his children, but he had been a cowboy all of his life and couldn't cook, wash clothes, or do the countless other household chores. He sure didn't have any idea how to

My 4th grade class at Aransas Pass
That handsome young devil on the far right in the second row is me.

take care of two young children. So when Grandma Viola died in 1923, Papa John and Mama Nellie brought Mother's younger brother Joe and sister Edith to live with them. Both were only a few years older than their own kids. My parents didn't think anything about taking them in. They simply considered it their duty, and that was the end of it. Another thing I know for an absolute fact: even if they could have, which they couldn't in the 1920s, they would never have turned to the government to help support them. They had too much pride for that. Grandpa Winslett continued to live in a small shack behind our house until he died.

In 1924, the year after Mother and Dad took in Joe and Edith, I was born; two years later, Laverne. Shortly after Grandpa Winslett died in 1930, Papa John realized he couldn't make enough money to support a family of six on a ranch hand's salary. As much as he loved being a cowboy, he loved his family more. His duty was clear: find something that paid better. Cowboying was always Papa John's greatest love, but that wasn't all that he could do: he was a pretty fair carpenter and all-around fix-it man. During his years around Aransas Pass, he had developed a good reputation for these skills. So when he checked around, he had no trouble finding a job back on the Gulf Coast in South Texas as a carpenter and maintance man with Humble Oil Company in Ingleside.[1]

We lived in nearby Aransas Pass, and until my junior and senior years, we stayed there all through my school days. Those last two years we moved back into the Ingleside School District. While in school, I did the normal things that boys who lived around ranches in South Texas did: chased girls, played football, roped cattle, and rode in rodeos.

I learned many things about life during my school years, but the single greatest lesson I learned was humility. That lesson was brought home to me in spades when I was in the tenth grade. I played left tackle on the football team and we had a good team—a darn good team, if I do say so. We were playing Rockport for the bi-district championship. When the Rockport team came on the field, we just knew this had to be some kind of practical joke. They were undoubtedly the most ragtag-looking bunch of players you can imagine. Most of them were actually wearing little more than rags and a few were playing barefooted! True, this was during the years of the Great Depression, but this was going a bit far even for those difficult times. There was no question in our minds: this was going to be a slaughter. And it was.

---

[1]This refinery was later torn down and moved to Baytown, Texas.

Final score 21-0. There was only one problem: we were the zero part of the score. And believe me, the game was not nearly as close as the score. We chased those Rockport boys up and down the field all day and never did catch them.

As much as I enjoyed football, it wasn't even a close second to my first love: horses. I got cowpunching in my blood early and it's still there. To this day, there is nothing I like better than horses, cattle, and the smell of saddle leather. As a teenager, I would spend every Sunday, weather permitting, at the Ingleside Roping Club with my cousin Orville Nicely, another relative who was living with us at the time. Between roping calves and trying to ride the bulls, those Sunday afternoons seemed to fly by.

If you think football is a rough sport, let me tell you: rodeoing wrote the book on rough. It was so rough it caused me to miss my senior year in high school. It happened like this. I was trying to hang on to the back of a bucking bronc, something he strongly disapproved of. He was as determined to throw me off as I was to stay on his back. Suddenly, he lurched forward and stopped dead in his tracks—I didn't. I flew over his head and landed in a heap. To my great sorrow, that old butt-buster wasn't through with me by a long shot. Up he went again and before I could move, that crazy jughead came down on my ankle and crushed it. That was the end of school for me. But I am proud to say that I didn't waste my time lying around. While I was laid up, I managed to get my GED[2] diploma through correspondence courses from American College in Killeen, Texas.

As soon as my ankle healed, I got right back on the backs of those old broncs and bulls. It was not until after the Second World War and several more busted bones before I finally saw the light: a man could get seriously hurt trying to stay on the back of a bucking beast.

The end finally came in Lockart, Texas, in 1946. I had drawn[3] a small Black Angus bull. Your ride—either a bull or bronc—is penned into a small, narrow opening called a chute. When your ride enters the chute, there is just enough room for the cowboy to get his legs down beside the animal's side. As soon as you're mounted and nod that you are ready, the chute gate is thrown open. When the gate is thrown open, your ride is supposed to come

---

[2]General Educational Diploma.

[3]The method used to pick a bronc or a bull is the same: luck of the draw. All the numbers are put in a hat, and each rider draws a number representing which animal he will ride--or try to ride.

flying out the chute, bucking for all he's worth. The trick is to stay on for eight seconds. Eight seconds. That doesn't sound long, does it? Trust me, those eight seconds can seem like an eternity when you are trying to stay on the back of a mad bull that weighs two thousand pounds and definitely does not want you on his back under any circumstances. Anyway, before the chute door opened, that old bull somehow got backward[4] in the chute. When the gate did open, I hung the toe of my boot on the chute and I heard my left ankle pop like a rifle shot. That was as far as I got. I hit the ground right there in the chute gate. I sat there looking at my ankle, afraid to try and move it. I decided one thing right then and there: it was time for me to find another hobby. I finally got up enough courage to try and stand up. I somehow managed to get on my feet—or rather I stood on my right foot. I looked up at the rodeo announcer and yelled to him to auction off my "war bag."[5] I got twenty-five dollars for the whole outfit. I taped up my ankle and hitchhiked home. From then on, I was a rodeo watcher. My days as a participant were over.

---

[4]Chutes are constructed so that when the animal goes in, he is facing the hinged part of the gate. When one gets turned around, he is facing where the gate opens. As narrow as a chute is, it still amazes me how an old bull or bronc can turn around in one, but they can. The minute the bull or bronc sees daylight between the fence post and the gate, he goes. When your ride is turned around, it squeezes the rider between the gate and the gatepost. That is how I hung my boot. The post is set in concrete and is about eight inches around. Something had to give: it was not the gatepost.

[5]A war bag is what you carry your gear in.

After boot camp in 1943

Greetings

I have no trouble remembering the year that first old bronc busted me up. My leg was still in a cast when the Japanese bombed Pearl Harbor on December 7, 1941. All of a sudden, jobs that had been scarce became plentiful. The military was building all around the Austin area, so we moved to Austin in order that Papa John could get one of those good-paying construction jobs. We had not been in Austin long before my ankle had healed enough for me to go to work. I was only seventeen years old, but I had no trouble getting a job as a helper with Papa John at the Naval Air Training Station that was being built just south of Austin in San Marcos. When that job was finished, we moved down the road to nearby Bastrop County to help construct the Camp Swift Army Base.

I know a lot of people from that era say that they could not wait to get into the service; they were afraid the war would be over before they could get into it. Not me. I never really gave it much thought one way or the other, but it sure got my undivided attention just after I turned eighteen. I got a real pretty-looking letter addressed to me from my Uncle Sam. I guess I was a naïve country boy back in those days, because I was shocked when I opened it and it said "GREETINGS." I had been drafted.

When I reported to Austin for induction, all the draftees were loaded on buses and hauled to Fort Sam Houston in San Antonio. Then began an ordeal that was almost worse than anything the Nazis would ever throw at us—the needles. We were lined up and I was stuck with so many needles

12

that I felt like a pincushion. Still feeling like porcupines, we were guided to the next section, just like the cattle I used to herd. There I had so many clothes stacked in my arms—with little or no thought given to sizes—that I could hardly see the ground. From there, I was directed to a barracks that would be my home until the Army decided differently.

At the barracks, I put my civilian clothes in a pillowcase and dropped them off where I was told. I gussied myself up in that brand new uniform, and I guess I was strutting a little bit when I walked outside and headed for the mess hall and my first Army chow.

I saw a group of men on the other side of the parade ground in the chow line. I was as hungry as a horse and I could see no reason to walk all the way around the parade ground when I could cut straight across. I found out right quick that raw recruits do not walk on the Army's grass. A PFC[6] started screaming at me at the top of his lungs, "Get off that grass, you moron!" I swear I tore up more grass trying to get off the field than I would have if he had not scared me so much. From then until I shipped out, I made it a point to steer clear of that PFC.

When I got to the mess hall, I saw a sight that made all of those screams by the PFC worthwhile—mountains and mountains of food. They put more food on my plate than I had ever seen in my life. And miracle of miracles, every table had a gallon of milk on it. I ate until I could hardly move. Papa John always worked at something, but none of the jobs paid very good and it seemed that we kids were always hungry. But what kid is not always hungry? In spite of all the work and never-ending exercise they put us through, by the time I finished basic training I had gained twenty pounds!

A day or so after our arrival, when the powers-that-be decided our arms and butts had healed from all the shots we had received, we were loaded on a train heading for Camp Roberts, California, and basic training. Camp Roberts is located about halfway between Los Angeles and San Francisco. I was assigned to the 88th Training Battalion and was issued a field pack, an M-1 rifle, sheets and blankets, and a cot that would be my home for the next thirteen weeks.

The North African Campaign was in full swing, and it was not hard to figure out that was where we were headed. The first thing the Army did was put us on a water ration. Every morning we would march out with a full

---

[6]Private First Class.

13

canteen of water and when we returned, the sergeant would run his finger into the mouth of the canteen. If he couldn't reach water, the next day you went in the field with an empty canteen. And let me tell you: it was hot in California. I was raised in South Texas and I thought I was used to hot weather, but I never saw it hotter in Texas than it was during that thirteen weeks of basic training in California. It was so hot and the humidity was so low that you did not sweat through your clothes: your body was using all its water. When you took off your backpack, you could see white streaks all over your clothes where you had sweated out salt. That was why we had to take salt tablets every two hours.

It didn't get any better with the passage of time, not with all the marching we had to do: twenty-five-mile marches with a few five-by-fives thrown in for good measure. Five-by-fives were forced marches where you are ordered to go at a trot for five miles and then walk another five miles. In that California heat they were real killers. All along the road, guys were dropping like flies and vomiting their guts out, while others just collapsed, totally exhausted.

Dark, moonless nights were special favorites with the DIs.[7] The darker the night, the more they loved forced marches. I know the last thing in the world they meant was for them to be fun, but to me that's just what these night marches were—fun. Being a country boy and used to spending most of my nighttime under the stars, I had developed a wonderful sense of direction. I knew how to find the North Star and pick out landmarks and sightings such as oddly sized large rocks, tall trees, or other high places or peculiar landmarks. So while many of the men were stumbling all over the place lost as a goose, I was having a ball.

The DIs put us into five-men groups with nothing but a compass to guide us. They would head us off in one direction and tell us how far we were to go. If we followed instructions to the letter, there would be a note there telling us where to go next. If we hadn't followed instructions to the letter, we were in for a mighty long night. As a matter of fact, it didn't matter whether we followed instructions or not; this exercise was designed to last all night.

One thing all DIs have in common (and it doesn't matter what branch of service they come from): they do not believe in letting recruits have one second of idle time. So if the instructors didn't have us marching, they had

---

[7]Drill Instructors

14

us dry-firing our weapons. The only thing I could figure out as to why we were dry-firing was that the Army didn't have enough ammunition for us to fire live rounds. So we pretended to fire mortars, pretended to load belts of ammunition into our weapons, and pretended to fire our machine guns and rifles. Since we were not firing real bullets and shells, obviously we weren't getting our weapons dirty. At least that made sense to me. Unfortunately, the DIs didn't ask for my opinion. They made us clean our weapons over and over. Did we get to use oil? Why, of course not! In that scorching California heat, they made us collect water and wood; then we had to build fires and boil our weapons. At least this was one of the few things they did that I could understand. In that hot, dusty area of California, if we had cleaned our weapons with oil, the dust would have stuck to them, causing more harm than good. So we broke our weapons down and boiled them. Of course you had to make sure that you got rid of every drop of moisture so they wouldn't rust. Then for good measure, if we had any "spare time," which the DIs made sure we had when they wanted us to, they would make us scrub the barracks floor using a GI brush and lye soap. That was loads of fun.

But we did have our moments of enjoyment, mainly on the bayonet field. DIs set up dummies filled with straw and instructed us as to the proper use of gutting a man. For example, if you hang your bayonet up inside a man, don't stand there trying to rip it out—shoot it out. Their final word on that subject was that "if you're close enough to stick him, shoot him." We were instructed to pretend the dummies were Nazi or Japanese soldiers. We definitely took our frustrations out on those dummies. We ripped them to shreds and tried our best to run not only the bayonet but the whole rifle through the straw men. This made our instructors happy. As far as they were concerned, the meaner and rougher they could make us, the better they were doing their jobs. I wouldn't be surprised if more than one of us imagined the dummy to be our drill instructor instead of a German or Japanese soldier. I know I did. But of course the DIs also knew this.

Sometimes we would forget, but I think we all knew that the DIs were trying their best to train us to survive against battle-hardened troops that had been in combat for years and would kill us without batting an eye. Those troops were more than capable of ripping us to shreds if we weren't ready. To even better acquaint us with what we would be facing in combat, for the last two weeks of basic training we lived in foxholes. That was tough enough without anyone shooting at me, and I didn't look forward to having to do it with someone trying to kill me.

15

It was a tough thirteen weeks, but we survived basic training and it was time to graduate—graduate, that is, after we marched twenty-five miles to our home base. That was one twenty-five-mile march that didn't seem long. It was one of the proudest moments of my life when I marched into our base camp with a band playing the National Anthem. Never have I felt prouder to be an American.

The following morning, they lined us up and started calling out names. When your name was called, you gathered up your equipment and climbed aboard a truck. This went on until only two men were left: me and another soldier whose name I forgot long ago. We looked at each other and both of us were thinking the same thing: we've flunked boot camp and are going to have to do it all over again.

Taken while I served as a drill instructor at Camp Roberts. I don't remember this guy's name, but we thought we'd flunked boot camp!

With no explanation, a six-striper[8] told us to get in a nearby jeep and report to the company command post. We loaded up and headed through the woods, convinced we were going to have to relive another thirteen weeks of boot camp. All I could think during that walk was, "Boy, you must be a real dummy. Only a real moron could flunk boot camp."

We hadn't flunked, but it was the next worse thing. They told us we were now corporals, and our new assignments were— drill instructors! And that was it—no *ifs*, *ands*, or *buts*. Our opinions were neither asked for nor wanted. We were DIs. We got back in the jeep and headed back to Camp Roberts.

One of our first assignments as DIs was to go to the railhead and meet a new batch of recruits. I don't see how I could have possibly been as green as these recruits, but thirteen weeks earlier, I guess I had been. These boys gave new meaning to the term *raw*. I tried

[8]In today's ranking, he would be a Master Sergeant, an E-7.

very hard not to scare any of them the way that PFC had scared me at Fort Sam Houston. Those days in San Antonio were only a few short months behind me, but in some ways it seemed like an eternity had passed.

I'm just fooling around in this picture taken during boot camp at Camp Roberts, California, in 1943. No machine gunner in his right mind would ever carry a bandoleer like this. Get one of those bullets out of line and it will cause a jam in your gun—often with fatal results.

We did the best we could. We trained these men just like we had been trained: the twenty-five-mile marches, the five-by-fives, the dry-firing, the whole works. Thirteen weeks later, they stood on the parade ground loading into trucks going to God only knew where. I felt good about the job I had done. I knew that I had done the very best that I could to make them ready. But ready for what? To this day, I have often wondered how many men I trained to die.

This was the only group I trained in California. About a week after my recruits graduated, I was loaded on a train at Camp Roberts headed for Camp Blanding, Florida. The North African Campaign was going strong, and that was what we had been training for in California. But I guess the brass was already looking past North Africa and was planning the D-Day invasion on some nameless beaches on the French mainland called Normandy. We were being sent to Florida to train men for that dance.

I don't know what happened between the group we trained in California and the group we had for thirteen weeks in Florida. That first group was a good bunch of boys, eager to do whatever was necessary to get the job done. Not the East Coast group. They were slackers, dumb as a post—or least they seemed to be. The main problem was their total indifference to learning anything. We just couldn't make them realize that not only their lives but also the lives of their buddies depended on what we were trying to teach them. Unlike the group of boys at Camp Roberts that I

17

possible death, I have never felt bad about this bunch. We did the best we could: the choice to ignore what we were trying to teach them was theirs.

When we finished with this group, I got a welcome ten-day "delay in route" furlough before having to report to Fort Meade, Maryland. With ten days of leave, I headed straight for Texas as fast as I could get there. While I was away, Papa John and Mama Nellie had moved to a ranch in the Hill Country northwest of Austin. I was in heaven. For a few glorious days I was actually on the back of a horse, working cattle. It just does not get any better than that.

Unfortunately, that ten-day furlough was over all too soon. It seemed I had hardly gotten home before I was hugging and kissing everyone goodbye. Mama Nellie held a straight face until I left. Only later did I learn that after I left, she went into convulsions and passed out. I was told she cried for days. I have often wondered what she did when my civilian clothes arrived from Fort Sam Houston. I imagine she did the same thing. I never asked.

When I arrived in Jacksonville, Florida, I boarded a troop train heading up the Eastern Seaboard for Fort Meade, Maryland. We were only in Fort Meade a few days before we were again loaded into trucks, this time pointed north to New York City. Passing through, glimpses were all of the Big Apple I got to see. I don't think we even slowed down as we went through the city to the port. Arriving at the port, I saw the biggest boat I had ever seen or imagined—the *Queen Mary*. I could not believe anything that big could float.

Well, at least we were going to war in style. The *Queen Mary* and her sister ship, the *Queen Elizabeth*, were the two greatest luxury ships in the world and both had been converted into troopships. Four gangplanks had been set up going into the ship and there was a steady stream of men on each of the planks. The beauty of the *Queen Mary* is not my main memory of that ship: it is the horrible smell that hit me when I boarded. It was a mixture of stale food and something I couldn't recognize. Later, I learned the smell was coming from the kitchen. The cooks worked twenty-four hours a day to feed the thirty thousand men on the ship. You would not believe food could stink so bad, but it did.

The first thing handed to us when we stepped on the ship was a small colored piece of cardboard. This was our meal ticket and it indicated when we were to eat. You might be served breakfast at midnight, lunch at six in the morning, and dinner at two in the afternoon—providing you could stomach that horrendous smell. But complaining was not allowed.

I don't know how many decks the *Queen Mary* had, but I know that I thought I never would stop going down stairs. With as many flights of stairs as I had descended, I just knew I was in the very bottom of the ship. So you can understand my amazement to find that I was billeted in a cabin that was still above the waterline in a room that had a window—or as they call it in the Navy: a cabin with a porthole. It was quite a sight looking at the Statue of Liberty as we sailed out of New York Harbor. Quite a sight, indeed.

Regretfully, many of us could not admire the sea or anything else for long. Seasickness is a terrible thing, just terrible. Imagine, if you can, thousands and thousands of men all throwing up at once. It hit me hard before we ever cleared the harbor. Men lay in their bunks and puked; they lay on the deck puking. Others managed to at least hang their heads over the rail, and some just walked around with a sick look. I guess there was one good thing about it, though: the kitchen smell didn't bother me anymore.

If I have ever spent a worst ten days in my life, including combat, I don't know when it was. It took ten days to go from New York to Plymouth, England. Thankfully, we didn't have to go in a convoy. That would have taken weeks and I don't think I could have survived. The *Queen Mary* was so fast that she could outrun any U-boat Hitler had. The *Queen*'s captain just put the spurs to that big old boat and we came across the Atlantic Ocean in a big hurry. I never saw a prettier sight than the shores of England. I know that today the *Queen Mary* is a luxury hotel in permanent dock in Long Beach, California, but I think if I walked on her today, I would immediately be sick. I don't see how they could have ever gotten that smell out of her.

By the time we landed in England, the Normandy Invasion had already started. We docked at Plymouth and went through England like a runaway freight train to Southhampton. We were not a unit, a battalion, or any other kind of organized group: we were just a group of replacement soldiers on a train. As soon as we hit Southhampton, we were loaded on Liberty ships and headed across the English Channel. At D-Day plus 4—June 10, 1944—we were sitting just offshore of Omaha Beach, behind the 29th Division. We were the cannon fodder to replace the killed and wounded of the first waves that had hit those beaches. The next eleven months for me would be a journey through Satan's Inferno.

Chapter 11

World War II
1943-1945

Digging Holes

It was about two o'clock on the afternoon of June 10 (D-Day plus 4)[9] when I went ashore at Omaha Beach. Our boat was filled with replacements who, like me, had not been assigned to any unit. D-Day was four days past, but the fighting was still very heavy. The artillery of the 29th Division was on the beach and putting a heavy fire on the German positions inland. That sounded really good and I liked that idea. Unfortunately, it was not a one-way street—Jerry[10] was answering us round for round. Not only were the Germans dropping shells on the beach, but even worse, at least from my standpoint, too many of those shells were coming really close to the landing craft that I was trying to board.

Disembarking from a ship at sea is serious business and extremely dangerous under the best of circumstances. When tied up to a dock, you simply walk up or down a gangplank—no problem. At sea, you don't have a gangplank: you climb down a rope ladder. This can be a big problem. Not only do you have your weapon and ammunition, but you are also loaded down with fifty pounds of gear strapped to your back. If that weren't enough, there are several more men trying to climb down the same rope ladder. If you aren't stepping on the hands or head of the guy below you, then the guy above you is stepping on yours. That was bad, but it still wasn't the biggest problem: that landing craft was bouncing up and down in the water like a basketball. Take all of this, and then throw in a bunch of Germans trying their very best to blow your head off, and you get the picture.

In order to provide some protection from the incoming shells, our ship had been turned so that the rope ladders hanging down the sides of

---

9 The D-Day Invasion was on June 6, 1944.

10 "Jerry" was one of many nicknames that American troops used for the Germans.

the ship were away from the beach and the incoming shells. Once we were able to get in the landing craft, then trouble really began. The way our landing craft bounced around reminded me of one of those old bulls I used to ride. The only difference was that that old bull didn't make me seasick. And yes, I stayed seasick until we reached the beach, but I wasn't the only one. As if we didn't have enough problems just getting into the landing craft and being sicker than dogs, there must have been a German spotter watching closely because the second our craft cleared the ship, shells started hitting all around us. Some of the landing crafts were hit, but most of us made it to land. There is no good way to get killed. It is bad enough to get killed in combat, but to train for weeks and then be killed sitting in a landing craft before even making shore somehow seems an even more outrageous way to die.

When our landing craft's gate dropped, we charged out of there like Old Lucifer himself was after us. The first thing I remember hearing was a machine gun firing—and it wasn't ours. It was no trouble telling which were ours and which were theirs. A German machine gun had a totally different sound: it had a slightly higher pitch and its rate of fire was faster. Later I learned that this was the sound of an MG-42. It fired thirty rounds per second, eighteen hundred rounds per minute! Bullets were hitting the water and sand all around us, but thankfully none hit our group, at least not right then. After what seemed like an eternity crawling over dead and wounded GIs and every type of equipment you can imagine, we finally made it to the relative safety of the sand dunes. At least, it was reasonably safe from small arms.

It had only been four days since the 29th Division had hit the beach on June 6, but evidence of the horror they had gone through was everywhere. I have tried to watch the movie *Saving Private Ryan* a couple of times, but can't get past the landing scenes. It is so real I feel the emotions start welling up deep down inside me and I have to leave the room. I can still see the bullets pinging off the tank traps and for some reason I can't explain, the boots on the dead GIs. I see all too vividly the helmets, rifles, and ammo belts strewn all over the beach, just like in the movie.

One memory that movie brought back that I had forgotten about was the dead fish on the beach. All the shells hitting the water had killed fish by the thousands, and there was a row of dead fish about three feet wide lying on the sand at the waterline as far as you could see. Graves Registration, the people who handle the dead, had cleared most of the bodies off the beach by D+4, and were working frantically to get the rest cleared away. As hard as they were working, there were still a lot of dead GIs and pieces of their bodies scattered all over.

As good as the movie is, there is one thing *Saving Private Ryan,* or any movie for that matter, can't capture—the smell. Some of the men had been dead for four days. Add the thousands of dead fish to that and awful doesn't begin to describe it. I don't think anyone can describe the scent of death. It has an odor like no other.

Try as they do, there is another thing the movies can't capture: the blood. You can't imagine the amount of blood there is on a battlefield. It's everywhere: all over the ground, all over the equipment, but mainly all over you. And I don't care if you live to be a hundred years old, you can never wash it all off and you can't get it all out of your mind.

As Civil War General Nathan Bedford Forrest said, "War means fighting and fighting means killing." He was right. But until I saw all my dead and maimed comrades and and even my enemies, it didn't really hit me just how real and brutal killing was. Never, even when I was a little boy playing cowboys and Indians, had I thought of war as anything but a game. And like most teenagers, then and now, I thought I was bulletproof—at least I thought I was until that moment. Youth gives you a feeling of invincibility. I suppose that is the reason the military wants young boys to do the fighting. Older heads know just how unbulletproof they are.

Before June 10, 1944, I had another great misconception (one that I shared with many): "It might happen to you, but not me." What a crock! Looking at that carnage and the destroyed bodies on that beach made me realize again just how wrong I was. Suddenly, like a bolt of lightning from God, I realized I was nothing but meat and bone and that there was a pretty good chance that before this war was over, I would be dead. Even worse, I might be shot to pieces and still be alive to exist—exist, not live—until merciful death could take me. Let me tell you, that'll wake you up. As I lay there in the sand looking at the dead and mangled bodies, I knew without a doubt that every one of those boys probably thought they, too, had been bulletproof. You learn real quick that bullets don't discriminate: they don't care who they kill or maim or if you are young or old, American or German.

I don't mean to preach, but unless you've been there, unless you've seen it, unless you have smelled it, you just cannot truly imagine what combat is really like.

Soon a tattered and wounded sergeant came over one of the sand dunes we were behind and told us to follow him. His arm was bleeding, but that wasn't stopping him. He got us up and we started running. Do you believe you can sprint—not run, sprint—carrying a full fifty-pound field pack and an M-1 rifle through sand? It's not easy. Before that day, if anyone had said I could, I'd have said they were crazy. But if you are as scared as I was—and I was plenty scared—you can flat pick 'em up and lay down. I'm sure I set some kind of speed record. I would run a short distance, hit the sand and try to make myself as small a target as possible for a few minutes: then jump up and make another dash. We all made it to an apple orchard and the sergeant motioned us to dig in. He didn't have to tell us twice.

Having dug more than my share of holes working around ranches in South Texas all my life, I thought I could dig a hole as quick as the next man. Lying there on Omaha Beach, I rewrote the book on how to dig a hole fast.

Thankfully, the shelling had stopped by dark and we were able to take stock of our situation. One of the men who had been in the boat with us was missing. Later he was found back down the road, hunkered down in a ditch, crying. That was the first grown man I had ever seen cry, but it wouldn't be the last. I remember thinking at the time that the man was a coward, but as the war drug on, I realized some men are more sensitive than others about the shelling, the noise of battle, and the fear of death.

In the first chapter I mentioned that I had been promoted to corporal. That brought a few advantages. The men in charge didn't have a clue what to do with me. I had been trained in heavy weapons: .30-caliber water-cooled machine guns and 81-mm mortars. There are five men in a machine gun squad: a buck sergeant[11] squad leader, a PFC gunner and his buck private assistant, and the two ammo bearers who were also privates. There were no corporals.

Headquarters had set up several blackboards at the command post. When you were assigned to a unit, your name would be posted on one of the boards. So I sat in a replacement depot (we called them Repple Depples, which was slang for replacement depots) in the middle of an apple orchard. Each day, I would go down to headquarters and check the blackboards, looking for my name. About ten days after landing, I guess they had finally figured out what they wanted me to do. I found my name on one of the blackboards. I went back to the apple orchard, gathered my gear, went back to the command post, and waited for a truck to take me to my new unit somewhere near St. Lo, France.

---

[11] The lowest grade of sergeant. In today's ranking, a buck sergeant is an E-5.

The first heavy action I saw was at St. Lo in France.
There wasn't much of it left when the battle was over.

To Do or Die

My new outfit was the 134th Regiment of the 35th Infantry Division. The motto of the 134th was "All Hell Can't Stop Us." And it couldn't. The 134th hadn't landed on Omaha Beach until a few weeks after the initial invasion. Because I wasn't assigned to any unit, the 134th was as good a unit as any. I said earlier that I had come ashore on D+4 and after the first day or so, I had settled in and felt relatively safe and sound in that apple orchard just off the beach. But once the 134th landed and I was assigned to it, my peaceful life came to a screaming halt. The regiment's assignment was to take St. Lo. To the brass in their dugouts in the rear, I guess that sounded easy enough. But to those of us having to do the doing, it was a killer. There would be a lot of hard fighting and spilled blood before that easy job was completed.

We loaded up in trucks and moved out. We hadn't much more than started when we began to hear machine gun and artillery fire ahead of us. A few weeks later, when I had become an old, grizzled, combat veteran, I would have gotten a good laugh looking at us tenderfoots[12] all hunkered down as low in that truck bed as we could get. But at the time, all I knew was that the truck bed's thin wooden sideboards were all that stood between me and a German bullet.

After a few miles, the trucks pulled off the road and stopped. We

---

[12]A tenderfoot is old cowboy slang for a rookie cowboy.

unloaded and began to walk. The more we walked, the noisier the sounds of battle became. The 35th Division was relieving what was left of the 29th Division. The 29th had been cut to pieces trying to take St. Lo and didn't have the strength left to launch another counterattack.

Tenderfoots we may have been, but we learned fast. I said earlier that every soldier ever born hated to dig worse than anything in the world. Well, that's true until someone starts shooting at him. In those times, I for one developed a passionate love affair with my shovel. When we stopped for our first rest, I started to dig. Before I had much more than hit my first lick, the sergeant yelled, "Move out!"

We hadn't gone far when we met a staff sergeant[13] coming down the road. He told our sergeant that he had a list of names of men who were to follow him. My name was on that list. He led us to an area where men had already dug foxholes. and he told us in a lifeless tone that if we wanted to live, we had better follow their lead.

I'll never forget that old sergeant. As we stood there, he started crying. He was crying for all the buddies he had lost in the fierce fighting, buddies he had trained and been with in the States. Most of them he had known for what must have seemed to him forever. Through tears he said to me, "Corporal, I know you have your rank, but I'm going to put you to carrying ammunition. But don't concern yourself with that. The way this war is going, you won't be doing that long. You'll be leading a gun squad soon enough." He pointed up ahead to a light .30-caliber machine gun and said, "Corporal, there is your gun and back there is the ammo dump. Get you a couple of boxes and dig in."

As I said earlier, I had been trained in heavy weapons, but in reality that didn't really make much difference. Heavy and light machine guns have the same mechanism, and about the only difference in them is that the heavy one is water-cooled and the light one is air-cooled and usually much closer to the front.

Sarge wasn't wrong. The way we were losing men, I started moving up in rank fast—too fast. I started out carrying ammunition, but within a week I was the assistant gunner. Almost as quickly, I was the gunner. A few days later, I was the squad leader. But I am getting ahead of myself.

---

[13]Staff sergeant—E-6.

Our first assault of St. Lo was on a place called Hill 122 on a military map. The big brass, from the safety of their positions far in the rear, decided the best way to take the hill was by a night attack. With seasoned troops, a night attack is, at best, organized mayhem. With green troops who have never fired a shot in combat, there could only be one ending—slaughter.

But I was only a lowly corporal and my opinion did not matter. I remember an old poem:

> Theirs not to reason why,
> Theirs but to do & die.[14]

We would eventually take Hill 122, but far too many men of the 134th would die doing it.

As I looked out over the field of battle, all I could see were rows of trees; at least I thought they were trees. When we got closer, they turned out to be what would go down in the history of the Normandy Invasion as the infamous hedgerows.

The hedgerows in Normandy are ancient. They had been originally planted by the Normans hundreds of years before and were used as fencing for the various fields they encircled. They had a dirt base anywhere from three to six feet high with hedges and other types of brush growing on top so thick you couldn't see through them. Everywhere you looked, all you could see were hedgerows zig-zagging all over the countryside. Of course we had no way of knowing it at the time, but it would take weeks to break through those hedgerows, and it would take buckets of blood to do it.

We had been fighting and moving constantly, but there was finally a brief lull. I got a chance to talk with an ammo bearer in our gun squad, or at least I tried to, but he was not very talkative. I later learned the man I replaced had been a longtime friend of his. They had trained together in the States and had become very close. As I talked to him, he suddenly began to cry and I shut up. I felt terrible.

Many a soldier has gotten a Secton 8[15] not because they were cowards, but because they lost a brother. In combat, that's what your fellow soldier is: your brother. I know this sounds hard, but I'm glad I didn't get to know that ammo bearer. Later he was hit by a mortar fragment in the left

---

[14] From "The Charge of the Light Brigade" by Alfred, Lord Tennyson.

[15] A discharge because of a mental breakdown.

134th's Motto and the Gospel: ALL HELL CAN'T STOP US

This says it all. Hell couldn't stop the 134th Infantry Regiment. This was copied from a mural drawn by Corporal Howard Droste of Seattle, Washington, which hung at the 35th Division Rest Area in Nancy, France.

side and leg. He was evacuated and I took his place as first ammo-bearer. I never learned his name or even if he lived or died.

But back to the story. Everyone began to dig. I may have been the tenderfoot in this outfit, but I was an old veteran when it came to digging foxholes. I matched them shovel for shovel. It was about dark and we had just settled in when the German machine guns began raking the bushes over our heads and mortar rounds began falling nearby. Thank God for shovels. My foxhole was deep and I was relatively safe, at least from the machine gun fire.

About nine o'clock, the shelling stopped and the squad leader came to my hole and briefed me on how to move among the hedgerows. He said to keep below the dirt bank and, above all, stay away from holes cut in the hedgerows. The Germans had cut the holes and had a machine gun trained on each one of them just waiting for some poor, unsuspecting GI to stick his head into the opening.

We were in the hedgerows for nearly two weeks. The brass tried everything in the world to get us through those things. They brought up high explosives and a Pioneer Platoon[16] and tried to blast a hole through,

---

[16]A Pioneer Platoon was a carryover from World War I. It was a special unit whose job was to keep ammunition supplied and to handle special taasks like blowing up bridges, hedgerows, etc.

without success. The ground under the hedges was so thick and solid from the root systems that were hundreds of years old, the explosives hardly made a dent in them.

Failing with the explosives, the leaders brought up a bulldozer and tried to push a hole through. The driver said this would work, provided we could keep him from getting shot and give him a week to do the job. That was no good.

So we would have to do what the Queen of Battle[17] has done since the beginning of combat: fight our way through.

And fight we did. And many of us died. Those hedges were so thick that we would climb over the top just like you would climb over a fence. The only problem was that once on top, you were exposed to enemy fire. That was as far as a lot of men ever got. If you survived the top of the hedges and got on the other side, your troubles were just starting. You were in open ground, and no sooner would you hit the ground than a machine gun would open up on you. You wouldn't believe how small an object you can crouch your body behind if it offers the least bit of cover from that murderous machine gun fire. If you moved a muscle, you could count on a burst of ma-chine-gun fire ripping up the ground around you— around you and not through you, if you were lucky.

You wouldn't be there very long before the mortar[18] shells would start dropping like rain. In a lot of ways the mortars were as bad, if not worse, than the machine guns. The Germans had zeroed in on every inch of those fields with their machine guns and mortars to the point that they could almost put a mortar shell in your hip pocket.

Occasionally, when I'm watching a football game on television and I hear an announcer say that a kicker is going to try a long fifty-yard field goal, my thoughts will sometimes go back to 1944. Let me tell you just how long fifty yards is: sometimes it's an eternity. It was common for us to fight all day and all night to get across a fifty-yard stretch of open ground.

---

[17]Infantry.

[18]A mortar is a lightweight, portable, muzzle-loading artillery piece used mainly by infantrymen. It fires low-velocity shells for short range, and is usually fired at a very high trajectory. For example, when we were in a ditch, we would fire into a ditch on the other side of the road.

Hedgerows
There was just no place to go.

German soldiers dead in the sunken roads of the hedgerow country in Normandy.

Our reward wasn't making three points: our reward was living.

A few days later, there was a welcome lull in the fighting. As I lay behind my machine gun, I got to thinking back to what seemed like forever, but in reality was only a few days ago. I had thought it was great to be a machine gunner. I hadn't seen how anything could stand up before the blistering rate of fire I could lay down. Now I realized just how foolish I had been. It was because of the machine gun's rapid rate of fire that the Germans usually made them the main target. The life expectancy of a machine gunner in combat was something like two minutes. I didn't much care for that statistic.

I had been thinking of some way to beat those odds. One day I told my gunner that I knew we had been trained to set up a position and stay there until we received an order to move, but I felt that one of the reasons the Germans killed so many of us was because we stayed in one place too long. Training or not, I wanted to do things a little differently. It seemed to me that by staying in one spot as the book said, it allowed the Germans to zero in on our position with the inveitable results. Those German mortar crews were so good that they could drop a mortar shell in a bushel basket at a thousand yards. I considered sitting in one place until ordered to move was pure suicide. I suggested that as soon as we got the gun set up and in firing position, we should immediately start looking for an alternate spot where we could still cover our assigned target and keep it under fire as per our orders. But instead of anchoring ourselves to that spot, after firing a few minutes, we should move to the new spot that we had picked out.

My gunner didn't see it that way. The book said we had to have permission from the squad leader to move. That was how my gunner had been trained and as far as he was concerned, that was how we were going to do it. Obviously, that wasn't what I wanted to hear. When I got a chance, I told our squad leader my idea. He, too, was out of the old school and vetoed my plan. He wanted us where he knew our exact location, not moving all over the front. That was all fine and dandy except for one thing: we had received no training for fighting in hedgerows. I don't guess anyone had ever thought of having to fight in them, even if those hedges had been there for hundreds of years. I decided right then and there that if I was able to survive until I made squad leader—rules or no rules—I would move my gun. But for now, I was the assistant gunner and my gunner said we would play by the book. Well, he followed the book and we stayed put. And he died.

Moving on the roads in those hedgerows was eerie. In a way, the roads reminded me of what the trenches in World War I must have been like. They were all sunken to a depth of five to six feet. I guess this is where the dirt came from to build the hedgerow bases. As for the hedgerows them-selves, they were an assortment of plants. Whatever the growth, everything seemed to have thorns—big, long thorns that would cause you to swell up like a poisoned pup. There were wild roses, black thorn locust, and some fruit trees. The fruit trees were mostly small apples, and there were some grapevines. As bad as it was on the roads, the fields were oftentimes worse. Once you stepped out from behind the hedges, you had no cover. Talk about feeling naked!

One day we had gotten about halfway across one of those little fields when a machine gun opened up on us. We all hit the ground. We hadn't been there for more than a few seconds when, sure enough, just like clockwork, the mortar shells started coming in. We really started to sweat. Sweating was all we could do. If you moved, you died. Any movements would have gotten the immediate attention of one of the German machine gunners. We lay there, being as still as possible, and played dead. We were hoping the Germans believed they had done their job and killed us.

I was utterly terrified lying there in that field. You don't have to see but a couple of arms, legs, and bodies go flying up in the air or have what

Never have I been as scared as I was when we were pinned down
by German machine guns and mortars in a field much like this one.
I knew I was going to die.

is left of what had been a brother seconds ago splattered all over you, and
you get so scared you can't think. I've seen men in this situation crying,
cussing, or praying—some all at once. I've seen men so scared that they
wet their pants or worse. I never did, even though I was so scared I couldn't
move. But I guarantee you one thing: if I had, I wouldn't be ashamed to
admit it. We all had one thing in common: fear. I said earlier that I don't
mean to preach, and I don't, but if you haven't been there, you can't imagine the fear. Death could be—is, probably—only a split second away. But
scared or not, you can't just quit. If you do, you die for sure.

I have never known fear the way I did that day lying there in that field.
As the bullets and the mortars slammed all around us, I was totally
convinced that there were only two types of men in that field: the dead and
those of us who would shortly be dead. We had to do something and we had
to do it quick. In the end, we really only had two options: lie there and be
killed or make a run for it and maybe, just maybe, a few of us would make it.
Given those options, there was really no choice. The sergeant went first. He
and one of the ammo bearers jumped up and, to our amazement, they made
it to safety. Once safely under cover, they sat up their machine gun and started
laying down some cover fire for the next group. Again to our amazement,
this group also made it. With more cover fire, the odds were getting better.
Hey, I might, just might, make it out of there.

The sergeant called out for me to make a run for it. I was so scared I couldn't think. I was shaking and I had my eyes closed so tightly that I'm surprised I didn't push them through to the back of my head. I was also grinding my teeth so hard it's amazing they weren't ground down to the gums. But scared or not, I jumped up and started running as hard as I could. I remember that run like it was yesterday. With every step, I expected to feel a bullet ripping through me. I don't remember, if I ever knew, if I was even being shot at or not. I assume I was. That run, even then, was just a fog in my mind. Like the other guys who made that run, I was almost blind with fear. All I know for sure is I ran harder than I've ever run in my life, and I made it!

The first thing I remember after the fog began to clear in my mind was hearing the sergeant yell for the last gunner to come on; we would cover him. But the gunner didn't move and my heart, along with everyone else's, sank. The sergeant yelled again, "Come on! We'll cover you." But the little guy still didn't move. We kept watching for the slightest movement but we saw none. We hoped and prayed against hope that he was playing possum, but I think we all knew the truth.

It was close to sunset and the sergeant said that as soon as it got dark, he was going to check on the gunner. Sarge had pushed Lady Luck to the brink of the grave getting out of that field once; to go back, even in the dark, was suicide. But, you know, it never entered any of our minds to try and stop him. How could we? And how could he not go? One of his men was down. Finally it was dark and, thank God, it was very dark. The sergeant pulled off his boots, dropped all his gear, and crawled out to where the little guy lay. He came back soon. After crawling back to us, he didn't say a word. He didn't have to.

One by one, all the original men of the 134th were being picked off and new men, like I had been, were replacing them. The 134th was an old National Guard unit from Nebraska, and almost everyone in the unit had known one another for years. They had trained together in the States, shipped over together, and many had been friends their whole lives. Some were neighbors and others played football, basketball, or baseball with and against each another. I knew how hard it was on them every time one of them was killed. To them, every time a man went down it was like losing a blood brother. Of course, I wasn't from Nebraska, but they treated me like I was. Because of those guys, I can't think of anywhere I'd rather be from, other than Texas, than Nebraska.

When you consider that in combat a machine gunner's life expectancy was two minutes, you realize that you advance in rank real fast. In no time, I was the gunner and a sergeant. The first thing I did was revise my old "move the gun" plan. I told my assistant gunner that we would move our gun from position to position and not give Jerry time to zero in on us, but never would we forget our assigned target. I would carry the gun and tripod while he carried a couple of boxes of ammo. He was the new man and I was the old veteran by now, and he agreed with me without question. Of course, it wouldn't have mattered if he didn't: I was the sergeant. To this day, I honestly believe that moving my gun around is what got me through all those months of combat. My sergeant never gave me permission to move around the way I did, but as long as I covered my assigned target, he didn't say anything.

Looking back, I don't think he was able to object to anything. That old sergeant had lost so many men so fast, he was mentally numb. I don't think any amount of training can prepare a man psychologically for the horrors of war. Instructors can teach and drill, but as I said earlier, you cannot imagine war in its rawest form until you see it up close and personal.

Days and weeks went by and we were still in the hedgerows. A successful plan was finally devised to deal with them. The artillery had a spotter plane overhead during all daylight hours, and this kept the German big guns silent. If one fired, the spotter plane immediately zeroed in on him and Jerry got back tenfold the number of rounds he fired at us, usually resulting in his demise.

But that didn't mean the fighting slacked off: it continued to be just as fierce as ever. We would crawl along the edge of the hedgerows hoping to spot the enemy before he saw us. Unfortunately, it did not always work out that way. Most of the time, we would not even see the Germans when they opened up on us, and then it was too late.

We avoided the sunken roads as much as possible. They were death traps for the enemy and us alike. If you were caught in one, there was simply no place to go. If you tried to advance, more likely than not an enemy tank would suddenly appear from around a corner with its cannon blazing and its machine guns wide open. If you tried to retreat, you still had the German tanks to contend with. The hedges were so tight and thick that going through them to get away was next to impossible. Needless to say, this was extremely costly in both lives and equipment. But costly or not, we got the job done, mainly using the old-fashioned method: we slugged our way through.

In the small town of Mortain, we made an almost fatal error. We didn't know it, but we bypassed a pocket of German armored infantry. What they were doing there is still a mystery to me. The only thing I could ever figure out was that they were possibly heading for the coast to plug a breach in their lines.

We were moving down a road that a spotter plane had advised us was clear for several miles. Then all of a sudden, it seemed we were engulfed in the fires of Hades. Behind us we could hear the squeak, squeak sound of a tank track. At first we thought it was our tanks moving up, but then we heard machine guns firing and the whine of the 88-mm cannons firing. We knew they were definitely not ours.

Worst of all, an 88-mm cannon on a tank meant only one thing: Tigers. The best tank the Germans had was the Panzer[19] Tiger tank. It was bigger and better than anything we had. It was literally a moving pillbox. Its diesel engine gave it the power plant for its massive size but above all, it had that 88.

An 88 had the most spine-chilling sound you can imagine. It was originally designed as an anti-aircraft gun but became so versatile because of its flat trajectory. The Germans started mounting it on tanks and wheeled vehicles and also using it as stationary artillery emplacements as well as in any other way they could think to put one into action. It made a dreadful whining sound when fired from a long distance and a awful swish-bang when fired up close. I know I am safe in saying that if any soldier who lived through an 88 barrage heard an 88 today, he would immediately recognize it. That gun was bad, bad news and very powerful: an 88 could shoot a hole completely through the four-inch steel turret of our Sherman tanks like a hammer hitting a pane of glass. Once it pierced a tank's armor, it would leave a mess of shrapnel behind ricocheting around inside the tank, usually killing all of its four-man crew.

We had run into a battalion of Waffen SS Panzers,[20] and this was definitely not good. The only thing that saved our bacon was the tremendous amount of firepower we had. The Tigers were tough, but they could be knocked out. Every company runner was sent to the rear to request that tank destroyers be dispatached at once. We hung on by our fingernails, waiting for them to move up. Bazooka teams from every company in the

---

[19]Panzer in German means "armored."

[20]SS troops were the elite German fighters. There were two units of SS: the death camp SS who murdered millions of innocent men, women, and children; and the Waffen SS. The Waffen SS were the toughest and best fighters the Germans had.

area started pounding the Tigers. Shortly, we heard the rumble of our tank destroyers. What a joyful sound that was!

Tank destroyers are light, highly maneuverable, and very fast armored vehicles that mount a 90-mm gun. They came up and moved into a flanking position on the Panzers and began to pound them with such a withering fire, the Panzers started pulling back. The bazooka teams and the tank destroyers were soon joined by a sky full of P-47s, P-51s, and strange-looking planes we later learned were P-38s. My little .30-caliber machine gun wasn't of any use against a Panzer's armor, but it was devastating against the cloth blouses of the infantrymen that moved with the Panzers.

We lost a lot of brave men that day. I lost a gunner, an assistant gunner, and one machine gun before that dance was over. By the following morning, I had a new machine gun and my first and second ammo-bearers were my new gunner and assistant gunner. But we had done the job: the Panzer battalion was completely destroyed and we moved forward to join the rest of the 35th Division.

We finally got the last German tank on the afternoon of August 12, 1944, and broke out of the hedgerows. Along the way, we took a mess of prisoners and shipped them back to the MPs in the rear. Most of them had run out of ammunition. They simply stood up as we approached and started pleading, "Kameraden nicht schiessen."[21]

When we broke out of the hedgerows, the commander of the Ameri-

---

[21]In German: "Friend, please don't shoot."

Many of the fine buildings of St. Lo and those of other areas in Europe were lost to future generations after the battles.

On leave in Paris, 1944

Heaven

can ground forces, General Omar Bradley, begged General Dwight Eisenhower, the Allied Supreme Commander, to bring in General George Patton. General Bradley needed a tank man in the open rolling country we were now in. This was classic tank country, and Patton was the absolute best we had. But there was one problem: General Bradley had to win a reprieve for Patton to get him out of Ike's[22] doghouse. In Italy the year before, Patton had slapped a GI named Charles Kuhl for what he considered cowardliness. It appeared that Patton had been mothballed for the rest of the war, but now he was needed. I guess Ike decided Patton hadn't really slapped that GI so hard after all. Patton came roaring (he never did anything quietly) into the fray in France and took over the Third Army, which included our 35th Infantry Division.

It was shortly after Patton's arrival that my squad leader, Sergeant McCoy,[23] a red-headed, whiskey-drinking Irishman who cared for his men, was wounded in the Mortain battle by machine gun fire. I became the squad leader and was promoted to buck sergeant.

When "Old Blood and Guts" Patton took over, we started moving—moving faster than anyone had imagined possible. Try as we might, we foot soldiers simply could not keep up with the tanks, and our com-

---

[22] General Eisenhower's nickname.
[23] I don't remember the sarge's first name.

38

manders complained to Patton. His solution was simple: "There is room on top of the tanks. Load 'em on." We climbed aboard and across France we went.

Patton has been called a self-centered *prima donna,* and I guess he might have been. I never met the man, and I like to draw my own conclusions about people. Patton was a tanker general and he knew how to get the job done. I always thought that he felt foot soldiers were good for only one thing: to protect his tanks. Inside a tank, the field of vision is extremely limited. With us riding on the top, we could furnish eyes for the tank crew, thus allowing them to keep the tank lids buttoned down and not have to expose themselves to enemy fire. It wasn't very comforting knowing we were the targets, but at the same time, it sure beat walking.

Our whole five-man squad climbed up on one tank. Besides being a sitting duck perching up there as pretty as you please, there was another big problem: you couldn't hear a thing. Usually you didn't even know you were being shot at until the bullets started ricocheting off the tank; or worse, you heard the dull thud of a slug hitting a man. When you heard that ping or thud, believe me, you fell off the tank in a big hurry.

On the ground, there was a phone on a holder, mounted on the back of the tank. Once we located where the firing was coming from, we

Patton told us infantrymen to jump on the tanks so that we could keep up. Until someone started shooting at you, it sure beat walking.

39

would pass this information on to the tank commander. The main thing was to stay under cover and let the tank do the shooting. To prevent giving the enemy a stationary target, seldom would the tank driver completely stop his tank. The tank would back up a little, then pull forward, and then back up again. Of course, he couldn't see us because we were as far under the tank as we could get or on the side away from the line of fire. It was strictly up to us to stay out of the way of the tank's tracks. And we did most of the time. When someone failed, it wasn't a pretty sight.

It was a truly inspiring sight to see that old tank's turret swing slowly around and then hear its .75-mm cannon roar. Then we would see bodies, arms, legs, pieces of equipment, or whatever weapons they were using go flying through the air. Our problem was over, at least for then. And, no, it didn't bother me the least bit, then or now. Just seconds before, those same Germans had been trying to do the same thing to me.

On D-Day, the German line of defense had been on the beaches. When that line was broken, they fell back to their second line of defense: the hedgerow country. Once we finally broke through the hedgerows, we were in open country and the Germans' next line of defense was hundreds of miles away—the Seine River. Apparently, all the Germans wanted to do now was to just get away. We were overrunning their hospital units, rear echelon repair areas, and the like. They had security personnel stationed around them but no real combat units.

One of the biggest problems we had was that we were taking so many prisoners. The main concern of the regular German soldier—not the SS boys—now appeared to be just surviving the war. They were surrendering in droves. We couldn't truck them to the rear as fast as they were conceding.

We had a Mexican fellow from San Antonio (I'll call him Pete) who had been wounded several times. He hated Germans with a passion. Someone made the mistake (I guess it was a mistake) of putting him in charge of the prisoners a couple of times. There was only one problem with that: as soon as he got out of sight, you would hear his gun open up. When he came back, he always said the same thing: "They tried to run. I shot all of 'em." It wasn't long before the company commander got wind of what Pete was doing and told us not to let him have any more prisoners. One other thing: what Pete did was not that uncommon.

We drove south of Paris to a resort area at Joigny and Montargis, meeting only light resistance along the way. Miraculously, we had not suffered any casualties lately in my platoon, but we still needed new equipment. Unfortunately, the big brass didn't seem to be in any hurry to provide us with new artillery, and the only thing we could figure out was that they must have thought the heavy fighting was over. Rumors were flying that Germany was putting out peace overtures, and word was spreading like a prairie wildfire that the war would be over by Christmas.

That made sense to us foot soldiers: Patton had literally shattered the German defenses in his mad dash for Berlin. But in doing so, some of his men—including one very tired buck sergeant—were worn to a frazzle. I did catch one bit of good luck, however. A few of us got three-day passes to Paris.

Paris almost made the front seem like a distant dream. It was really heaven. You could walk around without fear of a sniper killing you, or a Bouncing Betty[24] blowing your legs off, or, or, or. . . . The list of terrible things that could happen to a fellow in a combat zone could go on and on. I remember the Moselle River that runs through Paris was beautiful. Its water was so clear, you could see all the way to the bottom. I remember there were lots of fish swimming around. We looked at one another and we all thought the same thing: "Fresh fish sure would be good."

Unfortunately, we didn't have any fishing gear. Well, that's not quite right. We found some German potato mashers[25] and did a little fishing. Throw in a couple of those potato mashers and *voila!* We had enough fish for a real feast. The French had not had sufficient rations for some time while they were under German occupation. Almost before the grenade went off, they would jump into the water and gather up as many fish as they could carry. Seeing the fish floating all of a sudden brought the war back to me. It reminded me of the dead fish on Omaha Beach.

Like my ten-day leave to Texas before I left to come to Europe, my leave in Paris was over all too soon. We had orders to move out.

We moved out of the Joigny area in trucks. Joigny had been our first real rest since entering combat near St. Lo in what seemed like an

---

[24]A landmine.
[25]American nickname for German hand grenades.

eternity   ago but yet in other ways was only yesterday. The war hadn't waited on us while we were in Paris, but had moved on ahead. We rode trucks for several miles and then started marching. We were soon ordered into combat formation: staying spread out about twenty yards apart and in a staggered formation. If we were ambushed or came under an artillery barrage, we would not be bunched up and slaughtered.

We were part of a rifle squad of fifteen men broken into several teams or squads consisting of the squad leader, a scout, three riflemen, and a BAR[26] team. The BAR team was made up of three men: the gunner, who carried the rifle and an ammunition belt with ten clips of twenty rounds each; his assistant gunner, who carried an M1 rifle and an ammo belt with another ten clips for the BAR; and a third man, who also carried a rifle and another belt of ten clips. Then there were more riflemen and a bazooka team of two men: a gunner and a loader. Of course, there were also the machine gunners, who were usually assigned to the assault or lead company. We had lots of firepower.

There were three light machine-gun squads in a weapons platoon. There were two assault companies and one in reserve. A light machine gun squad was attached to each rifle company. Each group had its specific responsibilities. The bazooka team's responsibility was to knock out tanks. With their rockets, they could knock a track off and stop the tank. Then a rifleman would approach the tank and order the occupants to come out or die. It was their choice and we didn't really care which option they took. We also had an anti-tank company attached to us, but it only had a .37-mm gun. You could bounce those .37s off a Tiger tank all day and it would just keep coming. Occasionally, they would knock out a smaller German tank, but tanks were so mobile it was hard to get one of them in their sights.

We kept moving and meeting light resistance as we advanced on Nancy. I remember we captured a German field marshal[27] who could speak English better than most of us. It was rumored that he had been educated in some college in the States. We had occasion to talk with him, and he said if he had our artillery and Air Force, he could throw us back on the beaches of Normandy in two weeks. Seeing what our Air Corp[28] was doing to the Germans, I imagine he could have done just as he said.

---

[26] Browning Automatic Rifle.

[27] I don't know his name, if I ever did.

[28] During World War II, the Air Corp was part of the Army. After the war, it was spun into its own branch, the Air Force.

We finally got a break from walking or being human targets sitting on the top of a tank when we were loaded into trucks and rolled into Nancy. That the war was far from over was brought home to us as we approached. Our company commander, Captain Davis, was hit. His jeep hit a mine in the street going into the city. At least he was alive: his driver and executive officer were both killed.

That was just the start of the blood. There was a large canal running just east of Nancy and we were ordered to cross it. There had once been a bridge crossing the canal, but it had been blown up by the retreating Germans. Therefore, we had to cross in assault boats. We were lined up along the road and an engineering captain came down the line, counting us off in fives. Each boat held five men plus the two engineers who operated the boat. As soon as five men stepped out, another group of five would move up. For the last fifty yards, we did not have the shelter of buildings, so we ran to the bank of the canal behind a levee. When I got to the levee, there were five men already there. One was our section leader, Sergeant Potts, whom we had not seen much of during the campaign.

The engineering captain, who for some reason I remember was from Beatrice, Nebraska, was pushing us over the bank and into the boats.

It was in a boat like this that I was forced out of my regular place in line. The man in front of me got "weak-kneed" at the thought of crossing that river under an artillery barrage. That action ended up saving my life.

43

He ordered Sergeant Potts to hit the boat. Well, the sergeant froze and started screaming and crying. I was lying next to him, and the captain kicked me   and ordered me over the bank. I went wide open. My going instead of Sergeant Potts got us out of the five-count the engineering captain was barking out. I learned later that the next boat, the one I was supposed to be on, was hit by tank fire from across the canal. Both engineers and all five infantry- men were killed. As for Sergeant Potts, I don't know what happened to him. He is not listed as killed in action, wounded, or missing in action, so I as- sume he survived the war.

We didn't waste any time on the far bank. We charged right on inland and were able to capture a plane hangar. That ended our fighting for the day and we bedded down inside it. The next morning, the company runner crossed the canal and came to our site. When he saw me, I knew immediately something was bad wrong. His face turned ashy white and he asked me how I had gotten across the river. In my cockiest tone I told him, "In a boat." After giving me a real dirty look, he said I had been reported as missing in action when the boat I was supposed to be in was hit by the tank fire.

I'll never forget that company runner, Howard Spakes from Doyle, Tennessee. He carried messages from the company commander to and from the front when the messages were urgent. I told him to get a message back to the company clerk that I was not missing, and to do it quick before it got sent to Battalion. If that message had been sent to my home, it would have been devastating to my family. Thankfully, we got it stopped before it left Battalion Headquarters.

44

Let's Get Out of Here

We had lost our captain for a while in that little battle, but it didn't slow us down. We were quickly reorganized with a new temporary commander and immediately pushed out of Nancy. We marched until dark, stopped, and did what all infantrymen do who want to live: we started digging. Everyone was exhausted and after digging only a short time, it suddenly became very quiet. We had all dozed off. Artillery fire suddenly started falling like rain in our area and everyone started digging furiously. When the artillery stopped, the digging again stopped. Just about the time we got comfortable, shells started coming in once more and the furious digging started all over again. This went on all night. By daylight, the foxholes were so deep you had to walk up to them and look down to see who was at the bottom.

When the sun rose, we pulled out. As the light got better, we could see a very high hill jutting up out of the terrain. I was no military strategist, but even I knew that whoever controls the high ground usually wins the battle. Sure enough, we headed straight for that hill.

Unfortunately, the Germans also knew the importance of the high ground. We had gone only a short distance when a heavy German artillery barrage from the hill started hitting us. The closest cover was a small village that was really no more than a group of farmhouses off to our right. Reaching the village, we regrouped and started for the hill again. About halfway up, bullets from machine guns and small arms started hitting all around us. Thankfully, there was no artillery or none of us would have gotten off that hill. As it was, the lines of Companies A and C broke, and men started back down. I was on the right flank and I never liked to pay for the same ground twice. I got out in front of the men and started cussing and shouting at the retreating line. The retreat slowed, and soon the men turned around. Back up the hill we went, this time all the way to the top. Once there, I set up my machine gun with a field of fire to cover all of the hill and the surrounding territory.

Once sure that my men and gun were dug in and well placed, I picked out a spot and waited. Shelling and sporadic fire continued until dark. Then it got quiet—too quiet. About eight o'clock, mortar shells started falling on us, and suddenly German soldiers started pouring into our position. The fighting became hand-to-hand and very desperate, and it looked like we might be pushed off. The carnage and confusion became unbelievable, but that hill commanded all the surrounding area and it had to be held.

Our situation was already past desperate. Then it went from bad to worse. A mortar shell hit the company CP[29] at the base of the hill, severely wounded our company commander,[30] and killed his radio operator and a couple of S-2 men.[31] Besides blowing off part of the CO's hand, the force of the explosion totally addled him. He crawled over to the dead radio man, called battalion artillery, and told them to lay fire along the crest of the hill because it had been overrun by the Germans. Soon our own 105 howitzers and mortars started exploding on our position. That was too much for the Germans: these crazy Americans were shelling themselves! They broke.

I've already said that shells and bullets do not distinguish between American or German uniforms. There were two companies of Americans, less the wounded and dead, on the crest of that hill. All we could do was hunker down and wait for the barrage to stop. But the shells didn't stop: they just kept coming.

I was in my foxhole just trying to stay alive, when all of a sudden I went flying into the air like I had been propelled from a slingshot. Of course I didn't know it then, but a shell had hit close by and burrowed itself into the ground until it was almost directly under my foxhole. When it detonated, I

---

[29]CP - command post.
[30]I can't remember his name.
[31]Intelligence men.

flew up and then came down—without my helmet, rifle, pack, or my hearing. I lay there for a while trying to get the cobwebs out of my head. My mind finally emerged from the fog enough to operate to a small degree. I stumbled over to my machine gun, but it was out of commission with a piece of shrapnel wedged in the breach. The Germans had not been the only ones who broke and ran. I saw men on both sides of me running down the hill, at least those who could still run. I don't know how many were dead, and to be honest with you, right then I was not worried about them. I yelled at my gunner and his assistant, "Let's get out of here!" We left everything we had and joined the race to the bottom of the hill.

Some of us stumbled onto a road and ran into a staff sergeant. He told us to dig in along with other members of Companies A and C. I had picked up an abandoned rifle on the way down the hill and that was all I had—no extra clips, nothing. I was stiff and almost totally deaf, but by noon the next day I able to hear again. That was as close as I ever came to buying the farm. Thankfully, I guess the Germans had all they wanted for that day. If they had counterattacked, I don't think there's any way in the world we could have held.

The people of Nancy, France, were sure happy to see us when we liberated them from four years of German occupation.

47

Just as the sun started coming up, we saw a large group of German troops coming around the bottom of the hill straight at us. They had a half-track with them, and their infantrymen used the same tactic we did. So as to not give us a stationary target, they would move out and then retreat, move out again, and go back. I had just about decided we were in for another hairy situation when my gunner punched me and pointed to the rear. Several of our tank destroyers were coming up the hill. They moved through our lines and headed straight for the Germans. A half-track is no match for a tank destroyer, and the Germans knew when they were outgunned; so they pulled back. The fight around Nancy and the hill was over. I was ready for some R & R,[32] but that was not to be. As quickly as our guns and equipment could be replaced, we moved out again.

The mad dash across the open fields and small towns of the French countryside was over. From now on, it would be a day-by-day existence in mud, snow, ice, tears, blood, and death—lots of death—in the highly industrialized heartland of Europe. We had pushed the Germans back so fast that we actually thought that for once, the top brass actually knew what they were talking about: the war would soon be over and we would be home by Christmas! But the German Army was a long way from being defeated, and that was the only way it would quit: being totally and completely defeated. It didn't take them long to dispel our false feeling of euphoria. Now the only thing we cared about was just staying alive. At that moment, Texas seemed far, far away.

We moved out of residential Nancy in combat formation, headed for its industrial area. Company C would serve in reserve. We had only gone a short distance when we saw large smokestacks on the horizon. We halted frequently because of the fighting Companies A and B were having to do around those smokestacks. I am not sorry to say that the fighting was not hard enough to bring up the reserves yet.

It was in a brick factory on the bank of the Saar River where I got to spend several days in safety inside an oven. This factory was huge, and right in the middle of it was a large brick structure of some kind. None of us had the least idea what it was. I was none to happy when our section leader

---

[32] Rest and relaxation.

48

looked at me and couple of other guys and pointed at what turned out to be an oven and said, "Check it out."

Needless to say, we were more than a little apprehensive as we approached the door. We had no idea what or who we would find when we opened it: Germans, booby-traps, anything. Easing the door open and ready for anything, we found—nothing. It was a huge brick-baking oven. After making sure there were no booby-traps that would suddenly shorten our lives, we made ourselves at home. It took about a week before the whole factory area was considered secure. Our group got to live in the comfort of an oven that week. What made it even better was that we didn't even have to fight for it. It turned out that as we entered one side of the factory area, the Germans went out the other. As far as the other boys and I were concerned, that was how wars should be fought. But what did we know?

As it is with war, all too quickly the safety of the oven was over and it was time to go back to fighting. We were ordered to cross the Saar on a bridge that the retreating Germans had partially destroyed. This was another order that looked good to the brass in the rear, but in reality was impossible. The center section was sagging into the water, making it unusable for us. Working under heavy mortar and small-arms fire which killed many of them, engineers succeeded in building a footbridge for us. Then it was our turn to expose ourselves to danger. We dreaded what lay ahead, but we hit the bridge at a dead run—or as much as you can carrying full combat gear. We lost a lot of men on the bridge, but we managed to get across and into the town of Sarreguemines.

This wasn't Nancy. The Germans were determined that we would not stay in Sarreguemines, and they immediately mounted a heavy counterattack. Regrettably, enough of us had not been able to cross the river before the counterattack hit our whole line. After heavy fighting, we were forced to withdraw back across the river. The Germans blew out our little footbridge to make sure we did not make any further use of it. That was the end of that tune.

If any of us had any silly notions that the war would soon be over, that thought had completely vanished by now. It was obvious we had come up against a reorganized German Army. Patton had done a good job on his wild charge across France—probably too good. He had outrun his supplies and found himself with not only a badly over-extended supply line, but also exposed flanks. This was not good. If the Germans had been able to mount a major counterattack right then, they could have completely cut off and surrounded the whole Third Army. Thankfully, the German Army was still reeling from the battering the Allied Armies had been dealing it since Normandy. It was all they could do to barely hang on and mount an effective defense. They didn't have either the material or the manpower to pull off such an offensive maneuver. At least, that's what the boys with ranks on their shoulders thought.

Patton was fit to be tied when his tanks started running out of gas. He had done everything he could to keep the attack going, even parking half of his tanks and diverting all available fuel to the remaining tanks in order to keep attacking. But the supply shortages finally proved too much even for George Patton to overcome. He had to stop, reorganize, and let his fuel and supplies catch up. If the powers-that-be had supplied Patton the way they should have, who knows? The war might have been over by Christmas. But we'll never know, and of course all that grand planning was way above my lowly GI head.

While Patton, Bradley, Eisenhower, and the others planned, we pulled back to a heavily forested area we later learned was the Gremercy Forest. For the first time since the fighting around St. Lo, we were ordered into a defensive position. We had no more than settled in until it started raining. And it rained and rained and rained. I didn't think it was ever going to stop. It rained for days, and all the while the mud got deeper and deeper.

What I would not have given to have been back in that nice, dry oven at the brick factory instead of in that wet, mud-filled foxhole. It got so bad we had to dig sump holes[33] at the foot of our foxholes for the water to run into. Even that wasn't enough. We had to take our helmets and dip the water out of the sump holes and throw it outside so that the water in our foxhole would have someplace to go. I've seen pictures of American Doughboys in the mud of the trenches of World War I. They lived in that stuff for months and months. I don't know how they did it.

There had been a call for volunteers to go to the rear for a special assignment. I was so sick and tired of the rain and mud that I was ready for anything that would get me out of there. I talked to Ansalem Rumca, my best friend, about volunteering. We had not been told what this special as-

---

[33]In this case, a hole dug in the bottom of a foxhole to drain the water out of it.

If we were in a place warm and safe enough to undress to take a bath, it was like heaven.

signment was, but it didn't matter. The way I figured it, anything had to be better than the mud. And besides, they promised us a bath, clean sheets, and clean clothes. What more could I ask for? I don't think Rumca was as sick of the mud as I was, because he didn't think much of volunteering for anything, especially something he didn't know anything about. But I finally persuaded him that I was right, and we volunteered—me with enthusiasm, Rumca with a ton of reservations.

I guess everyone has heard that old Army saying: "Don't ever volunteer for anything." Trust me, that is good advice and I should have followed it. We did get the shower, the clean clothes, and a bed. For one whole night. Then we were told what our mission was: to take prisoners. When I heard that, my stomach did a flip-flop. And if looks could have killed, I'd be dead right now from the look Ansalem gave me.

You see, there's only one place you could find prisoners: behind enemy lines. I was having enough problems staying alive with the Krauts[34] in

---

[34] Another American nickname we had for the Germans.

front of me without going behind their lines looking for more trouble. But one thing about it: if it's true that misery loves company, then I had lots of company. All of us "volunteers" had the same look that said, "Maybe the mud wasn't so bad after all." Well, too late now. We were broken into four- and five-men teams and assigned different nights for each unit to infiltrate the German lines.

Our group drew the first night and, thankfully, it was dark as sin because the first thing we did was walk right into a barbed-wire trap. The Germans had filled tin cans with rocks and hung them on the barbed-wire entanglements lying in front of their line. You had to be there to appreciate the noise those rocks made banging around in those tin cans. There is no way Big Ben striking high noon could make more noise.

Indians used to have a saying: "He who runs away today, lives to fight another day." We ran like Satan himself was after us for the ditch we had just crossed coming across No-Man's Land. Thank goodness, the German machine gunners apparently mistook the direction of the rattling cans, because they were firing tracers off to our left. There was no doubt in our minds that a German patrol would be coming to investigate shortly, so we hunkered down and waited for the fight we knew was on its way. Thank the Lord for small favors. They went the same direction the machine guns were firing. We lay still, trying not to move a muscle until they gave up and went back to their lines. Then we got out of there and went back to our lines.

There was one other thing while all of this was going on: Rumca never stopped cussing me. He called me every name you can imagine, not counting some new ones he invented. But he wasn't making a thing on me. I was already calling myself most of those same names.

When we got back without any prisoners, our status with the brass dropped like a rock. Our clean sheets and nice warm beds became clean hay in a barn. That was still better than the mud on the front lines. But our days operating behind enemy lines were over. I guess they decided that anyone so dumb as to walk into a barbed-wire entanglement couldn't be smart enough to capture prisoners. We were loaded up and sent back to the front line. And the mud.

Dead Dog Lying in the Snow

We got back to our outfit just in time to help break camp and get ready to move out. The brass was finally going to turn Patton loose. Ever since he had been forced to stop his assault, he had been chomping at the bit—so much so that Ike had called him on the carpet yet again and told him to calm down. Patton's mouth had gotten him into trouble many times, and for once, he kept his mouth shut—at least as much as he was capable of keeping it closed.

When the day finally came for the attack, the 134th (by luck of the draw, I suppose) was assigned to be the reserve regiment while the 137th and 320th drew the assault positions. Our reserve position didn't last long, however. Early in the morning of the first day, the 134th was ordered to attack on the right. We moved into position. Companies A and B led the attack, with my Company C in reserve. It looked like the gods were smiling on Company C, but soon their smiles turned to frowns.

By now, it was December and the weather started turning very cold—much colder than anything I had experienced. Remember, France is on a line with Canada and, trust me, Canada gets a lot colder than Texas. We began to receive winter overcoats, new equipment, gas masks, and the never-ending stream of replacements. Shortly thereafter, large trucks began pouring into our area, and we loaded up and headed north. The Battle of the Bulge had started.

If you saw the movie *Patton,* you will recall that when Patton was called to Allied headquarters to discuss strategy for meeting the German assault in the Ardennes, he told those assembled he could have a well-equipped fighting force on the move north within twenty-four hours. Most of the generals thought he was letting his huge ego overload his mouth. Their reactions were dubious, to say the least. Evidently, they didn't know old "Blood-And-Guts" Patton nearly as well as they thought. The fact was, we were already in trucks heading north!

Even Patton couldn't come up with enough trucks to move us all at the same time. It was important that we not be led into battle piecemeal, because to have done so would have invited disaster. A shrewd plan was devised to allow us to strike the enemy in strength. We rode about fifty miles, were unloaded, and started marching. The trucks then turned around and went back to pick up the rest of the regiment. At least this was the way our regiment moved, and I assume other regiments did the same. We leap-frogged like this all the way to the battle zone. The thing I remember most about that forty-eight-hour march was the cold. The farther north we went, the colder it got. Our overcoats felt good while we were riding in the trucks, but when we were marching, they got hot and heavy. We began to see them discarded by the side of the road. Not mine: it stayed with me all the way.

We kept moving farther and farther north toward the battle. We didn't line up into formation until we reached a small village whose name, if I ever knew, I have long since forgotten. It had been totally demolished. When we did form, we were smack in the middle of the Battle of the Bulge. I guess the brass decided we needed a good meal before going into battle, because we were served a hot Christmas dinner. I'm not saying it was any good, but it was hot.

We fought in that sector for nearly a month, trying to break through the Germans guarding the flanks of their armored units. They were fighting hard to keep their supply route open. The fighting was so fierce that the 35th Division had been reduced to the strength of a battalion. Truckload after truckload of replacements kept rolling in.

Our forces were divided into a northern and a southern command. Every unit north of the German penetration was placed under the command of the British *prima donna*, Field Marshall Bernard Law Montgomery. Those south of the penetration remained under General Patton. Guess who got transferred north to serve under the *prima donna*? You got it. The 134th was one of the unlucky units. We caught every dirty detail Montgomery could think of, and then I think he made some up.

Monty, as he liked to be called, would have tested the patience of Job. He rewrote the book on how not to rush things. If we drew fire from, say a building, his idea was to pull back and level the house with cannon fire regardless of how long it took and how much it slowed the overall advance.

British soldiers were good; they just had, in my opinion, a sorry commander. Another thing I remember distinctly about the British was their peculiarity about tea. They had tea every afternoon at three o'clock regardless of what was going on. If there was shelling, a firefight, or whatever, at three o'clock they had tea! Night or day, you had no trouble knowing when a column of British troops went by: it sounded like a herd of cattle, with each one being a bellwether. They hooked their teacups to the bottom of their pack and it sounded like bells banging against their equipment.

This may sound strange, but the Germans were not our biggest enemy, not by a long shot. Our worst enemy was the cold. We were losing men from frostbite faster than we were from combat. One of the worst scares I ever had was because of the cold. One time I fell asleep in my foxhole and when I awoke, I couldn't feel my feet! A shot of fear went through me. I jerked my boots off and started frantically rubbing my feet. Finally, they started to sting and a few minutes later, they began to hurt. Never had pain felt so good! I knew that the pain meant my feet were not frozen to the point of having to have them amputated.

It was incredibly tough, but both the battle and the cold continued. I guess it's a good thing we didn't know that our commanders, from Ike on down, were frantic over the German winter offensive. There was a very large supply dump at Liege, Belgium, and I heard that was one of the main objectives of the Germans. They didn't have enough fuel to go all the way to Antwerp, which was their primary goal. They had to have the fuel and supplies from Liege to have any hope of victory. All I knew for sure was that Germans were in front of us, it was still cold, and both had to be dealt with. We pushed through the timber and snow to the little town of Lutrebois, sustaining heavy casualties as we went.

Once in Lutrebois, we commandeered a house and my squad and several infantrymen were able to get in out of the cold. We had just settled in comfortably when the Germans launched a counterattack. We repelled the first attack, but the Germans soon regrouped and attacked again. Even though we mowed them down like a knife cutting through butter, they kept coming, and some finally got through.

I heard the door crash open and in came a squad of German SS troopers. These boys were bad news—very, very bad news. They were tough and they were mean. They ran down the hall, grabbed several of our boys, and hustled them back toward their lines. We heard them, but we were in a small room off the main part of the house and the door leading into the room looked like an outside door. I suppose that is all that saved us that day.

None of us dared to breathe while the SS troops were in the house. I had picked up a little loot, and if we were captured, I sure didn't want to any of that on me. I was lying on the floor, and I started emptying my pockets and shoving my money under a dresser in the corner. I had a hand grenade with the pin pulled and an M1 carbine that I had grabbed. They were at the ready and on full automatic. I had made up my mind that whether they captured me or killed me, I was going to take a bunch of them with me. But our luck held and the SS left the building without trying our door.

The SS were pure bulldogs when it came to fighting, but the same cannot be said of all of the enemy soldiers. To our great surprise, we discovered we weren't just fighting Germans: we were taking Dutch, Poles, and Frenchmen prisoners who had been fighting with the Germans. One day an entire platoon of Germans—at least they had on German uniforms—all of a sudden burst out of a house, jabbering something that was not German. They obviously wanted to surrender, but I never did figure out what language they were speaking.

When we entered the house they came out of, we found a dead SS officer. From our broken French, what little English they knew, and a lot of hand gestures, we learned the SS officer had been holding a gun on them. If they didn't shoot us, he was going to shoot them. This turned out to be a common occurrence during the rest of the war.

There was no letup in the fighting. It was vicious, the resistance was brutal, and we suffered a lot of casualties. Two of those losses were ammo-bearers from my squad. With the fighting as heavy as it was, we were using up an incredible amount of ammo. I was the squad leader, but this was no time to stand on ceremony, and I started carrying ammo to help out.

By now, nearly half of C Company was down, but we dished it out better than we received. We killed so many Germans, they were stacked up like cord wood by the side of the road. The killing was unbelievable, but we got the job done. We cut the road to Bastogne, and the German supply route was severed.

With their supply line cut, the Germans started retreating. Unfortunately, this didn't mean the end of the battle. There was still a lot of fighting to be done before the Battle of the Bulge was over. The Germans who managed to get out of the Bulge alive gathered in the Ruhr Valley, several miles to the northeast of our position, and prepared to counterattack. When the attack came, we did our part to help thin the ranks of their assault troops. We did a very good job, I might add.

We had just entered a small village in the Lorraine area, and our section leader pointed to a house and told us to take a couple of infantrymen and set up our machine gun in it. When approaching a building in a combat zone, you always assume that it is occupied by the enemy and that you will have to fight for it. Anytime we didn't have to fight, like this time, was a pleasant surprise. We dropped our gear, set up our gun, and started looking for something to drink: vodka, schnapps, wine—it didn't matter, just so it poured.

One of the infantrymen who had come into the house with us found a trapdoor in the corner of the big room we were in. It led to a cellar—a wine cellar? He reached down, grabbed the handle, and yanked the door up and open. There was a blast from the cellar, and he was hit full in the chest and face with fire from a German burp gun. A burp gun was a small, hand-held fully automatic weapon with an extremely fast rate of fire. When you got hit with a burst from a burp gun, you didn't get just one round. It fired so fast, you usually got hit with at least four or five rounds.

The other two men and I all hit the floor together. The floor was made of heavy wooden planks so we didn't have to worry about bullets ripping through. For what seemed an eternity, but was probably only a minute or two, we hugged the floor, not daring to move a muscle. After getting my thoughts together, I pulled a grenade and motioned for the other men to do the same. We crawled up to the trapdoor that had fallen open when the rifleman went down, and on the motion count of three, all of us tossed our grenades into the opening. Only seconds later—Boom! Boom! Boom! All was silent, but I had played this game too long to take any chances. To be absolutely sure we had finished off the Germans, we lobbed three more grenades into the cellar. Boom! Boom! Boom! When we went down the stairs, we found one of the ghastliest sights I've ever seen in my life. A man, a woman, two small kids, and two SS officers were literally dripping off the walls and ceiling. The only thing we could figure out was that the SS officers had apparently taken the family hostage and forced them into the basement when we entered the town.

That incident bore on my mind for weeks. I have asked myself countless times why one of the parents or one of the children didn't cry out when that SS man fired. If we had known the children were in the cellar, we wouldn't have tossed the grenades. But they didn't, and we did. The parents had lived some of their lives, but the children . . . that was something else.

We had been in the house only a short time when we got orders to move out. Men in combat handle fear differently. Most confront their fears and handle them, but some can't—or won't. I remember a young man sitting in a corner cleaning his rifle. Only problem was, it was already clean and freshly oiled. He kept pointing the muzzle at his foot. I knew what he was getting ready to do and I didn't want any part of it. I moved under a stairwell and got some heavy timber between him and me. I couldn't see him, but all of a sudden there was a loud bang and he started screaming and rolling around on the floor. Someone called the medics, and after they got his boot off, they found a huge blood blister between his big toe and the toe next to it. He couldn't even do a good job of shooting himself: the bullet had gone between his toes. When the company commander came in and saw what had happened, he grabbed the slacker by the collar, shook him like a rag doll, and cussed him unmercifully. He called for the Military Police, and they led him away, hopping on his good foot: the CO refused to allow the coward a stretcher. I suppose about the only punishment he received was a court marshal. I doubt if they did more. Ever since Patton had been forced to apologize to Private Kuhl when he slapped him back in Italy, discipline was not as harsh as it had once been. If it hadn't been for the slapping incident, this weasel would probably have been shot on the spot.

Over the years, I have often pondered that thin line that separates a coward from a brave man. One night at the annual Texas Ranger Reunion in Waco, my co-author was talking to C. J. Havrda, our Senior Ranger Captain, about some of his experiences in combat. The captain had been an infantryman in Vietnam, wounded in combat, and awarded a Purple Heart. Captain Havrda gave the best description of courage I have ever heard: "The biggest fear a brave man has in combat isn't getting killed: it's letting his brother down. A coward is only concerned with his own well-being." The more I think about that, the truer I realize what he said is true. A coward puts his own life and well-being above that of his brother. In a way, it's like a football game. As Captain Havrda said, "You're a team, and if you don't do your job, your team loses." In the game of war if you miss an assignment, the team isn't just thrown for a loss: someone usually dies. How could anyone ever look at himself in the mirror if he knew that he was alive only because he thought so much of himself that he was willing to sacrifice his brother's life? How could anyone live with himself, knowing what he had done? I couldn't.

Thankfully, we didn't run into many SS troops until late in the war. When Hitler got desperate, however, he turned them loose. It's true that they were fanatics of the first order, but they were also the best fighting men Hitler had. We knew when we ran into them, we were in for a hard fight. When we crossed the Rhine River, we started running into SS troopers regularly. Nearly every time, they acted like they were drunk or on dope. Whether they were attacking or defending, they were suicidal in their fighting.

One day a group of SS men, accompanied by a half-track, attacked the First Battalion's left flank. The Germans were outnumbered ten to one, but they kept coming, yelling and screaming like crazy. My squad was off to the left about one hundred yards when we heard the commotion. I told Rumca to swing our little .30-caliber machine gun around and start firing into their flank. They fell like mowed weeds, but they still kept coming. They got within twenty yards of our lines and were still advancing when the last one fell. The really sad part was there there had been no reason for the attack. They would have gained nothing even if they had been successful.

When you have seen as much death as I have, you sometimes become indifferent to it. I remember one episode in particular that shows just how insensitive I had become. The Graves Registration people were gathering American bodies from the snow for burial. When they put this one poor little guy on a stretcher, I recognized him. But like I said, I had seen so many men I knew killed, I had become hardened to the sight. What was so bad was that I knew this should bother me, but it didn't. I felt nothing. I didn't think any more about seeing him than I would have looking at a dead dog lying in the snow.

In a way, the snow was a blessing. It covered a lot of trouble. It put a soft, gentle covering on the blood bath, not allowing us to see things as they really were. We were numb to the massive slaughter that we were constantly confronted with. Every time you woke up, the first thing that went through your mind was, "Am I in a hospital or on a battlefield?"

Men learn to cope with the stress of battle in different ways. One of the ways I coped was never allowing myself to become close to anyone. It was just too hard to lose them. The exception was Ansalem Rumca. I didn't want to get close to him, but I did. Another thing you learn is that simple things become supremely important: a hot meal, a hot bath, a clean bed, a woman, or that letter from home.

Even though the resistance wasn't what it had been during the Battle of the Bulge, plenty of men were still dying. I was still moving my gun or having my squad move theirs from place to place. As I described earlier, when we were assigned a target—whether it was a house, a woods, or whatever—I would direct my gunner to set up the gun and I would find a secondary position for him to move to after his initial bursts. Many, many times we moved and had no more than gotten set up in our new position than a mortar shell would hit within a few feet of our old position. I still give myself credit for saving many lives in my squad because I moved our gun frequently.

There are three machine guns in a light machine-gun section and three .60-mm mortars. This was the makeup of every American combat company in World War II: six squad leaders, one section leader, and the first sergeant. We had a new section leader, whose name I'm sorry to say I have forgotten, and we saw him much more frequently than we ever did Sergeant Potts.

For more than two weeks, the slaughter continued until we finally won the day. We were constantly being resupplied with men and materials because our losses were so heavy. During those two weeks, I lost an assistant gunner and five ammo-carriers. But Rumca and I seemed to lead charmed lives and just kept plugging along doing whatever we could to survive.

We were still under Monty's command when we were finally ordered to move northeast toward the Rohr River. At one time, we were within five miles of the American lines on the opposite side of the Bulge. I guess Ike wanted to teach the Germans a lesson, because he ordered a frontal assault on the leading German column and pushed them back until they were in the original starting area of the Bulge. I don't know how many men we lost, but it was a lot. I was only a dog-faced infantry sergeant with no knowledge of grand strategy, but I do know we could have cut off the head of the Bulge, surrounded the Germans, and starved them out. But I suppose that is why Ike was a Five-Star General and I was a lowly sergeant.

After that dance in the Ardennes I thought, "Old boy, you ain't coming out of this war alive and that's a fact." I could see that the Germans still had a lot of fight left in them.

The ending of the Ardennes Campaign, the Battle of the Bulge, had left the 134th Regiment behind the main war. The Battle of the Bulge wasn't officially over, but it had been slowed to almost a standstill. We rode trucks for several miles, dismounted, and started marching. We hadn't been marching long before the order came to "spread out." That could only mean one thing: we were within range of the enemy artillery and during an artillery barrage, one of the last things you want to be is bunched up. If one well-placed artillery shell landed . . . well, you can imagine. We crossed a couple of small streams and saw a welcome sight: open country. I remember there was one field of about a thousand acres littered with knocked-out American and German tanks. From the smoke rising from the tanks, it was clear that a big tank battle had only recently taken place.

No one needed to tell us we were back in the war; a blind man could have seen that. We stopped in an area of woods and were told to remove all division and regimental insignia. Shortly after our arrival, several GIs arrived with paint and began to mark out the insignia on all of our equipment. I don't have the faintest idea why they did this, but it looked like we were going into battle incognito.

We moved out and, sure enough, artillery fire started hitting all around us. It was heavy stuff, the heaviest we had heard in a long time. You could hear those shells coming from a long way off, rumbling like a freight train. They passed over us and exploded somewhere in the rear area. Evidently, the Germans had spotted something big moving toward the front. I was glad someone else was on the receiving end of those monster shells.

Artillery batteries have to have protection, and that means infantry. Patrols were sent out to scout the area to our front. When the patrol returned, we were not given any information but were told to move out slowly and quietly. Something had to be up; we had never advanced in this manner before. Soon, small artillery started dropping in our midst, and we stopped and dug in. We waited until dark and then moved out again, still in the blind as to what we were doing. I always hated night marches. Daylight moves are bad enough, but a night march is worse. There we were in enemy territory with no insignia and skulking along like thieves.

Suddenly there was a burst of German machine gun fire up ahead, and we all dropped to the ground and froze. Our section leader came back and got my squad. We moved forward, veering to the right of where the German gun was firing. We finally reached a small stream and set up our gun. All was quiet for about ten seconds; then the German gun opened up again, but that was his mistake. We zeroed in on his position and put about five hundred rounds of .30-caliber bullets there. We heard nothing more from that battery.

We were still holding this position when some German flares went off. Shortly thereafter, the mortar fire started. We dug in between mortar rounds until we were well below ground. We suffered few casualties but to add to our misery, we spent the night in ankle-deep water. It turned out we had dug in so close to a river that the water seeped through into our foxholes. About two o'clock in the morning, we heard some engineers coming up behind us. They were fully equipped with their bridge-building equipment and ready to build us a bridge over the river. When the sun broke through the eastern sky, we could see the small river in our front that had caused us such discomfort the night before.

Our section leader and a cameraman took our picture guarding the river while the engineers built the bridge. They told us this was the Rohr River and that all those buildings in the distance with the smoke rising from them were in Hilfarth, Germany—what was left of it. Our artillery was re-

Hilfarth, Germany, was another town almost completely destroyed after we captured it.

ally laying it on Hilfarth. Watching the artillery blow that town to pieces. you wouldn't have thought anything or anybody could possibly survive. But I had been around way too long to believe that nonsense: I knew that enemy soldiers would be waiting for us. Only now, they would not be fighting just for their homeland: they might possibly be fighting for their own homes.

No one had to remind me how hard we had fought all across France, but I also knew it was going to get a lot tougher. My thoughts returned to Ingleside, Texas. Yes, if I was in those Germans' places I would fight harder knowing I was fighting for the lives of Papa John, Mamma Nell, and my brother and sisters. Yes, indeed. I would fight much, much harder.

Orders came down that at 0600 the following morning: our advance was to start. A brigade of engineers with assault boats was to ferry us across the river. There would be no reserve status for us this time. Companies A and C would be leading the assault, and my machine gun had been assigned to A Company. We had no more than entered the river when the German artillery and mortars started falling all around us. Thankfully, six o'clock in the morning in that part of Germany was still fairly dark, so they didn't have us zeroed in. It didn't take them long to correct that. I think our boat was one of the last to make the far bank before the artillery started slamming into us.

I can't imagine a more lonesome or helpless feeling than sitting in a small, lightweight boat with heavy artillery and mortars tearing everything to pieces all around you. There's not one single, solitary thing you can do about it but keep your head down and pray. I didn't know land could feel so good as it did when that little boat bumped the far shore of the Rohr River.

We hit the shore running and we didn't stop until we reached the cover of one of the nearby houses. Looking back at the river, I saw a terrible sight. The water was a roaring mass of mud, debris, blood, and bodies. About a hundred yards down from where we crossed was a blown-out bridge. Lodged firmly against what was left of the bridge were the remains of many of our boats and the bodies of more men than I wanted to attempt to count.

But I didn't have long to think about those dead men unless I wanted to join them. We had barely secured our position and pointed our guns toward the enemy when the Germans counterattacked. Many a German soldier lost his life in that futile battle. They kept coming and we kept firing. The bodies began to stack up higher and higher. Looking back, it was almost like a bad dream; there were so many of them. But finally, their attack broke and they fell back. Later, when we moved forward, we saw the reason for the ferocity of their attack: these had been SS men.

Funny what you hear in the heat of battle. Throughout the attack, I heard a German machine gun rattling away in our rear. I remember thinking, "Somebody better take that gun out." But when the Germans retreated, it stopped firing. It turned out that when we had occupied the house, Lieutenant Malacheck of C Company had climbed to the house's top floor and found a German machine gun with a lot of ammunition. He had turned the gun, with devastating effect, on its former owners.

A deathly silence settled over the field, and then I saw a white flag. Actually, it was a sheet. We were ordered to hold our fire until we found out what the Germans wanted. We all looked at one another: we were mystified. That they might be surrendering never entered our minds. These guys were SS, and the only way to make them quit was to kill them. We were right: they didn't want to surrender. They wanted a truce in order to gather up their dead and wounded. We needed to do the same thing, so we agreed. True, our losses were nothing compared to those of the Germans, but we still had a lot of dead and wounded that needed caring for. Soon stretcher bearers began to appear from both sides.

When the truce ended, the Germans pulled out, leaving us the field. As soon as the new replacements came up, we again prepared to move out. It was hard to realize that I was younger than many of these men. It seemed like an eternity since I had been one of them, but it had actually been only a few short months.

In a way, we were happy to see the replacements because while waiting on them, we were able to sleep. And sleep we did. You might say we slept the sleep of the dead. We were worn out and our nerves were shot. We looked fresh and ready to go after a few days' rest and clean clothes, socks, boots, pants, and underwear. Looks can be deceiving.

Pulling out, I looked at a handbill that the Germans had left scattered throughout Hilfarth:

WELCOME men of the 35th Division! Considering you are new-comers, we would like to do everything to make you feel at home. We extend to you a cordial welcome and greetings from the Ruhr Valley. You have tried to veil your arrival here by doing such things as removing your divisional insignias. Nevertheless a little bird told us all about it. Before you arrived, there were other divisions here who didn't fare so well; namely the 84th, the 102nd, and the 29th not to mention the British. They all got knocked about a bit. You can see you won't have an easy time of it against the Ruhr defense lines. As we said before we will do our best to make you feel at home. We will try to make every day here seem like the "Fourth of July." There'll be plenty of fireworks.

They didn't lie. There were enough fireworks to last me a lifetime.

Looks Like We Made It

In the last few weeks of the war, Germans surrendered by the tens of thousands.

We knew that troops from the First Canadian Army were approaching from the north. The First Battalion, with tank support, was sent to make contact. That was us. We mounted the top of the tanks and moved out. We arrived at a small creek in front of some nameless town and immediately started drawing fire. A German Panzerfaust[35] hit a tank to our right and killed two men. Answering fire was given *en masse*. Soon the firing was heavier than ever, but it turned out that none of it was from the Germans. When things finally quieted down, a very British voice yelled, "Point them bloody guns the other way, lad!" We had made contact with the Canadians.

Captain John Davis had finally recovered from his wound and resumed command of our outfit, now as a major. Major Alfred C. Boatsman had been in command until Major Davis could arrive and take over command of the First Battalion.

We were soon reunited with our regiment, but we didn't have anything to shoot at. It was obvious that German resistance was breaking down all along the line. The race to the Rhine was on, and it was a short race.

For the first time since D-Day, the entire division was pulled out of the line and put in reserve. That's not to say we weren't busy. We even had some close-order drill: you know, hut two, three, four; hut two, three, four.

---

[35] A bazooka.

66

What a load of nonsense. After being in combat for so long, this routine was not only boring, but insulting. There were certain privledges that went with being a sergeant, however. I would march my men until we were out of sight of the CO and then order everyone to sit down.

This peaceful existence was too good to last. One day we received orders to be ready to move out in thirty minutes, but at the last minute the order was canceled for the remainder of the night. We did move the next morning, and that is when I saw the Rhine River. When I first saw it, I said to myself, "Now *there* is a river!" Up to now, what everyone had been calling rivers were just creeks. It looked almost exactly like Omaha Beach on D-Day. There were balloons overhead and aircraft filled the sky, flying back and forth. Trucks, jeeps, and men were all over the place. We had built a bridge across the Rhine without any resistance and it was ready to receive troops, trucks, and tanks. By nightfall, elements of the advance units had penetrated two thousand yards into Germany.

The war was all but over except for mopping up small pockets of resistance. It was now an all-out race to the Elbe River. Our regiment wiped out a pocket of resistance in Gelsenkirc and took off for the Elbe, riding tanks again. We reached the Elbe and set up our gun pointing across the river. Like the Rhine, the Elbe was a real river. We received no orders from anyone to do anything, so we just sat.

Early the next morning, we saw a man on the other side of the river waving a big, white bedsheet. He was a German, and the order came down the line to hold fire. We did, and the man walked down to the water, dropping off equipment as he came. He waded to the water and never stopped. The Elbe River is wide, but not very deep. This soldier just walked across the river and someone to our left took him into custody. He was the tip of the iceberg. After he appeared, the woods on the opposite side of the river came alive with surrendering German soldiers. We were there only seven days and took thousands of prisoners. We received orders to sit and wait for the advancing Russian Army.

May 8, 1945. The war is over! Unbelievably, the war is over! I looked at Rumca, and he looked back at me and said, "Tex, it looks like we made it." Then we both started crying.

In my life I've known many brave men, but Rumca was without a doubt one of the bravest. Back when we were still in the hedgerows, I saw him perform one of the most courageous acts I have ever witnessed. Rumca and I had been ordered to take up a defensive position and to hold our line until reinforcements arrived later in the day. We dug a foxhole and camouflaged our position with brush. Not knowing just when the reinforcements would arrive, we had taken a couple of extra boxes of ammunition with us. Each machine-gun belt held one hundred fifty rounds, so all together we had about one thousand rounds. We busied ourselves replacing the tracer[36] rounds in all of the gun belts. Every fifth round was a tracer that was great for zeroing in on your target, but it also allowed the enemy to zero in on your position. And that wasn't so great.

At 0600 hours, the Germans struck with a strong artillery attack. When it stopped, I looked up and it was just Rumca and me—and a squad of Germans moving straight toward us, spread out in attack formation. Right behind them were at least two more squads.

Rumca knew what to do. He loosened the clamp on our gun's tripod so that he could swing it in any direction as far as he needed to. He lined up the Germans on the far left of their line and let loose. Three men dropped like a rock. He just swung that gun right on down the line and kept firing. It was all I could do to keep feeding ammo into the gun. To this day, I don't know what in the world kept the barrel of our machine gun from literally melting. I guess it would have if we hadn't run out of bullets.

Yes, we ran out of ammo. Rumca looked at me and asked, "Any suggestions what we do now?"

"Yeah. Yank the bolt[37] and let's get out of here."

"They'll shoot us in the back if we do. Tex, I don't know about you, but the way I see it, we might as well die facing the enemy."

"Yeah. I guess so."

All Rumca had left was a Colt .45 with three clips. I had picked up an M-1 with several clips. I poked my rifle through the brush and started shooting at anything that moved. Rumca stood up! I never knew if he was just mad or scared, but he stood up and started shooting Germans as fast as could pull the trigger on that old .45. As soon as one clip would empty, he would eject it and slam home another. The whole time, naturally, he was cussing like a banshee. Well, more accurately, he was cussing in English and

---

[36] A bullet that leaves a trail.

[37] You never wanted to leave an operable gun for the enemy if you could help it.

Polish and screaming like a banshee—all at the same time. Just as he finished his last clip, the Germans decided they had enough of this crazy man and the whole German line started retreating.

Shortly afterwards, we were relieved. I told our company commander, Captain John Davis, what Rumca had done. I said that he surely deserved some kind of medal. Captain Davis agreed and said he would recommend a commendation and send it through channels. It came back as a Silver Star.

The war was over and the two of us had made it! How do two men make it through such an ordeal and come out alive? Looking at each other, the tears turned to grins. He grinned and I grinned, and then we grabbed each other and laughed and giggled like school kids. It was over, and we were alive! The whole time I was in Europe, Rumca was the only man I ever allowed myself to get close to, and we had both made it.

POW's were pouring in from everywhere, but fortunately, Rumca and I did not have to process them. We headed for the rear area. There was a vacant spot, I would guess about six or seven hundred acres, that was solid with Germans, Poles, Russians, and numerous other nationalities. They were being separated and loaded on trucks as fast as the trucks could get there. We found an MP who sold us a bottle of vodka, and Rumca and I got so drunk they had to haul us back to our gun position in a jeep. I don't remember it, but the crew we left there told us how we arrived. The next morning, my head felt like it was as big as a pumpkin, and it was throbbing like crazy.

Shortly thereafter, we started moving back toward the French coast. We took a different route than the one we fought for. As we traveled, I couldn't help but think of all the men who had died for this peaceful-looking land. When the unit ahead of us moved out, we would move into their place. This went on all through the French countryside until we reached the coast of France. There we were put up in a very large tent city. We also got a new company commander, one of the so-called "90-day wonders."[38] He was a spit-and-polish guy. This shavetail second lieutenant had us standing guard duty, doing close-order drill, and undergoing inspections of our tents and

---

[38] A man with a college degree could attend war college for ninety days and be commissioned a second lieutenant.

bunks regularly.

But what goes around comes around, and revenge can be oh, so sweet. One day we were walking along the beach and we caught a huge blue crab. It had the largest set of pincers any of us had ever seen. We took the crab back to our company area and sneaked it into this 90-day wonder's cot. About nine o'clock that night, after lights-out had been sounded, we heard a blood-curdling scream coming from his tent. We didn't dare go out to investigate. How could we? He had ordered us all to go to sleep, and we followed orders—we were all deep in slumber in our bunks. Some of the staff officers bunking with the lieutenant told us the story later. They said he came out of his cot with that huge blue crab on his foot, screaming at the top of his lungs. What goes around, comes around.

Shortly after arriving at the coast, we boarded a Liberty ship and sailed across the English Channel. When we arrived in England, however, we could not disembark. There were so many of us, we had to wait three days for the troops ahead of us to move out before we could. When we finally did get ashore, we headed for a bar in Camp Norfolk and got roaring drunk. A couple of "Bobbies"[39] got us by the scruff of the neck and threw us out of the bar and into the street. We complained about how ungrateful the British were because we had saved their bacon in France, but that was the whiskey talking. They fought as well as we did and a lot longer. They also   lost more men than we did, not to mention all the civilians killed in the air   raids throughout the war. We finally returned to Southhampton, and there was a boat as large or maybe even larger than the one I came to Europe on. On the side, in big bold letters, was the name *Queen Elizabeth*. We went home in style.[40]

Going home, I was only seasick four days. That's because it only took four days instead of the ten it had taken coming across on the *Queen Mary*. Of course, this time we weren't zig-zagging to avoid giving any U-boat a target. The *Elizabeth*'s captain just pinned that old boat's ears back and set sail for New York. Docking at New York Harbor, we looked down on a wharf alive with pretty girls and bands playing. I didn't get to spend any time in New York before I was sent to Fort Meade, Maryland. I didn't much more than hit Fort Meade than I was on a train headed for Fort Sam Houston in San Antonio, Texas.

---

[39]English policemen.

[40] There were 22,000 of us on board the *Queen Elizabeth* that trip. Among us was my co-author's father.

Crossing a footbridge

Sitting behind a heavy .30-caliber machine gun.

Still posing, this time behind a .50-caliber machine gun.

Medics didn't need to pose for anything. They saw as much combat as any rifleman.

A Dream Come True

As soon as I got to Fort Sam Houston, I requested and received a thirty-day convalescence furlough. I had hardly started walking toward the Austin Highway when a cab stopped and a man in the backseat asked me where I was going. I told him Austin. He said get in and I'll give you a ride. The guy was a pilot, and we drove to a local airport and flew to Austin. After we landed, I thanked him and quickly caught a ride to South Austin to my Aunt Edith's house. In those days, people could not do enough for men in uniform. If you were in a uniform, your money was no good. You couldn't pay for a ride or a meal because everyone wanted to show appreciation. They sure didn't spit on you like they would at the next generation of soldiers.

When I got out of the car, I saw the prettiest sight I have ever seen in my life. Sitting there in my aunt's yard were my dad's pickup truck and horse trailer. There was nobody home, but I heard what sounded like a rodeo going on across the road. A rodeo! This would be too good to be true. I walked over to the old roping arena and there it was—an honest-to-goodness rodeo.

I walked up to the gate, looking for a familiar face. I felt a gentle tug on my sleeve. I looked down into the beaming face of Aunt Edith. Then I was swarmed by my family. I was home!

I was surrounded by my cousins, my brother, my sisters, my aunts and uncles, my friends, and by Momma Nellie. My dad was sitting in the arena on a beautiful sorrell mare. He let out a yell like a panther, and here he came around the back of the bucking chutes. He did a wild dismount and grabbed me around the half-dozen or more who already had ahold of me. Weeping, praying, and yelling were all going on at the same time.

When things settled down, my dad handed me the reins to his sorrell and said, "Here she is, boy. Her name's Kitten and she's all yours." I had to make a round in the arena with everyone cheering and clapping. I don't know how many times I dreamed of this while I was in Europe. It was a dream I didn't think would ever come ture, but it had!

After I dismounted, we went to Aunt Edith's house and visited until late in the night; then we loaded up and headed for Mom and Dad's house. Dad was working on a ranch about forty miles from Austin, but it didn't seem to take any time at all to get there.

I slept like a rock for the first week, and then the nightmares began. The first time I woke up with Momma Nellie trying to hold me down as I screamed and tried to climb the wall. The nightmare was always the same: Germans were coming at me by the hundreds and no matter how many I killed, they just kept coming and coming and coming. I couldn't kill them all.

The healing began when I started riding with my dad as he checked the cattle. I credit that with saving my sanity. We were five miles from the nearest neighbor, and it was about fifteen miles to the nearest store. I would ride out into a lonely pasture, get off my horse, sit under a shade tree, and just listen to the quietness of nothing happening. Try to imagine the quiet: no machine guns, no mortar and artillery rounds falling all around me. And nobody trying to kill me. It was pure heaven. After about a month or two, the nightmares began to get farther and farther apart, until they finally went away.

The war was over and it was time for me to get on with my life.

Co-author's note: Two things struck me as Ed and I prepared this chapter. The first was a note he had put in the margin when he was describing one of the firefights he was involved in: "Please forgive my typing. I can do better, but I get nervous writing this stuff. It all comes back so vividly." The other was his telling me that as he prepared this part of the manuscript, he had a nightmare for the first time in fifty years—the same nightmare he had suffered after the war. Thankfully, that also passed quickly.

Chapter III
The Highway Patrol
1949-1957

I Loved Being a Cowboy

I worked with Papa John at the Hill Ranch, located in the corner of Hays and Travis Counties, for about a year before he left for another job. John Winkley, the owner of the ranch, was trying to cash in on the post-war home-building boom and was constructing a subdivision in Austin. He knew Dad was a very good carpenter and he asked him if he would head up the construction. With the job would go a nice increase in pay, so Papa John took it.

Mr. Winkley asked me if I would take Papa John's place as the foreman of the ranch. I didn't have to give the offer a second thought. For a year and a half, I'd been working beside Dad, so I was already well-versed in how to operate the day-to-day functions. I found myself in charge of a six-thousand-acre ranch and thirteen hundred head of livestock. This was a great responsibility that I didn't take lightly.

Movies and TV have so misrepresented the cowboy and ranch life that it's hard for most people to comprehend how hard the work really is. There is always something that needs fixing: a fence, a corral, or a leaking roof. In the winter, in the middle of a drought, or during the blazing heat of a Texas summer, the cowboy has to carry feed to the cattle or drive the herd to the feed. Either way it's hard, back-breaking, and never-ending work. I polished more than my share of saddle leather with the seat of my jeans in the next couple of years checking the herd, riding fence, and generally doing what cowboys have to do every day to keep a ranch going. I promise you that not one time did I single-handedly fight off a band of blood-thristy rustlers

76

or scalp-hunting Indians with nothing but a trusty six-shooter. I sure didn't save a poor widow's ranch from being foreclosed on by either evil bankers or large ranch owners who wanted the poor woman's land for the water rights. No, sir. It was hard work with not a nickel's worth of excitement. I loved it more than anything in the world.

When you're not mending fences, carrying feed, or helping a cow birth a new calf, then there are always cattle down with some kind of disease. Medical research in the last few decades has not only advanced in humans. Medicines to fight diseases in livestock have developed so much that cattlemen today take for granted easily cureable diseases that were real killers in the 1940s and 1950s.

One of the worst killers I ever faced was the tiny screwworm. They came in the summer, and if not watched closely and fought to the death, they would destroy a whole herd before you could turn around. Screwworms were carried by flies, and in those days there was no screwworm irradication pro-

Me with my horse Kitty; Bully, a Brahma bull; and Papa John on the Hill Ranch in Hays County shortly after I returned home from Europe. Kitten was very special to me. All during the war, I sent money home to help Papa John and Mama Nellie. Somehow, Papa John saved five hundred dollars of that money and bought Kitten. When I got home, she was broken and ready for me. I loved that horse.

This was made on the Hill Ranch right after I returned from the battlefields in Europe.
L-R: John Reimer, Me, Artie Grumblis, Kite Myers, John Gooding on Kitten.

gram: you had to check every head of stock at least once a week. If a cow received any kind of wound that broke the skin and you failed to find or see the wound and treat it within a week, all too often you would find the cow had literally been eaten by the screwworms. Not only was that a terrible sight, but the poor cow also died in agony.

From 1946 through 1948, I worked with a cowboy named Kite Myers. Kite had been cowboying for a long time and had a ton of experience. To this day, I know of few men that I admire more than him. Even after I became a Highway Patrolman and then a Texas Ranger, I kept in touch with Kite whenever I had an opportunity. As of this writing (2001), he is ninety-three-years old and lives with his daughter at Bee Caves, Texas. I am proud to be able to call Kite Myers one of the best friends I've ever had.

I've sometimes wondered if I would have remained a cowboy if Mr. Winkley had not sold the Hill Ranch. I'll never know, but I do know one thing for an absolute certainty: those two years on the ranch saved my life. I was a mental wreck after the war and those wonderful days on that ranch gave me the time and solitude to cure myself. I loved being a cowboy almost as much as I did being a Texas Ranger later. I hated it when Mr. Winkley sold the ranch, but he did and I had to find a job. I moved to Austin and went to work in construction with Papa John.

Little did I realize that when I moved to Austin, my life was getting ready to take a huge turn—a turn I had never given a thought to. My sister Loma had gotten a job in Austin as secretary for the sheriff of Travis County, an ex-Ranger named Rip Collins. It's hard to believe today when everyone has a car that cars were still a rarity in the 1940s. Loma didn't have a car, so I carried her to and from her job at the courthouse. During these trips, I became aquainted with two Highway Patrolmen whose names have long since escaped me.

It was in June or July of 1948 that the patrolmen told me that a Highway Patrol school would be starting in Decmeber and that veterans were getting preference and extra points on their test scores. With my military background, they said I stood a better than excellent chance of being accepted and that I should apply.

Construction work was okay, but I was tired of it. And even though I loved horses and cattle, I knew I didn't want to end life as a full-time cowboy. As I said earlier, cowboying isn't a bit glamorous: it's hard work. It's not romantic riding fences in freezing weather one day and scorching heat the next. And let me tell you: worming cattle, goats, and sheep is about as nasty a job as you can imagine. Building fences from rocks you find lying in the pasture is hard on the back, and dipping cows that don't want to be dipped . . . well, it's just not a bit glamorous. When I compared all of that hard work to riding around in a car and getting paid for it—well, give me that application!

I filled out the application and sent it in. I honestly didn't think I would ever hear anything from it. To my surprise, I was invited to go to Austin and take the entrance examination. The test was held in the senate chamber in the State Capitol. The exam was tough, but somehow I managed to pass. However, that didn't automatically mean acceptance into the Highway Patrol. Until I heard whether or not I was going to have the opportunity to be a Highway Patrolman, I had to go back to work.

I'll never forget the day I was accepted. We had been working in cement all day. Not only is that tough work, but it's also filthy. My whole body was covered in cement dust, my hands were split and bleeding from blisters, and I had on a pair of laced-up work boots and work clothes all covered in cement. I was getting ready to clean up when someone yelled to me, "There's a police car sitting out there! The officer is looking for you, Ed. What have you done now?"

"I haven't been doing anything but working."

I went out to the patrol car to see what the officer wanted. Sergeant K. B. Hallmark was sitting in the car and he told me to get in. Not only was I filthy, but it was hot and I had been sweating. I knew I smelled worse than a wild boar. I said, "I hate to get in your car as filthy as I am and stinking the way I do."

Sergeant Hallmark looked at me and said, "Don't worry about that. We're looking for people that aren't afraid of work. Get in."

Sitting there in that patrol car, with me nastier than a bear and stinking worse than a polecat, Sergeant Hallmark gave me an oral interview. When he finished he said, "I'll send this in and you'll probably be hearing from us." I could hardly believe it when a few weeks later I got a letter from the Department of Public Safety to report to Camp Mabry on December 1, 1948. Training school would be for thirteen weeks and school pay would be one hundred dollars for the whole thirteen weeks. I was told to report with a pair of black boots, two pairs of khaki pants, two shirts, one pair of black gloves, and a motorcycle helmet.

At that time, Camp Mabry was just several old Army barracks on the outskirts of Austin. The ground floor of our barracks was the mess hall, while our bunks were upstairs. Another building housed the classrooms and headquarters for the colonel and his staff.

For the next thirteen weeks, our routine never changed. We rolled out at five o'clock in the morning. Burl Avery was in charge of our physical conditioning, and Burl knew as much about physical training as I did about birthing babies, maybe less. But every morning he made us run from our barracks over to a machine shop, to the airport hangar, to the armory, down to the front gate, and then back to our barracks. That circuit was a good two miles if it was a foot.

The first morning was the worst. It was December and it was cold. Some of the men got about halfway around the circuit and started throwing up and falling out with cramps. Avery told us, "If you don't come in as a bunch—if there are any stragglers—you're going to have to run the whole thing again."

There were several stragglers and we told him, "Man, we can't run that far. Give us a break. This is the first time most of us have ever had to run to amount to anything." Too bad—run. Having been in construction, ranch work, and the Army, I was in pretty fair physical shape and I made it around the course, but I was pretty winded when I finished. Fortunately for me, so many men were choking down that I didn't have to run very fast. If it had not been for that, I'm not a bit sure I could have made it. Somehow we all finished, but not in a tight bunch.

For the next thirteen weeks, our routine never changed. After our morning run and breakfast, we would spend the rest of the morning in the classroom studying a little criminal law, but mainly traffic law. In the afternoon, it was two hours on the pistol range, one hour on motorcycles, and another hour of physical training. Then more running. We started school with one hundred five recruits and finished with seventy-three.

About a week before graduation, W. J. Elliott, chief of the Highway Patrol, came in to talk to us. Chief Elliott was a grizzled old man who chewed tobacco while he

Highway Patrol Chief W.J. Elliott

talked. He was a one-man operation as head of the Highway Patrol. With one secretary, he personally ordered all the department's cars, uniforms, weapons—everything. Just him and one secretary! Today you have a whole staff of who knows how many people just to handle any one of the things he and his secretary handled by themselves.

I'll never forget the speech he gave us that day. It was short and, boy, did he ever get straight to the point: "Just remember two things—first, the badge can get you girls, and girls can get your badge. Second, it took a three-cent stamp to get you here and we can replace you with another three-cent stamp!" And that was it.

We were handed a slip of paper with three blanks on it. We were to state our choices of three places we would like to be stationed. Those of us who were single were told that preferences to duty stations with the best housing and schools would be given to the married men. We single men would get whatever was left. I knew then it didn't really matter what I put down; I was going to be sent wherever they wanted. First, I put down Austin because my family was there. Second, I wrote Balmorhea out in West Texas near Midland so that I could be close to ranching. Third, since I knew that they were shorthanded in Houston and that nobody wanted to be stationed there, I put it down. I figured I might as well because that's where they would probably post me anyway. I was right. I was ordered to report for duty in Houston on March 1, 1949. My starting pay was two hundred and thirty dollars a month.

With Lena, 1953

My first partner on the Highway Patrol was an old-timer named Ed Carmichael. A rookie like me never drove until his partner, the lead man, saw fit to let him drive. The lead man was totally in charge of the "black and white"—that's what we called our patrol car. He decided when to

83

stop, when and where to eat, and everything else. I was fortunate to have Ed as a teacher and I learned a lot from him.

I had ridden second seat for about two or three weeks when Ed threw me the keys and said, "You ain't ever going to learn any younger. Now you go where you want; stop and eat when you want to eat. You're in the lead. All I'm going to do is witness if you have to kick somebody's butt. If you get in a shooting scrap, I'll be here to help you." We worked that way until Ed said I was "broke in." When the next group of rookies came out of patrol school, I got a partner to break in myself. He was a fine young man named Heston Thomas.

I worked Heston like Ed had worked me. We worked wrecks, chased speeders, and did routine patrol work. Besides our regular monthly pay, when we were on patrol we were given a meal allowance that worked out to about thirty to thirty-five dollars a month. As was usual in those days, we worked at least ten hours a day, six days a week. After about four weeks, I felt Heston was ready to lead and I started letting him drive. Heston was a good man and made an outstanding Highway Patrolman. He and I got along fine.

I enjoyed my time in Houston, but I wasn't destined to stay there long.

It was in Houston that I met the prettiest little girl that God ever put on the face of this earth: Lena Richardson. Nine of us patrolmen were living in the same boarding house. One of my roommates, Joe Mladenka, was dating a young lady named Jean Richardson. One day he tried to call Jean for a date. Jean's older sister Lena answered the phone and when Joe asked to speak to Jean, Lena wanted to know what he wanted to talk to her about.

"I want to ask her for a date."

"No, she can't go unless you bring me and our other sister Bobbie a date. I know you've got nine patrolmen out there and we want a date or Jean's not going a step."

Joe wanted a date with Jean pretty bad, so he grabbed Ernie Scholl and me and told us we had dates that night whether we wanted them or not! Ernie and I didn't have anything else to do and it sounded pretty good to us, so we got dressed and went over to the Richardson's house.

I learned later that Lena had already seen me. She had spotted me in passing one time when I was with Joe as we stopped by to see Jean. I had a habit of wearing my hat pulled down over my face, and I guess I looked like I was seventy years old. Before we arrived, Lena had told Jean, "I'll bet you a dollar that I get that old man!"

When we arrived at their house, I was bareheaded and all dolled up in my Sunday-go-to- meeting suit. Lena and I hit it off from the first. After that first date, we'd go dancing a lot at a local nightclub called the Plantation Club. We just had a wonderful time together. Nine months later, on September 8, 1950, Lena and I were married. That was the happiest day of my life.

Lena and I wanted to take a long weekend in Austin for our honeymoon. In those days, though, you didn't work a five-day week: you worked six days a week. A long weekend was Saturday and Sunday, so I had to ask my captain, Glen Rose, for the extra day off. He said, "No. I'm not giving you permission to get married. You're making a big mistake getting married." Needless to say, that didn't set too well with me. I told him I was getting married whether he approved it or not. I guess he realized I was serious. He finally said, "I'll give you the weekend off, but that's all I can afford. We're short of men and cars, so that's all I can give you."

Police officers are noted for their practical jokes and some can be pretty stout. I got word from a friend, Dub Cowen, that an elaborate joke was being brewed for Lena and me on our wedding night and that we had better get out of town. Some of my "friends" were going to arrest us and put us in jail. I love a good joke as well as the next person, but that was going a bit far. Lena and I slipped out of town and we were married in nearby Hempstead, Texas.

In 1950, only single officers were stationed at the headquarters office in Houston. I guess they thought the single officers needed a little closer supervision. So as soon as Lena and I were married, I was transferred to nearby Baytown, effective October 15. I didn't ask for Baytown: I was assigned Baytown.

Baytown is a few miles east of Houston, right next to the San Jacinto Battlefield. Having just gotten married, Lena and I didn't have much to move and I could get everything we had in my patrol car. Her cedar chest and my uniforms were about all we owned. On the positive side, that meant that we didn't need a very big apartment. It didn't take us long to settle into Baytown. I worked out of there until 1957, when I transferred to the Rangers and we moved back to Houston.

Baytown

My partner in Baytown had already been working for some time, so I didn't have to break in another man. I had gotten along great with Ed Carmichael and Heston Thomas, but I regret that I can't say the same about my new partner. We just did not like one another. He was small man and I think he suffered from "small-man syndrome." It seemed like he was determined to prove to the world, but probably mainly to himself, that he was a tough guy.

We had been told in recruit school that we might have a partner we didn't get along with. The answer to that problem then was much different than it is today. As I said earlier, the chief of the Highway Patrol, W. J. Elliott, was crusty. He had a simple solution when partners clashed: get somewhere out of sight and go at it until one of you whipped the other; then get back in the car and go to work. Can you imagine a commander telling his men to work out their problems like that today? The lawsuits would never stop.

I took my new partner's guff for about six months. Then one day he said something that hit me wrong and made me mad as the devil. I didn't say anything. I was driving, and when I came to a logging road that went back in the woods, I turned into it. After I got down the road far enough so that no civilians could see us or interfere, I stopped the car and invited him out. I told him, "Get out. I've had enough of your gruff. I'm going to whip you from one end of this field to the other." Not only was I about a foot taller and fifty pounds heavier than he was, but also I still had the muscles I had built working in construction for the better part of a year. He wisely declined to get out of the car. After that, we got along just fine. However, he shortly thereafter asked for and received a transfer to another station.

The last man I worked with on the Highway Patrol was Gene Lockhart. He was a shy boy, but he was a truly nice guy and as good a partner as a man could ever want. He was single and briefly lived with Lena and me. We had been riding together for nearly six weeks, and I decided it was time for Gene to lead. One afternoon we had just finished doing our reports and were walking to the car when I did the same thing to him that Ed Carmichael had done to me. I tossed him the car keys and told him he would never learn any younger; it was time for him to lead.

The Case of the Stolen Ford

It turned out that I had picked quite a night (Saturday, November 25, 1956) for Gene to earn his spurs as lead driver. We drove over to US Highway 90, which was our was main patrol area and also our primary problem. In the years before Interstate 10, Highway 90 was the main artery between Houston and Beaumont and was known as Blood Alley. In a single one-year period, I had twenty-two people killed in my twenty-mile stretch of Highway 90 alone. I don't know how many more were killed on other parts of the highway, but I imagine the numbers would be about the same.

On this particular night, we had just sat down to eat supper at Butch Hillard's Cafe when a wild-eyed man came running into the café, shouting that there had just been a terrible wreck a short distance up the road. He said that a bunch of people were dead and added, "There's one laying covered up with a sheet. A big truck and a car hit head-on up there."

Supper was forgotten. People naturally think that the wreck they've just witnessed simply has to be the worst ever. They mean well, but usually their imagination gets the better of them. But sometimes they're right. This was one of those times. I would not have let Gene lead that night if I had known we were headed for the worst single night in my Highway Patrol career.

As we drove, I told Gene to just remember what he had learned in patrol school and what he had learned driving with me for the last six weeks and everything would be fine. Arriving at the wreck, I knew immediately that this was a bad one.

A sixteen-year-old kid, Delano Zwahr of Crosby, had been driving a farm tractor, heading home. Joe Frazier, 24, of Kountze, was heading west when he attempted to pass Zwahr. He did not swing out far enough and clipped the left rear wheel of the tractor, tearing it off. Frazier's car flipped and veered across the road straight into the path of an eighteen-wheeler loaded with oil-field drill-stem pipe. The trucker had locked down his brakes, but he still hit the car at about the door post on the passenger side and shoved it down the road about twenty feet. Frazier's car was totally demolished.

Gene took his accident investigation notebook and walked around the rear of what was left of the car. When the car had hit the truck, it threw the driver down into the passenger side of the floorboard. As the car was pushed down the road by the truck, the door had come open. Frazier's body was lying in the open door. His chest was crushed and there was blood everywhere. When Gene looked down, the dead man's eyes were staring Gene right in the face. Gene whirled around saying, "I can't look at that."

I guess I had seen too many mutilated bodies in the war. Dead bodies had little effect on me. I took the accident form and wrote out a report. After I finished the accident investigation, Gene and I drove to the hospital in Baytown to question the kid, Delano Zwahr, who had been driving the tractor. He was fortunate: he only had a broken arm. The truck driver wasn't hurt at all.

Finishing at the hospital, we started back to Highway 90 with Gene still driving. I told him not to feel bad about his reaction to his first fatal accident. It was natural. In time, he would be able to handle what he had just seen and much more. If he couldn't, he would never make it in the Highway Patrol.

We had barely left the accident scene when our radio started blaring. Buddy Bean and A. L. Roberts, two Highway Patrolmen from nearby Liberty, had recognized a 1957 Ford as stolen and had attempted to stop it. Upon seeing the patrol car, the thieves took off. Bean and Roberts were right on their tail, but because of the heavy oncoming traffic, they were not able to pass. Soon both cars were roaring down Highway 90. At times—when traffic allowed—they were reaching one hundred miles per hour and more. Gunshots came from the Ford, blowing holes in the patrol car's windshield and knocking off the rearview mirror. Bean and Roberts returned fire, but were not able to stop the fleeing car thieves. We were requested to set up a roadblock at the intersection of the Crosby-Lynchburg Road.[9]

I looked at Gene and said, "Stand on it."

Just as we came into the intersection, I saw headlights coming fast. Gene asked me if I wanted him to put the car across the road.

"No."

I reached under the front seat and unzipped the boot where I kept my 12-gauge shotgun. I walked to the center stripe of the highway and waited. Why I walked into the middle of the road, I have no idea, because it really wasn't a very smart thing to do. Soon I could see both sets of headlights and they were really moving. The patrol car was still on the fleeing Ford's bumper.

They were coming so fast that I was only able to get off one shot at the driver's window before they were past me. They went by me so fast that at first I thought I might have hit the patrol car. Fortunately, I didn't. Later, Gene said he had fired once with his revolver.

About a quarter of a mile past our roadblock was a curve. The Ford was going so fast that when it went into the curve, it started sliding. It side-swiped a Ford station wagon, fortunately hurting no one, and then slid directly in front of a Cadillac, matching headlights head-on. The impact with the Cadillac, which had been traveling at about thirty-five or forty miles per hour, was so hard that it drove the much bigger and heavier Cadillac backwards six or eight feet.

As soon as the suspects passed us, Gene and I jumped into our car and headed for the accident scene, arriving right behind Bean and Roberts.

As I got out, I saw that the engine of the Cadillac was on fire. I ran over to it to get anyone out that I could. There were two people in the front seat: a man and woman, both dead. Two women were in the backseat, but they were still alive—barely. I pulled on the lady that was on the passenger side. She took a couple of breaths, stiffened in my arms, and died with me holding her. There was nothing more I could do for her, so I laid her down and headed around to the other side of the car. The other lady was behind the driver. By now, the fire was getting hot and I was afraid it would hit the gas tank and cause an explosion. I grabbed the lady and pulled her out of the car. Even though her legs from the knee to the hip were badly broken and crushed, she would survive. As gently as I could, I laid her in the grass in the ditch. While I was doing this, Gene was calling for an ambulance.

Having done all I could at the Cadillac, I went to the stolen Ford. The driver, obviously dead, was lying on the ground just outside the door on the driver's side. In those days, most cars had a chrome hornring inside the steering wheel. The hornring had broken and gone through the roof of the driver's mouth and was sticking out the top of his head. Another man, one of the shooters, was in the backseat and still alive. I had seen enough men die to know he wasn't going to make it.

I got in the backseat with him and could see that he was bleeding around his skull along the hairline. I took his hair and lifted it. I could see his brain pulsating every time his heart beat. He had hit the overhead light in the roof of the car and broken his skull. He took two or three breaths and died.

Buddy Bean was also in the car, trying to extricate the other man who was also still alive. His head had gone through the windshield and one of his eyes was almost completely ripped from its socket. When Buddy lifted him up to pull him out of the car, the guy stuck a small pistol in Buddy's face and tried to shoot. Buddy jammed the suspect back down on the dash and put his knee on the back of his neck, cussing all the while. By then, a crowd had gathered and I told Buddy to watch his language: "We've got an audience."

He said, "I don't care. I'm going to kill him. Here I am trying to save this thug's life and he's trying to kill me."

"I know, but just settle down."

Buddy took a deep breath and said, "I'm okay."

Between Buddy and the wreck, the lowlife didn't have any fight left in him. Buddy raised the guy up a bit, and I ran my hand under his chest and got the pistol. By then, the ambulances had arrived, and the workers gathered up the dead and injured and carried them to a nearby hospital in Liberty.

When we finished with the accident scene and things calmed down, Gene and I headed back for our patrol area. I decided to try to lighten the night up a little. I told him that our captain, Glen Rose, would "probably want to talk to you about tonight."

"What about? I haven't done anything wrong."

"Gene, you've just had six people killed. You're the lead man and this area is your responsibility. I promise you, Captain Rose will want to talk to you."

"Well, I don't know what I could have done about it."

"Hey, you're the lead man. Those people were your responsibility."

This had definitely not been one of Gene's better nights, and I figured I had carried this joke as far as it needed to go. I told Gene not to worry about it. He had done nothing wrong, but with this many people dead, the captain would be out tomorrow.

Captain Rose did come out and conduct an investigation. Of course, he found that everyone had acted properly and that was the end of it.

As for Gene, he retired several years ago after a truly outstanding and distinguished career in the Highway Patrol. As of this writing, Gene lives in Huntsville and I occasionally get to talk to him.

Helpless

I worked many very bad accidents during my years as a Highway Patrolman, but none affected me as much as the one my partner Perry Dickerson and I worked near the San Jacinto River Bridge on Highway 90. It was late in the evening when we got the call that two eighteen-wheelers had collided. One was lying on its side in the roadway and the other was hanging over the bridge's guardrail. The only thing that kept it from plunging into the stream was that it was still connected to the trailer by the fifth wheel. The situation was critical: not only was the truck on fire, but its fuel tanks had ruptured and fuel was pouring over the truck cab feeding the growing flames.

Suddenly, somebody yelled that the driver was still in the cab and couldn't get out. We got down the embankment as fast as possible. Looking up, I saw the most horrible sight I had seen since the war. The impact of the wreck had jammed the truck's doors closed and the driver was frantically kicking and hitting at the windshield and door glass. He was trying to either kick out a window or kick open one of the doors.

The truck cab was so far above us we couldn't reach it and due to the fire, we couldn't climb down to the cab from above. Never have I felt as helpless as I did standing there not being able to do a thing but watch and, even worse, listen as that poor driver burned to death. Thankfully, smoke soon covered the cab and we didn't have to witness the driver burn. I sincerely hope that the smoke suffocated him before the flames got him.

I had seen people burn to death before. It is one of the most horrible sights you can imagine. Inspite of my war experience, it was difficult for me to stand helplessly by and watch a man die such a death. If this had been during the war, I would have shot the poor guy and been patted on the back for showing him mercy. But this wasn't the war. Even after the flames finally burned themselves out, there was nothing we could do until the cab cooled enough to be touched.

Meanwhile, we called for a wrecker to get the rigs back on their wheels and out of the right-of-way. The wrecker we got was from Crosby and was not big enough to get the job done, so we called Duke's Wrecker Service in Houston. Since Duke's had a contract with Greyhound Bus Company to handle all their wrecked and disabled buses, his wreckers were big enough. They arrived about midnight.

Even though the wreck had happened several hours earlier, the cab that had burned was still too hot to touch, so we started on the other rig. We got that truck upright and Duke pulled it over to the side of the road and out of the way. Then we started on its trailer. The trailer and its freight weighed about fifty thousand pounds. Duke hooked his wrecker to the trailer and started his winch. It wound and wound, but instead of the trailer lifting, we saw the wrecker starting to slide backward. Duke stopped the winch and pulled his truck up to a huge tree just off the roadway. He put a giant chain around the tree and hooked it around his bumper. He got back in the cab and started the winch in low gear. Then he jumped out of the cab and ran around to the front of the truck. When we saw him put the truck between himself and the cable, we didn't need any encouragement. We joined him, double pronto. Considering the tension on that cable, if it had snapped, it would have gone through the cab of the wrecker like a red-hot knife through melted butter. It didn't snap, but it kept pulling. I began to wonder if Duke was going to pull his wrecker into. The wrecker and the cable held, and the trailer finally came upright. Duke kept pulling until it cleared the road.

Then it was time to work on the other truck. I wasn't looking forward to this job. I don't know where the ladder or the pry bar came from, but they appeared and I climbed up to the truck cab. At the cab's door, I took a deep breath and forced the door open. If you have ever smelled burning flesh, you know what I faced. The weather was cold, and I had on a pair of gloves lined with rabbit fur that my wife had given me for Christmas. I reached in and pulled the driver out of the truck.

About that time, the truck's owner arrived from San Antonio. This truck had been loaded with bananas. A few had been burned, but most were in good condition. All the truck owner wanted to know was if his load of bananas was ruined. Duke told him, rather pointedly, that he had just had a driver burn to death in as horrible a manner as he could imagine. The owner couldn't have cared less. His only worry was the bananas. He made me sick. But Duke extracted a little bit of revenge. He walked over to me and whispered in my ear, "He doesn't know it yet, but that attitude just cost him another hundred dollars." In the 1950s, a hundred dollars was a lot more than it is now.

Luckily, there was an old bypass that ran around the bridge where traffic could be diverted. Otherwise, we would have had a big mess. We finally got everything cleared away and Duke pulled the trailers and trucks away.

We finished about ten o'clock the next morning. I was exhausted. When I got home, I hit the bed and collapsed.

As for the gloves that Lena had given me for Christmas, I left them under the bridge.

Kicked, Stomped, and Clawed

During my years on the Highway Patrol, I worked just about every kind of case that a patrolman can work. They were not all on the highway.

For a long time, there was one beer joint after another just outside the eastern city limits of Houston. Inevitably, we would get two or three calls a week to handle a fight, usually between eleven and one o'clock in the morning. Working ten hours a day, six days a week, about the last thing you wanted to work was a fight between a couple of drunks at some old honky-tonk. But orders are orders, so we worked the fights.

The first call I got concerned a gang fight at the Dew Drop Inn. That particular night, I was working by myself. Trust me, it's a big mistake to handle a gang fight by yourself. A huge mistake.

As soon as I got the call, I headed for the Dew Drop Inn, running wide open. I don't know what I thought I was going to do when I got there, but I'm sure I didn't plan on things working out the way they did. Pulling into the parking lot, I saw what looked like a sea of people fighting. Everybody was hitting somebody, knocking first this one down, then another. I jumped out of my car and grabbed the closest person to me. Just as I grabbed this guy, somebody hit me over the back of the head with a beer bottle. It didn't break, but it left a knot on the back of my head as big as a person's fist. I went down. By the time I got on back my feet I had been kicked, stomped, and clawed. Obviously, my badge and uniform didn't impress them in the least.

I still don't know how, but I managed to get out of there with my gun, my badge, and my handcuffs all intact. But that was all that was in one piece: my britches were ripped to shreds and the seashells that covered the parking lot had skinned my boots up so bad I didn't know if they could ever be repaired. I was dirt, mud, grime, and blood from head to foot. That was enough for me. I do not consider myself a coward, but I'm no fool, either. If they wanted to beat one another to death, that was fine with me. I headed for the house. I needed a little rest, a bath, and a complete change of clothes bad.

When I got back on duty, the first person I met was Deputy Sheriff Fats Brown. Fats was stationed in Baytown as a resident deputy. I'll never forget what he said to me: "Boy, what in the world was your hurry to get to that fight?"

"Fats, tell me if I'm wrong, but we are supposed to break them up, aren't we?"

"Yes, but there's ways to handle it. In the future, when you hear of a gang fight like that, go over to Crosby and then come through Lake Houston and come around that way. Let 'em fight awhile. That way, by the time you get there, they will have fought themselves out, they'll be easy to handle, and no one can say that you didn't obey your orders."

"Fats, I sure wish you had told me that before I got the crap stomped out of me."

A Texas Ranger

I worked as a Highway Patrolman for eight years, but in the back of my mind I always hoped that a vacancy would come up in the Texas Rangers and that I might join that organization. I had grown up listening to Papa John talk about the old Rangers that he used to ride with back in the 1920s while he gathered cattle to be dipped.

The number of Highway Patrolmen in those days was pretty small. If a prison break occurred at, say, the Sugarland unit or at any of the prisons in our area, we would drop whatever we were doing and chase convicts for as long as it took to catch them. With my ranching background and abilities with horses, I was usually assigned a horse and followed the bloodhounds chasing the fleeing prisoners. I became well acquainted with the Ranger captain of Company A headquartered in Houston, Hardy Purvis, and his sergeant, Johnny Klevenhagen. It was not an intimate relationship, just a casual acquaintance. However, I never passed up an opportunity for them to see me. Understand that in those days, becoming a Ranger was totally different from what it is today. There were no written tests, no interview boards, no nothing. If the captain had an opening in his company and he wanted you to be his Ranger, you became a Texas Ranger. That was it.

In the late 1950s, there were only fifty-one Rangers to cover the entire state. Company A had only eight men, including the captain and the sergeant. They may have been few in number, but they covered all of the ground they stood on. Company A's territory was the same as Region I of the Highway Patrol: forty-two counties in the southeast corner of the state. This ran from Houston to Beaumont, Port Arthur up to Woodville, St. Au-

Colonel Homer Garrison had just sworn me in as the newest Texas Ranger moments before this photo was taken on May 15, 1957, at the DPS's headquarters in Austin.
(Courtesy of Texas Ranger Hall of Fame and Museum in Waco.)

gustine across to Huntsville and on up to Bryan, then down to Columbus, Bay City, and Galveston, then back to Houston. With six men plus the captain and sergeant, that meant each Ranger had an average of seven counties to work. I don't have any idea how many people this included. Many of the small counties only had the sheriff and a few deputies to enforce the peace and solve crimes in the whole county.

About the only thing the Department of Public Safety could offer the larger cities was the crime lab in Austin, which was as good a state lab as any in the nation. This was in 1957, long before all the modern technology of today. As we used to say, we did everything by hand.

My chance to become a Ranger came when Captain Hardy Purvis retired. At that time, all a promotion involved was that everybody moved up a notch. Johnny Klevenhagen was Captain Purvis' sergeant, so he moved up to captain and Eddie Oliver was made sergeant. My Highway Patrol sergeant, James Engleand, was a good man and a friend and he knew that I wanted to be a Ranger. One day he came out to my area and told me that the Rangers had a vacancy in Houston and if I still wanted to be a Ranger, I should drive over to Houston talk to Captain Klevenhagenn. I asked him when I could go and he said, "There's no time better than now."

I didn't need any more encouragement: I left immediately for Houston. The Rangers have always had an open-door policy, and I had no trouble getting in to see Captain Klevenhagen. We had a nice visit and I told him I wanted to be a Ranger and why.

He told me he would love to have me and had been hoping for several reasons that I would apply. He said that having been in the area eight years, I already knew the territory well and I knew most of the officers. He said that he knew that if he brought in a new man from out of the county, it would take much too long to train him. He was going to Austin the next day and would put my name in the pot for the position.

I drove back to Baytown floating on cloud nine. At least I had a chance. As the weeks wore on and I did not hear from anyone, I had just about decided that Captain Klevenhagen had changed his mind and didn't want me to be one of his Rangers. I had been working nights, and one day as I was helping Lena clean out a flower bed, Captain Rose called. He asked me how long it would take me to get to his office in Houston. I was dirty and muddy from digging and I told him I would need time to clean up. He said, "Just forget it, then. A Ranger captain has just been in my office and he wanted to take you to Austin to be sworn in. But if you don't have time . . ."

That was as far as he got. I dropped the phone, showered, shaved in record time, and was on my way to Houston. As soon as I got there, Captain Klevenhagen loaded me in his car and we set sail for Austin, where we spent the night. Early the next morning, we went to the office of Colonel Homer Garrison, the director of the Texas Department of Public Safety. After a few pleasantries, he had me raise my right hand and swear to uphold the laws of the state of Texas and the Constitutions of the United States and Texas. When I finished the oath, he pinned the badge of a Texas Ranger on my shirt. I nearly lost it at that point, but Rangers don't show that kind of emotion, at least not in public. I thanked him and said I would try my best to make him a good hand. He said that Captain Klevenhagen was the man I was working for and he was the man I had to please.

We drove back to Houston—I think. I don't remember much about

100

that trip. I do remember looking at that badge at least a hundred times, probably more. My duty station was to be Houston. It was May 15, 1957, and I was a Texas Ranger!

Chapter IV

The Houston Years
1957-1963

Hey, Boy

It took Lena and me a couple of trips to Houston to find a house. Ben Garret, a retired Highway Patrolman who was currently working for Humble Oil[41] as an investigator, told us about a house across the street from his home. The house would fit us perfectly and we bought it. Lena and I packed up the goods we had accumulated during our eight years of marriage and moved to our new home in Houston. It turned out to be a really great move. The Goodings and the Garrets became the best of friends.

When I took up my station in Houston, I did little the first few weeks but attend schools and ride with detectives from the Houston Police Department. I tried to observe and learn as much about criminal law and procedures as I could.

My first official function as a Texas Ranger was to attend a barbeque at Lake Houston that was being given to welcome me to the Rangers and to Company A. What a day that was! The first thing I was told was that I would be the "hey boy" until a newer man joined the company. Anytime anyone wanted anything, he would yell out, "Hey, boy!" That was fine with me. I couldn't have cared less. I was a Texas Ranger and that was all that mattered. Next to being alive at the end of the war and marrying Lena, this was the happiest day of my life.

I'll never forget that barbeque. I met some true giants in the law enforcement business: Buster Kern, the legendary sheriff of Harris County and Captain Klevenhagen's best friend; Ug Williams, Sheriff Kern's chief deputy; and Woody Stevenson, a captain in the Houston Police Department.

One of the guys said, "Hey, boy! Go out to Captain Klevenhagen's car." He wanted me to get something that he had forgotten, and I don't re-

---

[41] Humble Oil is now Exxon.

member what it was. The captain's car was parked right beside Jim West's car. Jim was an oil man for West Productions and a very close friend of the Rangers.

Walking past West's car, I saw more radio equipment than I had seen since the war. He had a state-of-the-art communications system. The dashboard looked like the control panel of a superjet. I just had to get a better look at that equipment, so I opened the door. What I didn't know, but everyone else did, was that his car was also rigged with an elaborate alarm system. This was long before police scanners, but he had gotten a police radio. He could listen in on not only our calls, but also the frequencies of all the police forces—including the sheriff's office and the DPS offices.[42] Anyway, when I opened the door, every light on the car started to blink and the horn started blowing. For a second, I thought I was back in Europe.

Mart Jones
(Courtesy of The Texas Ranger Hall of Fame and Museum, Waco, Texas)

Rangers are notorious pranksters, and I had been set up but good. Everyone had a good laugh at my expense. If the old saying "misery loves company" is true, I had plenty of it. I wasn't the only target of pranks: everybody was fair game. Mart Jones and R. D. Holiday, whose nickname was naturally Doc, were the most notorious jokesters in the company. If you had an Achilles heel, these guys would find it.

Mart Jones had a big Achilles heel: he was scared to death of snakes. In Southeast Texas, snakes are about as common as grass. More than once, I've been driving while Mart was riding shotgun and I would run over a snake. Invariably, Mart would pick both feet up like he was afraid the snake was going to come up in the car.

When I was a youngster growing up on the coast near Aransas Pass, there had always been plenty of rattlesnakes, water moccasins, and copperheads around. One day, two of my cousins, Shorty Nicely and Herman Wil-liams, and I killed a particularly large rattler. It so happened that Herman was taking a mail-order taxidermy course, so we took that

---

[42]The Texas Department of Public Safety.

big old snake home for him to mount.[43]

After being the brunt of more than one of Mart's practical jokes, I decided two could play that little game. You know, there's that other old saying: "What goes around, comes around." I got that old stuffed rattlesnake from Mama Nellie and took it to Houston. Mart loved hats, so I put the snake in a Dobbs hatbox, covered it with tissue paper, took it to the office, and put it on my desk for the next company meeting on the first of the month. Everyone was in on the joke and they all grabbed a chair. That left only one chair available for Mart: the one at my desk.

Mart had no more than sat down until he began eyeing the box. You could tell he was dying to open it and look at the hat. He would tap on the box with a pencil and then look off as if he weren't interested. Finally, his curiosity got the better of him and he asked me if it was my hat. I said, "Yes. My wife bought it for me for Christmas."

He asked if he could look at it.

"Of course, you can."

He put the box in his lap, pulled the top off, and yanked the tissue paper out. He then let out a curse and threw the box—snake and all—across the room. He jumped up, jammed his hands down in his pockets, and stormed down the hall. All this was to the hoots and hollers of the entire company. Mart was good at dishing it out, and after he settled down, he was just as good at taking it. It wasn't long before he was laughing as hard as we were.

However, we weren't finished with Mart. One day, Ranger Pete Rogers, who had flown a fighter in World War II, flew the Ranger plane[44] into Houston from Lufkin. He called for a ride to the office. He had landed at the H & H Guest Ranch, where Houston's George Bush International Airport is now located. When Mart and I got to the airport, Pete got in the backseat. Mart was riding in the passenger seat. Pete, as we drove along, undid part of a seat belt, threw it around Mart's neck, and started yelling, "Snake!" Mart got down in the floorboard, yanking at the "snake" and trying to get it off. Finally, he realized that the snake was a seatbelt and regained his composure. Pete and I were laughing so hard, I almost had to pull off to the side of the road. Mart wasn't laughing. In fact, he didn't see any humor in it at all. It didn't take Mart long to get over it, however.

---

[43] My nephew, Randy Taylor, still has the thing on a mantle in his home.

[44] When Hardy Purvis, Sr., was captain of Company A, we confiscated a pile of money from the Galveston gambling dens. Colonel Garrison authorized Captain Purvis' purchase of a plane. It was used mainly in manhunts.

Popularity

It was the first part of June 1957. I had just assumed my duties when Captain Klevenhagen called and said he wanted to see me. When I arrived at headquarters, every Ranger in the state except two—Hardy Purvis, Jr. and Charlie Miller—was present. It didn't take the captain long to get to the point: we were going to raid the Galveston gambling establishments.

Galveston was notorious for its gambling operations. Some of the clubs, like the Balinese Room, were known all over the country. For years, first one politician and then another would campaign, promising to clean up the city. But that presented a problem: most of the people who lived there didn't want it cleaned up. Galveston sits on an island in the Gulf of Mexico, and in those years, except for a few fishing boats and and even fewer tourists, gambling was about all Galveston had. It brought in jobs and money— lots of money. Few people were worried about anyone being hurt. As far as most of the locals were concerned, if a few fat cats got hit in the hip pocket, they had plenty money to lose anyway. When it came to gambling, I think most of Galveston would have subscribed to what an early twentieth-century mayor of New Orleans, Martin Behrman, said about the Crescent City's prostitution problem: "You can pass laws making it illegal, but you can't pass a law making it unpopular." And gambling was very popular in Galveston.

It wasn't any of our business to pass judgement on the morality of gambling. Our job was to enforce the law and obey the orders of our superiors, even if their motives were sometimes questionable. Traditionally, the attorney general's office is a stepping stone to the Texas governor's office. Attorney generals are first, last, and always politicians. Not surprisingly, they want as many of the high-profile cases as they can get. In 1957, Will Wilson was our attorney general. True to form, he had his eye on the governor's chair. He was looking for something that would get him a boatload of favorable press. What better way than cleaning up the infamous Galveston gambling dens?

He planned a huge raid that was designed to sweep down on Galveston and break the backs of the gambling dens. Well, it sounded good. About three weeks before the scheduled raid, Wilson put an undercover team in Galveston under the command of the chief of intelligence in the Houston area, George Reed. In the ensuing weeks, Reed's team compiled a list of sixty-five gambling halls they wanted to raid. Once their list was completed, they set up temporary headquarters on Bissonet Drive in Houston and brought in the Rangers and several carloads of assistant attorney generals.

The plan was simple and effective. After search warrants had been secured, three lawyers would team up with two Rangers, and each team would go to the targeted gambling halls. There they would serve their search warrants and seize all the illegal gambling equipment they could find. I was teamed with Ranger Pete Rogers, and we were dispatched to Galveston to secure the sixty-five search warrants. That sounds simple enough, but it wasn't. The club owners had lots of money at their disposal, and they didn't mind spreading it around buying protection from the local police and judges.

However, there was one district judge in Galveston County, Donald Markle, that we knew we could trust and count on to do the right thing. Pete and I drove to Judge Markle's house, showed him why we had probable cause for the search warrants, and explained our plan to him. Judge Markle signed the warrants.

When we got back to the Bissonet Drive headquarters, we found everyone moping around like whipped dogs with their tails tucked between their legs. Just as we walked in, I heard Wilson say that the raid was off because information had been leaked by one of the Rangers. That was a big—no, a huge—mistake by Wilson. Captain Klevenhagen operated on a short fuse anyway, and when he heard that ridiculous statement, he blew what little fuse he had. It didn't matter one iota that Will Wilson was the attorney general of the state of Texas. The captain was not going to let anyone or anybody talk about his Rangers. He let Wilson have it with both barrels. Seldom have I ever heard anyone talk the way Captain Klevenhagen did. Really, *yell* would be a better word for it. He roared at Wilson like he was an illegitimate stepchild.

"Don't you dare accuse my men of leaking information! You better clean up your own backyard before you start accusing my Rangers of anything."

Obviously not used to being talked to in such a tone, Wilson feebly tried to defend himself and muttered, "What do you mean by that?"

"How many women did you have typing these affidavits in Austin?"

"Fifteen or twenty. So what?"

Not backing up an inch, Captain Klevenhagen continued blasting Wilson. He asked the AG if he knew that women talked over their back fences.

"What?" asked Wilson, with a look of total mystery on his face.

"My Ranger in St. Augustine, Tully Seay, lives beside the lieutenant governor.[45] About a month ago, their wives were visiting in their backyards[46] and Mrs. Ramsey told Mrs. Seay to watch for something big that was going to happen in Galveston around the first of June. Now if the lieutenant governor's wife was telling her neighbor about the raid all the way over in St Augustine, then anyone with ears could have heard about it." Klevenhagen said all this in a tone like, "I can't believe I'm having to explain anything this basic."

Attorney General Wilson didn't like it one bit, but he had a little crow for dinner. I can understand and certainly appreciate a boss standing up for his people, but the AG was wrong. As bad as he hated to admit it, he knew it, too. He and the intelligence people had put a lot of time and effort into this venture just to see it go down the drain. But it did: the raid was cancelled. Regretfully, countless man-hours with no positive results are common in police work.

The raid had not come off, but Captain Johnny Klevenhagen was not the type of man to let something like this just quietly slip into the past, not by a long shot.

The day following the busted raid, Captain Klevenhagen and I went to Galveston and talked to Sheriff Frank Biaggne. After explaining our situation to the sheriff, the captain told him that he had two choices: help us close the gambling dens or stay out of our way while we closed them down. Either way, the Galveston gambling houses were going to be busted. Sheriff Biaggne listened and said he couldn't help; the gambling interests were just

[45]Lieutenant Governor Ben Ramsey
[46]Thus, talking over their back fences.

too strong. If he helped us, he might as well resign right now because he would never be reelected. Captain Kelvenhagen said, "Fine. Just stay out of our way!"

We left Galveston and went directly to Beaumont. Though it never had gotten the publicity, Jefferson County was just about as bad as Galveston County as far as gambling was concerned. The captain made the same speech to Charlie Meyer, the sheriff of Jefferson County, as he had to the Sheriff Biaggne. Sheriff Meyer had more backbone, at least on the surface. He told Captain Klevenhagen not to worry about it; his department would take care of Jefferson County. He assured us that there would be no more gambling in his county. When we got into the car, the captain asked me if I had ever heard such a load of crap in my life. He was right: Jefferson County continued to be a major headache for us.

Galveston was more than enough work without having to worry about Jefferson County. At that time, Company A consisted of only eight men. Mart Jones was stationed in Huntsville, Pete Rogers in Lufkin, Harvey Philips in Woodville, Tully Seay in St. Augustine, and Hollis Sillivan in Burton. Captain Klevenhagen and Sergeant Eddie Oliver were headquartered in Houston. I was the only Ranger private there. Of course, in those days, officers still worked cases, so I didn't have to work all of Houston by myself.

A few days later, Captain Klevenhagen called a company meeting and explained the situation we had in Galveston. He didn't want to request any men from outside companies unless he absolutely had to. Having so few men meant that we would be putting more hours in than ever, and sixty- to eighty-hour weeks were already the norm.

The captain explained his plan. With all the gambling places' high-placed connections, it was clear that search warrants did no good. However, there was nothing to stop us from going into the Balinese Room, the Turf Club, and the other big gambling establishments and just sitting around like any other private citizens.

The Balinese Room was far and away the biggest, fanciest, and best-known of all the gambling halls in Galveston. That's where the captain set his sights for us to start: right at the top. Of course, knowing Johnny Klevenhagen, I would have been shocked if he had wanted to start anywhere else. He explained that from that day forward, two Rangers were going to be at the Balinese Room every afternoon when they opened. We were to go in, find ourselves a good table, put our boots under the table, and make ourselves at home. And we were to also leave our hats and gun belts on—

It doesn't look like much now, but in its day, the Balinese Room, hanging into the Gulf of Mexico in Galveston, was one of the finest showrooms and gambling casinos in America.

conspicuously on—for everyone to see.

The Balinese Room is built on a pier hanging far into the Gulf of Mexico. Not only did this make it unique among the clubs, but it also allowed approach from only one direction. Officially it was a supper club, and it was—one of the best ever. Just about every big name in show business performed there at one time or another: Frank Sinatra, Phil Harris, and Jack Benny, to name a few. Being a supper club wasn't its claim to fame, however. It was *the* premier gambling casino on Galveston Island.

Being situated the way it was on the pier made it impossible to surprise the gamblers. You entered through doors fitted with electric locks at the seawall. A lady was stationed in a booth at the entrance and would be smiling very sweetly at you as you walked past her. All the while, she was standing on a buzzer, warning the occupants that we were on our way. There were actually drills, just like school fire drills, where the employees practiced putting the gambling equipment away. They could hide that stuff almost as fast as you could blink an eye. You could see the indentations in the carpet where the tables had stood, but the room would be clean and everyone would be sitting around playing dominoes or checkers, acting as innocent as a newborn babies.

Rangers Hollis Sillivan and Tully Seay drew the first assignment to

Galveston. None of us dreamed that it would be three and a half years before we finally completed our mission. We were to work two weeks on and four weeks off. The four weeks off didn't mean that we had vacation and didn't have to do anything. It simply meant that we had to go back to our regular duties and do six weeks of work in four! We kept up a full workload in addition to the Galveston duty. At least once a week, some of us would go to Beaumont to make sure that the gambling clubs in Jefferson County were staying in compliance the way the sheriff had promised they would. Needless to say, after a couple of months everyone in Company A was worn to a frazzle.

Captain Klevenhagen realized we couldn't keep up this killing pace. He contacted Colonel Garrison, director of the Texas Department of Safety, and asked for help. Homer Garrison is the best friend the Rangers have ever had in the director's chair in Austin. Anything he could do to help us, he did. Garrison saw to it that Klevenhagen got the help he needed. From then on, one man from Company A would work with a man from one of the other five companies throughout the state. This way, you worked one week with one Ranger from some other company, and then the next week you caught another Ranger from another company.

At first, the clubs didn't take us seriously. I guess they thought they would kill us with kindness. The Balinese Room had a five-piece band and a small dance floor. When we walked in, the band would play "The Eyes of Texas." All of the clubs tried to treat us like kings by offering us steaks, shrimp, and all sorts of food and drinks. But we were fooled. They were trying to have us bought and paid for, but we didn't take anything. Whatever we ate or drank, we paid for. I can't imagine how many gallons of coffee we drank. Clearly, they thought they could simply wait us out. They were wrong. We were prepared to stay in Galveston however long it took to break them. And we did.

When the patrons walked in, the first things they saw were our boots, hats, gun belts, and badges. Their reactions seldom varied. They would sit nervously for a while, have a drink, talk in hushed voices, and then leave.

After about two weeks, the management of the Balinese Room started calling Captain Klevenhagen, complaining that we were ruining business. "Couldn't some kind of deal be made?"

No, it couldn't. We kept the pressure on.

Then on Wednesday night, June 19, 1957, we broke their backs.

During that week, we started ripping the guts out of the gamblers.

Company A, 1957, right after I became a Texas Ranger

Bottom: Captain Johnny Klevenhagen, Sergeant Eddie Oliver, Harvey
Phillips, Quincy Lowman

Standing: Mart Jones, Me, company secretary-Mrs. Marshall, Hollis
Sillavan, Tully Seay, Pete Rogers

Courtesy of Randy Sillavan

The casinos had stashed their gambling paraphernalia before we came, and they were waiting for us to pull out. The only problem was that we *weren't* pulling out. To their horror, we started finding their equipment. In the few days immediately preceeding June 19, we had found and destroyed eight hundred thousand dollars in gambling equipment. As great as this was, we still had not hit the mother lode—the Balinese Room's equipment. We knew hundreds of slot machines and gambling tables were there, but search as hard we could, we had never been able to find them. They had hidden it really well, but not well enough.

The forerunner of the Balinese Room had been the Hollywood Supper Club. I never saw it when it was open, but I was told that it was really something to behold. It put anything currently in Galvestion, including the Balinese Room, to shame. In fact, the Balinese Room only came into being after a court injunction permanently closed the Hollywood Supper Club back in the late 1930s. In 1957, what was left of of the club was in pretty bad shape, but you could tell that it had once been a magnificent palace. I guess the gamblers figured that it would make the perfect place to hide their gambling machines until we left town. You can imagine the pleasant surprise when Hollis Sillavan and a couple of the attorney general's people happened to look in the Hollywood Supper Club and saw slot machines, pinball machines, roulette tables, and blackjack tables stacked to the ceiling.

Pete Rogers and I were working together when two AG agents ran up to us saying, "Man, we've found their stash!" Pete and I took one look and called the captain. After we explained what had been found, the captain hightailed it to Galveston. As soon as he got there, the captain and I headed straight for the old Hollywood Supper Club where we met Pete, Hollis, and several men from the attorney general's office.[47]

The agents had literally hit the jackpot: 1.2 million dollars—that's 1957 dollars—of gambling equipment. There were fifteen hundred slot machines, roulette wheels, blackjack tables, dice tables, and box after box of chips and dice. Many of the chips were hundred-dollar ones with Balinese Room inscribed on them. That seemed to open Pandora's box. Within a week, we confiscated more than two million dollars in gambling equipment.

I remember it all as though it were yesterday. As we stood there looking at the mountain of slot machines, I heard Captain Klevenhagen mutter to himself: "Man, I don't know what in the world I'll ever do with all this stuff. I wish I had a boat big enough to load it on, haul it out in the Gulf, and just dump it."

Cecil Rotsch, first assistant to the attorney general, overheard the captain and said, "That sounds like a wonderful idea to me."

Until now, whenever we confiscated equipment, we had taken it to the city dump and burned it. That was when we only grabbed a few machines, and even that had been a real pain. Now we had a mountain of stuff. As usual, we would have to have the fire department present to make sure the fire didn't get out of control. We would have to arrange our schedule to meet theirs, and that was clumsy and very time-consuming. The more Rotsch thought about dumping the equipment in the ocean, the better he liked the

---

[47] The assistant attorney generals were Cecil Rotsch, J.L. Smith, B.H. Timmins, Ed Horner, and Richard Stone.

idea. Rotsch looked over at the captain. "I think the attorney general will like this idea, too. Let me check with him."

Captain Klevenhagen hadn't been serious and didn't like the plan. He told Rotsch that he had only been mumbling to himself. But Rotsch was convinced it was a good idea, and the captain wasn't having any luck changing his mind. Finally, Klevenhagan said to Rotsch, "Well, that's fine, but until the AG tells me different, I'm going to start burning this stuff."

We hired a moving company to come in and load all the gambling paraphernalia onto trucks, and then we headed for the city dump. It wasn't long before we had a roaring fire going, and we started feeding it with the slot machines. We had only been burning a short time when I heard a voice from the captain's radio saying, "Eighty-eight to unit six." "Eighty-eight" was an airplane from Austin.

Captain Klevenhagen grabbed the microphone and said, "This is six. Go ahead."

"This is Joe Fletcher. Could you meet me at the airport?"

Rotsch had hit the right chord with Attorney General Wilson. Joe Fletcher was Colonel Homer Garrison's number-one man. If Colonel Fletcher was here, that meant something big was going to happen.

Rotsch had been right. The attorney general had liked the idea of dumping the whole mess in the Gulf. That would get him lots of free front-page coverage. When Fletcher joined us, he told us that on the trip from Austin, he had thought about the ferry at nearby Port Bolivar. It had a capacity to carry about sixty cars and would have plenty of room to hold what we hadn't burned. It was also big enough to sail a short distance into the Gulf, where the water would be deep enough to bury the gambling equipment forever.

Captain Klevenhagen told me to make the necessary arrangements for the ferry, but until I did, he was going to keep burning. I arrived at the dock just as the ferry was pulling in. I went aboard, climbed up to the pilot-house, and told the captain what we needed.

He said, "I'm sorry Ranger, I would really like to help you, but I can't. I'm not licensed to go outside the bars.[48] I can only sail inland waters. If I went into open water, the Coast Guard would pull my license."

I went back and reported this to the captain. But by then, the idea had taken on a life of its own. The attorney general personally came to Galveston.

---

[48] Into the open sea.

Among him, Colonel Fletcher, and a reluctant Captain Klevenhagen, they came up with what they considered to be a wonderful idea. The AG's office rented a tugboat to haul some of the slots into the Gulf. Tugboats are nothing but floating engines designed for one thing only: to supply power to move huge ships. A tugboat only has about a foot of walkway on each side of the pilothouse, so we couldn't put many slots on board. Nevertheless, we managed to stack about fifty machines all over that thing. Slot machines were hanging over the sides, on the pilothouse, just everywhere you can imagine. We didn't have much room for slot machines on board, but we had plenty of space for the newspaper reporters and cameramen!

We sailed about five miles into the Gulf, close to Pelican Island. Near a sunken ship, we pushed the machines into the water. We had left out during the night, and we were back to shore by three o'clock in the morning.

It had been marveleous fun. News reporters had sailed with us and had recorded it all. It made all the papers. Yes sir, it was great. Great, that is, until the next day. It seems the Army Corps of Engineers considered the ship channel their private domain, and they didn't want so much as a napkin thrown in their water, let alone a boatload of gambling equipment. Most of the machines had sunk to the bottom, but some were made of plastic and wood and those had popped back up and were floating all over the channel.

Cecil Rotsch was frantic the next day when he called Captain Klevenhagen: "Captain, what are we going to do? The Corps of Engineers is having a cow. They're threatening to file charges on us for fouling the waterways."

Keeping a straight face, Captain Klevenhagen said, "I don't know what you're talking about. I burned all the slot machines I was responsible for."

The battle with the Balinese Room would continue for several more months, but the haul from the Hollywood Supper Club had broken them. They had had enough, and the world- renowned Balinese Room closed its doors. Most of the big gambling establishments saw the handwriting on the wall and followed the Balinese Room into history.

Get Yourself an Axe Handle

The big clubs may have closed, but there was no shortage of other clubs for us to work. When the Balinese Room closed, we moved on to the next club, then the next, and then the next. We would go into a club and rip it apart. Naturally, the owner screamed like a wounded hyena, but that didn't cut any ice with us.

Captain Klevenhagen had given us very clear orders: "Get yourself an axe handle, go in rough, and take care of your business. If anyone gives you any lip, put a boot up his butt and show him the working end of your axe handle, and then throw him in jail. And keep doing it until I tell you differ-ent." As an extra gift, he bought each of us a nine-pound sledge hammer that we called "the key." That was an appropriate name because it would open any door on Galveston Island.

I can hear you now: "This type of law enforcement would not be tolerated today." No, it wouldn't. But this was 1957, and that was the way we did things back then for three-and-a-half years. During the entire time, we kept the same room at the old Buccaneer Hotel rented. In the end, we tore up the old Galveston gambling establishment.

It was slow going, but our work in Galveston gradually bore fruit. The Galveston gamblers were slowly dying on the vine. Finally, in 1960, there was a shakeup in the city government. The city began electing its mayor instead of letting city commissioners appoint him. The new city government put the hammer to what was left of the gambling dens. After three and a half years, we checked out of the Buccaneer Hotel. We were finished with Galveston.

That sure sounded nice, but never have we ever been more wrong about anything. It wasn't long before we started getting rumors that as soon as we had left, Galveston started running wide open again. This time the gamblers were trying to be cute. They were thinking they would fake us out by spreading the action around among the clubs. Some of the places had the dice tables, some had the roulette wheels, while still others had the black-jack tables, and so on. I don't know why they thought spreading it out like that would confuse us. But if that made them happy, that was fine with us. It didn't bother us in the least.

I don't guess any of the captains were willing to put their men back into Galveston. Captain Eddie Oliver, who had succeeded Captain Klevenhagen, didn't seem too keen to spare many men from Company A. That left two Rangers to handle Houston and all of Galveston Island: Skippy Rundell and Ed Gooding. Skippy and I would go down to Galveston at least once a week and raid one place or another, to little effect. They'd open back up before we could get off the island. It didn't take long before Skippy and I got tired of raiding the same place over and over, so we decided to do something about it. We still had those sledgehammers that Captain Klevenhagen had given us. We decided that from then on, whenever we raided a place, we wouldn't leave anything behind to be used in the future.

In those days of party lines, phones were anything but secure, so we worked out a code with Captain Oliver to let him know how a raid went. When we left Galveston Island, we would call the captain and report. When we raided a joint, that was one hit; if we arrested someone, that was one run; and if we had any trouble, that was one error. And, trust me, Eddie Oliver was not one to tolerate many errors.

Everything was going along just fine until Skippy and I hit the Silver Moon Club in nearby Dickenson. It had a new owner and he took exception to our method of operation. When we approached the Silver Moon, there was the usual watchdog at the front door. You had to go through two locked glass doors to enter the club, and this old gal who was working the office knew both Skippy and me. She should have: we had been there enough. On this particular raid, we pulled our hats off and eased in behind a large group that had gathered at the door. When the doors opened, we made a mad dash and got through both doors. We didn't slow down as we ran up the stairs at full speed. Of course, when the second the woman in the office saw us, she started pushing the alarm buzzer for all it was worth. We kept on running.

We had been in the Silver Moon many times before and knew the

118

floor plan well. We charged into the bar area, and without slowing down, we turned into the gambling room. I saw the club owner heading for his office. As he ran, the dice, chips, and money he had in his arms were falling all over the floor. I rushed him and stopped him before he could make it to his office.

True to our agreement, Skippy and I started the process of putting the Silver Moon out of business. We confiscated everything: equipment, TVs, leather furniture, even the carpet off the floor. Then we went back into the bar area. Behind the bar stood a man with one of those short waiter jackets that bartenders wear. My eyes focused on the nine-foot mirror behind him. I just didn't like that mirror. I

Skippy Rundell, as good a friend as I ever had. He ended his career as the Assistant Senior Ranger Captain, a job he deserved. We lost Skippy a few years ago, and I still miss him. *(Courtesy of The Texas Ranger Hall of Fame and Museum: Waco, Texas)*

swung the hammer and let it go. It hit right in the middle, and the bartender briefly disappeared in a shower of shattered glass.

We took the names of everyone in the club, arrested the owner, and put him in jail. We also told him he would be responsible for the fines of everyone in the club. About three blocks away, we found the lady who had sounded the alarm. And let me tell you, she was really hoofing it and crying at the same time. We offered her a ride. Through the sobs, she said she had rather walk: she was scared to death. I think she thought that if she got into our car, we would arrest her, which we wouldn't have done. After depositing the club owner in the city jail in Dickenson, we called Houston. One run, one hit, no errors.

The next morning, Captain Oliver got a call from the chairman of the Public Safety Commission, Eddie Dykes. He asked the captain to join him for dinner. He said that he needed to talk to him about Galveston. Captain Oliver hung up the phone, walked to the door of our office, and looked over the top of his glasses at us. We were sitting at our desks trying to look as pure and innocent as a freshly fallen snow. Captain Oliver asked, "What did you two get into in Galveston last night?" We fessed up, and the captain just shook his head and left. We fessed up because when there is the least bit of possibility for trouble, the last person in the world you want to lie to is your captain. Most of the time, he's the only help you're going to get.

We sweated bullets until he came back, but the commissioner was not sympathetic toward the gamblers. He did request that we let up a little bit with our sledgehammers, but he wanted us to keep the heat on the gambling halls.

Thankfully, a new district attorney had been elected in Galveston who was also not in sympathy with the gamblers. The Silver Moon owner complained to him, and the new DA told the club owner that he had been dancing for a long time and to consider what he had just lost as a down payment to the fiddler.

And what did the general population of Galveston think of us? Judge for yourself. Illegal gambling was in the open so much there, a tax was actually collected on the gambling machines. Before we came, the clubs paid a tax to the county and city on each machine they owned. After we had been there a year, we reduced the tax base in Galveston by three million dollars.

I had many experiences in Galveston. Most were good and a few were not so good. I would not take anything for those three and a half years. Except for Charlie Miller, I got to work with just about every Ranger in the state as they rotated through Galveston. I wouldn't take all the money in the world for the privilege of not only meeting, but also working with all these great professionals.

Today, I'm sure there is probably as much, if not more, gambling in Galveston. However, now it has been legalized. You see, you can't pass a law. . . .

September 15

Tuesday, September 15, 1959, is a black-letter date in Houston. The sound of the explosion that rocked Edgar Allen Poe Elementary School at about ten o'clock that morning had not been heard in Texas since the terrible New London School explosion in which more than 300 had died eighteen years before. Poe Elementary School, located near the campus of Rice University,[48] had become the target of a madman.

Journalists today would lead us to believe that school terrorism is a modern-day experience. I've heard people say that Charles Whitman started it all when he climbed into the Tower at the University of Texas in Austin and started killing people on August 1, 1966. Well, Whitman wasn't the first. At Poe Elementary, Paul Harold Orgeron murdered an innocent teacher, a custodian, and three seven-year-old boys—including his own son—in 1959. I suspect that there were other acts of cowardly mayhem even before this.

Poe Elementary School principal Ruth Doty was walking down the hall when she met a shabby,[49] middle-aged man and a young boy. Paul Orgeron told Mrs. Doty that he wanted to enroll his seven-year-old son, Dusty Paul, in school. She said that was fine. If they would follow her, she would take them to the school office to fill out the necessary paperwork. At the office, Mrs. Doty asked Juanita Weidner, a secretary, to give Orgeron the necessary enrollment forms.

---

[49] Other witnesses said Orgeron was neatly dressed. I suspect that the shabbily dressed description may have been slanted after-the-fact.

Ms. Weidner asked Orgeron where he and his son had moved from, what school his son had been attending, where they were currently living, and what he did for a living. She wasn't asking officially; most of that information would be covered on the enrollment papers. She was just making conversation. Not surprisingly, she became suspicious when he couldn't remember the name of the school his son had been attending or the name of the town. All he could remember was that it was in New Mexico. As for their current address, he couldn't remember that either. They had been in Houston only a few days and until the previous Monday, they had been living in a boarding house at 2720 LaBranch Street. The best he could recall, the street they had moved to was Bissonnett Street. However, he definitely remembered that he was a tile contractor by trade.

Parts of Orgeron's story later turned out to be true, sort of. When the address was checked with the owners of the boarding house on LaBranch Street, the E. C. Adamses, they identified the pictures of Orgeron and his son as former boarders who had lived at their house from September 10 until September 12. They said the man and boy were very quiet and never made any trouble. But they didn't know the man as Paul Orgeron: he had given his name as Bob Silver.[50] As for being a tile contractor, this was also true. But he was also a convicted safecracker.

Ms. Weidner told Orgeron that she was sorry, but since he didn't have Dusty's birth or health certificates with him, she could not enroll Dusty. Taking the enrollment form, he said they would return the next day with the needed certificates. Later, Ms. Weidner reported that Orgeron had talked rather loudly and fast, but that he appeared neither angry nor upset.

It was now almost ten o'clock and near the end of the period. Students from five first- and second-grade classes were getting ready to return to their rooms from their recess on the schoolyard. Just as Patricia Johnston, a ten-year teacher (three of them at Poe) was preparing to take her second-grade class into the building, she was approached by Orgeron and Dusty. Orgeron was carrying a brown, fabric-covered suitcase. The small, freckle-faced boy also carried a similar small bag. Orgeron stopped in front of Ms. Johnston, handed her two pieces of paper, and said, "Teacher, read these." Ms. Johnston said that the penmanship was so bad that the notes were almost unreadable. While she studied them, Orgeron kept mumbling something about the will of God and " . . . having power in a suitcase." All the

---

[50] We never did find out where that name came from.

122

while, he was moving the suitcase up and down. She noticed what appeared to be a doorbell-type button on the bottom of the bag.

Orgeron kept urging Ms. Johnston to gather all the children around them in a circle. She wasn't having any part of that until he could explain to her why he wanted the children and what he had in the suitcase. Still unable to make out what the notes said, Ms. Johnston was by now thoroughly alarmed. She was worried that the children that had joined her might be in terrible danger, and she wanted to get them as far away from this strange man as possible. She told two of the children to go find Mrs. Doty and James Montgomery, the school custodian. The rest she told to immediately go back inside the building.

Two other teachers, Julia Whatley and Jennie Kolter, were walking out the door when they saw their colleague talking to the strange man and small boy. It was the school policy not to let a teacher stand by herself with suspicious-looking people. They were already heading toward her when they saw Ms. Johnston signaling them to join her. Ms. Johnston handed the note to Ms. Kolter. Meanwhile, Orgeron continued rambling about "power in the suitcase" and that he had to "get to the children."

A few moments later, Ruth Doty and James Montgomery joined the group. No longer being needed, Ms. Whatley returned to her students and started moving them into the school building, with the girls leading the way. Pat Johnston also left the group and started toward her students to also get them into the building.

Mrs. Doty told Orgeron he would have to leave the school grounds immediately. Paying no attention to the principal, Orgeron kept rambling and repeating, "I have to follow the children to the second grade." He also kept waving the suitcase around.

That was the last thing any of them remembered. Suddenly, there was a tremendous explosion and six people were dead: Jennie Kolter, teacher; James Montgomery, school custodian; seven-year-old students Billy Hawes, Jr. and John Fitch, Jr.; and Paul Orgeron and his seven-year-old son Dusty.

The only word to describe Edgar Allen Poe Elementary School when I arrived is bedlam—absolute bedlam. Parents were swarming the school grounds, frantically searching for their children. Law enforcement officers were fighting a losing battle trying to keep order and, of course, the curiosity seekers were out in full force.

I joined officers from the Houston Police Department, the Harris County Sheriff's Department, and the FBI. The devastation was unbelievable. The blast had occurred directly under a maple tree. If you had gone by the looks of the tree, you would have thought it was the dead of winter: there was not a leaf to be found anywhere on it. All that hung from the stripped branches were bits of human flesh and a few shreds of clothing. There was a hole six inches deep at the spot of the asphalted playground where Orgeron had detonated the bomb.

Several bodies were lying on the playground, but one I remember in particular. One of the boys was totally nude. The force of the explosion had ripped every piece of clothing off the poor child.

Soon, we tentatively identified the bomber. Juanita Weidner said he had given his name as John Orgeron when he and his son had been in her office earlier. There was still one big problem: we weren't sure that he was dead. There wasn't a body, at least not one that was identifiable, and we were afraid that the bomber was still on the school grounds with another explosive.

There is only one way to cope with violent death when you have seen as much of it as I have: harden yourself to it and do not under any circumstances let yourself become emotionally involved. Sometimes you even laugh about it. It's not funny and you're not belittling the horror and pain, but that's one of the ways you learn to cope. However, no matter how much you steel yourself, you never get to a point where innocent children thrown into the path of violence doesn't unsettle you. Orgeron's son and the other slaughtered children bothered me more than anything I had seen since the time we had lobbed the hand grenades into the cellar back in Europe. Like that incident, this would bother me for a long time. At that moment, however, I had to put that aside and do what all the other officers on the campus were doing: our jobs. That was easier said than done. I really felt sorry for those officers who had not seen as much death as I had. They were having a really difficult time with it.

We evacuated the school to determine that there was not another bomb in the building. Then we asked all the children and teachers return to their classrooms so the teachers could conduct a roll call. Except for the dead and wounded, everyone else was soon accounted for.

I have to say right here that I have seen hardened combat soldiers not act as bravely as these teachers and children did. It was really incredible. There was one little nine-year-old boy, Costa Kaldis, that I especially re-member. He would have been awarded a medal for extraordinary bravery if he had been in the service. The school had supposedly been cleared of all the children when young Kaldis heard a child crying. A small polio victim had been unable to leave the building with the others and had inadvertently been left behind. Without a second's hesitation, little nine-year-old Kaldis ran back into the room and carried his schoolmate to safety. Remember, no one knew at that time whether or not there was another bomb still in the school. I have often wondered whatever happened to Costa Kaldis. He was as brave as anyone I've ever known.

Once everyone was accounted for, we started a search of the area around the blast, looking for anything and everything: bodies, wounded, or any clues as to what had happened and why. I was walking down a row of hedges along North Boulevard when I saw a man's left hand hanging on one the hedge's branches about sixty feet from the spot of the explosion.

Lloyd Frazier, assistant chief deputy of the Harris County Sheriff's Department, was an explosive and fingerprint expert and a better-than-average crime-scene chemist. Lloyd was a real student of his profession and could do just about anything concerning law enforcement. He took the hand for fingerprint identification, and we soon had a positive identification. We didn't have to worry about Orgeron setting off any more bombs.

Orgeron, 47, had a long police record, dating back to 1930. He had served two terms in Texas prisons and one in Louisiana. He was an old-time safe burglar, which accounted for his knowledge of dynamite.

Orgeron's left hand wasn't his only body part we found before completing our search of the area. His severed foot was found near the bomb site. The following day, the owner of a two-story building across the street from the school noticed a terrible smell coming from his roof. He found Orgeron's missing right shoulder and arm. Another man who also lived across the street from the school found a piece of flesh in his backyard.

We also found the notes Orgeron had given to Pat Johnson:

Note 1:
Please do not get excite over this order I'm giving you. In this suitcase you see in my hand is fill to the top with high explosive. I mean high high. Please believe me when I say I have 2 more (illegible) that are set to go off at two times. I do not believe I can kill and not kill what is around me, an I mean my son will go. Do as I say an no one will get hurt. Please.

P. H. Orgeron
Do not get the Police department yet, I'll tell you when.

Note 2:
Please do not get excite over this order I'm giving you. In this suitcase you see in my hand it fill to the top with high explosive. Please
do not make me push this button that all I have to do. And also
have two 2 more cases (illegible) high explosive that are set to go
off at a certain time at three different places so it will more harm to
kill me, so do as I say and no one will get hurt. An I would like to
talk about god while waiting for my wife.

The sheriff's deputies and I continued to search the school grounds
while several Houston police officers started looking for Orgeron's vehicle. They found his 1958 green and ivory Chevrolet station wagon parked
along North Street across from the school. Several sticks of dynamite were
under the hood, lying on the upper side of the wheel well and a box of
dynamite fuses was located in the car's glove box. Coils of wire, batteries,
and BB-gun pellets were found in the backseat. In the trunk, they found a
child's cowboy book, another book titled *Children At Play*, a toy airplane,
a toy submachine gun, and a toy six-shooter.

Also found at the blast scene was a sales ticket in the amount of
$41.94 for blasting caps, fuses, and one hundred and fifty sticks (approxi-
mately fifty pounds) of dynamite from the Bond Gunderson Company in
Grants, New Mexico. This gave us a whole new problem. As big as the
explosion was, it wasn't nearly as big as it would have been if Orgeron had
used one hundred and fifty sticks of dynamite. Where was the rest of the
dynamite? We never did find it. I suspect Orgeron passed the dynamite on to
some safecrackers.

Just like today, there are a lot of nuts in this old world. The dust
hadn't even settled before sickos started calling, claiming they had planted
bombs in other schools all around Houston. Finally, the National Guard was
called out and placed at schools throughout the area. One school in San
Antonio even received a threat from what turned out to be three teenagers.
Thankfully, they all proved to be pranks. Some people have a real sick sense
of humor.

Dead and mangled bodies from the bomb blast were not the only
things that reminded me of the war. While searching the blast area, I developed a terrible headache from breathing the glycerin fumes from the dynamite. This had happened to me all during the war. In a heavy firefight when
a lot of ammunition was fired, I usually developed a headache. I don't know
what it is about the glycerin fumes that gives me a headache, but it does.

After completing our crime scene investigation, we bagged as many body parts as we could find and sent them to a local Houston funeral home. We notified all of Orgeron's next-of-kin possible, many of whom lived in the Houston area, that they could claim the bodies. Dusty was terribly mutilated, and the only way a relative could make a positive identification of the boy was from a small scar under his chin. As far as I know, none of the relatives ever claimed Orgeron.

We discovered that Orgeron's former wife Hazel lived in Houston. It turned out that they had been married and divorced twice. She said she had tried to make a go of it both times, but since he liked to use her for a punching bag, it had been impossible. The last time she had talked to him was at Dusty's seventh birthday party the previous Saturday, at the home of his maternal grandmother Maude Tatum. He claimed that he had found God, had no malice for anyone, and was a changed man.

Continuing, she said that Paul and Dusty had been devoted to one another and that they had been inseperable ever since the divorce in July of 1958. She said they wandered from place to place, never staying in any one place for long. All she knew about their travels was that they had been in Altus, Oklahoma, shortly before returning to Houston. Upon investigating, we discovered that in July and August, Orgeron had worked as a tile contractor for James Scarborough in Altus. During the whole period, it appears that Orgeron and Dusty had slept either in the back of their station wagon or in a tent. When questioned, Scarborough said that for some reason that he never gave, Orgeron had insisted that he had to leave Altus no later than August 25. He also didn't say where he had to go or why. He had, in fact, left a few days before August 25. We knew he was in Grants, New Mexico, on August 25, when he bought the dynamite from the Bond Gunderson Company. We were never able to say for certain where the Orgerons were between August 25 and September 10, when they moved briefly into the Adams' boarding house at 2720 LaBranch Street in Houston.

Today, if you drive to 9710 Runnymeade in Houston, you will find the Jeannie K. Kolter Elementary School; at 4000 Simsbrook you will see the James Arlie Mongtomery Elementary School. Both are fitting tributes to a school teacher and custodian who loved their children.

On Monday, March 6, 1961, at the dedication of James Arlie Montgomery Elementary School, there was a custodian from every school in Houston in attendance. Ruth Doty, still the principal at Poe, related that James Montgomery ". . . above all, was a man who loved children." Another teacher said, "He was never too busy to climb a tree to retrieve a child's ball." Perhaps one student summed it up best when he wrote to Montgomery's widow the day after he was killed: "We all miss him very much—but someday we'll meet him again."

Don't Mess Around with Him

Legendary Hall of Fame Texas Ranger,
Captain **Johnny Klevenhagen**
*(Courtesy of The Texas Ranger Hall of Fame
and Museum: Waco, Texas)*

I don't like to speak ill about fellow law-enforcement officers, but we were having trouble with the FBI in Houston during the late 1950s. I guess the special agent in charge of the Houston office thought he could advance his career if he could hang a Ranger scalp from his belt, especially if the scalp belonged to a Texas Ranger captain. Did he ever take on the wrong one when he set his sights on Johnny Klevenhagen!

A Houston gambler had been shotgunned to death by someone who had pulled up beside him as he drove home. Lloyd Frazier of the Harris County Sheriff's Office had gotten a tip on the triggerman, but if we hoped to catch him, we had to move fast: the assassin was headed for the Houston Airport.[51] Captain Klevenhagen and Buster Kern, the Harris County sheriff, caught up with the killer at the airport and he surrendered without resistance. Catching him was one thing; getting him to talk was another. He didn't break easily, but after several days of intense questioning, he finally confessed to the murder. It wasn't anything personal: he had simply been hired to do a job. After he started talking, he gave us the name of the driver and the location where we could find the shotgun he had used.

In the early 1960s, the civil rights movement was just getting started and was getting lots of attention by the press. If there was one thing the FBI loved in my era, and I suspect it's still true today, it was a high-profile case. This one particular agent thought he saw an opportunity to advance his own career on our backs. He started making noises that we had brutalized the shotgun killer and violated his civil rights by hiding him from his attorney.[52] Of course this was nonsense, but it made great headlines and the district attorney was obligated to investigate. He called a meeting at his downtown office to evaluate the situation. That didn't help a thing. Before the meeting was over, we had to pull Captain Klevenhagen off the special FBI agent in charge.

During the ensuing trial, it only got worse. The prisoner suddenly came into a very large bankroll from an unknown source and hired one of the best criminal attorneys in the country, the renowned Percy Foreman. Foreman's MO was to attack the police and put them on trial instead of trying the facts of the case. When Captain Klevenhagen got on the witness stand, Foreman started trying his antics on him. There he made a big mistake.

Foreman called Captain Klevenhagen a liar. Faster than a speeding bullet, Captain Klevenhagen came over the rail of the witness stand, charging straight at Foreman. I'll give the devil his due: Foreman was no fool! He cut and ran. For a man his age, he sure could run! He flew out the back door of the courtroom and down the hall, with Captain Klevenhagen hard on his heels. All the while, the judge was going crazy, pounding his desk with his gavel and yelling over and over, "Order! Order in the courtroom!" With most of the courtroom emptied and chasing after Foreman and Captain Klevenhagen, the judge called a fifteen-minute recess to a vacant room.

---

[51] This is Hobby Airport today.

[52] If you believe defense attorneys, all of their clients are hidden from them. In East Texas, the press calls this the "East Texas Merry-Go-Round." In our part of the state, they call it the "Milk Run."

To the immense good fortune of Foreman, he was fast and able to outrun the captain.

When court reconvened, in limped Foreman with a bandage around his head, walking with a crutch. Looking pitiful and keeping a straight face the whole time, he addressed the jury and said, "Ladies and gentlemen, this is what happened to me in that fifteen-minute recess. Think what could have happened to my client after days of questioning by these Rangers."

Needless to say, we lost the case.

Jim Ray was a former Ranger captain and chief of the Criminal Law Enforcement for the Department of Public Safety. He said about Captain Johnny Klevenhagen: "If you were smart, it didn't take long to figure that you better not mess around with him."

I never saw a man with a fire burning inside him like the one in Captain Klevenhagen. He drove himself unmercifully. He finally drove him-self into a much too early grave, but the captain would not have had it any other way. To Johnny Klevenhagen, there was no middle ground: just one hundred miles an hour, flat out, every second of every minute of every day. Not once did I ever hear him say, "You go." It was always: "Let's go."

I don't think Klevenhagen ever slept or took time off; that just wasn't in his makeup. Many a time I have seen him work all day and night, stopping only long enough to wolf down a mouthful of food or take a quick shower and shave. Then it was right back at it. Most Rangers had to work like this—a lot more than any man should—but it was a way of life with the captain. Something down deep was driving him like a man possessed.

He just couldn't stop. I didn't think anything or anybody could ever stop him. No person ever did, but some *thing* did: a massive heart attack. Captain Johnny Klevenhagen, one of the greatest men in the glorious history of the Texas Rangers, was forty-eight years old when we buried him in San Antonio on Thanksgiving Day, 1958. I will be forever grateful that I had the privilege and the high honor to have worked for him my first year as a Texas Ranger. Only thirty men out of the thousands who have been Rangers have been elected to the Texas Ranger Hall of Fame in Waco, Texas. Captain Johnny Klevenhagen is one of the thirty.

Don't Cut a Gut

With Captain Klevenhagen gone, his sergeant Eddie Oliver became captain. My old friend Pete Rogers from Lufkin was promoted to sergeant. To fill Pete's place, Captain Oliver hired his former Highway Patrol partner J. L. Rundell (known by everyone as Skippy) to join us in Houston. That was good news to me. I was still the only field Ranger in Houston, and I more than welcomed the help. I had known Skippy since my Highway Patrol days and I liked him very much. We worked well together. Skippy was a stickler for detail, a trait that I wasn't exactly known for. Also, Skippy really liked to argue. I didn't.

Skippy was fairly new in the Rangers when we got a call from the sheriff in Montgomery County requesting our assistance. Captain Oliver called us in and told us the sheriff was having trouble with one of his commissioners. The captain wanted us to go up there and help, "but whatever you do, don't cut a gut." That was one of Captain Oliver's favorite expressions. It simply meant: "Don't mess up."

When we got to the Montgomery County Sheriff's Office, he laid his problem out to us. His county commissioner, T. J. Peel, had whipped up on a man and then refused to come in for questioning. He hoped we could understand the predicament this put him in. Peel was a thorn in the sheriff's side, but thorn or no thorn, he controlled much of the sheriff's department's annual budget. The sheriff couldn't afford to make him any madder than he already was.

The problem stemmed from the pending divorce between Peel and his wife. Mrs. Peel was a smart lady, and she was determined to have her ducks in a row before she filed for divorce. Peel had a violent temper, and the first thing Mrs. Peel had done was obtain a restraining order to keep him away from their house. A lot of money and real estate were involved, and she wanted to make sure she got her share. Accordingly, she had called their

132

Company A 1958-59
Back: Clay Bednar, Me, Hollis Sillavan, Everett Smith, Tully Seay
Front: Mart Jones, Pete Rogers, Skippy Rundell, Harvey Phillips, Eddie Oliver
Courtesy of Randy Sillavan

bank in Houston and asked them to send a land appraiser to evaluate their holdings.

The bank was more than willing to send an appraiser. They wanted to make sure their interests were protected, so they had wasted no time. After the appraiser had arrived, he and Mrs. Peel got right to work. They left his car at her house and went in her car to look at the land and livestock.

By chance, they had met Mr. Peel. He thought she was out riding around with a strange man. He didn't care that they were getting a divorce or that he had a passenger with him or that he was in his county pickup. Mrs. Peel saw him turn around and head after them. She didn't wanted any part of Peel's temper, so she pulled into a small filling station and got out, leaving the bank examiner on his own. Peel came sliding up beside his wife's car, pulled out the shocked appraiser, and started beating him on the head with

133

his fists.

The appraiser had finally been able to break free and got to his feet. Looking around, he grabbed a shovel and told Peel that if he tried hit him again, he would cut his head off. The service station owner tried to calm things down. He told Peel that he had already called the sheriff, and that Peel better leave before the law got there. Peel was a hothead, but not a fool. He left.

While all of this was going on, Mrs. Peel had cut out, leaving the land appraiser not only high and dry, but also afoot.

When the sheriff had arrived at the service station, the appraiser explained what had happened. He said that he had left his car at the Peel's residence and asked the sheriff to accompany him to pick up his car. But at the Peel home, the appraiser's car was gone.

It was at this point that the sheriff had called us, asking for our assistance. We told the sheriff we would try to handle his problem as best as we could. I called Commissioner Peel and told him to get his lawyer and come to the sheriff's office, because we wanted to talk to him. By the time Skippy and I got to Conroe, the commissioner and his attorney were already there. We asked Peel for permission to search his property for the bank appraiser's car. He agreed, so we were on safe ground when we started the search. What Peel didn't know was that just before we had left for the sheriff's office, we had received a call from an informant saying that the appaiser's car was in a stock tank (pond) on the commissioner's farm.

We drove out to the tank and, sure enough, we could see the top of the appraiser's car about three feet under water near the center of the pond. We drove around the pond and found where the car had been pushed in. I sent Skippy and the sheriff to town to get some plaster of paris. We wanted to make an imprint of the tire track we had found near where the vehicle had been pushed into the tank.

I also asked Skippy to request a wrecker while he was in town so we could pull the car out of the tank. As for me, I was going to stay there and guard those tracks and make sure no one disturbed them. All the while, Peel kept driving back and forth at the pond, yelling at me and asking if we had found the car yet. If his objective was to get under my skin and make me mad, he was sure successful.

Skippy soon returned with a wrecker. As soon as we finished making a plaster cast of the tire track, we pulled the car out of the tank. Meanwhile, Peel had gone up the road and was working on an old truck with three other county employees. I told Skippy we needed to match the treads of the right front tire of the pickup the commissioner was driving with the cast we had. I also told Skippy that he had better do the talking. If the commissioner so much as looked at me wrong, I was going to "cut a gut," and I knew that would cause me nothing but grief with my captain.

We drove up to Peel and his helpers, and Skippy asked him for the tire. It was a county truck and Peel didn't have the right to refuse our request, but he did. Skippy started arguing, and I was getting madder and madder. Finally, I had enough. I asked Skippy if I could talk to Peel for a minute. I had, shall we say, a rather vigorous discussion with the commissioner. After the "talk," Skippy and I checked the tire treads with our plaster-of-paris imprint. They matched the other tracks perfectly. For good measure, we put Peel in the county jail for assaulting the appraiser.

We held Peel in jail until we could find the man who had been riding with him when he whipped up on the appraiser. We found our man, and he wasn't about to take a fall for the commissioner. He started talking almost before we asked him the first question. He said that there had been three young boys working in the commissioner's yard at the time of the crime. Peel had told them to get in the appraiser's car and guide it to the tank as he pushed it in with the county pickup.

When things calmed down, I faced reality. Not only had I cut a gut, I had stomped on it. I called Sergeant Rogers and fessed up to my treatment of Peel. Pete went into the captain's office and said, "Captain, Ed's done gone and cut a gut." Later, Pete told me that Captain Oliver just glared at him, turned beet red, uttered a few unprintable oaths, and told Pete to haul it to Conroe.

When Pete arrived and heard our report, he was sympathetic but he said we had better cut Peel loose. We did, and Peel made a beeline for the hospital. He checked himself in, claiming injuries from us. He may have had a bump or two, but nothing like what he should have had. Of course, nothing came of this. He wasn't hurt in the least: he was just doing this for show.

We filed a destruction of private property charge on Peel and got it set for trial. That was as far as it ever went. We went to the Montgomery County Court in Conroe three times, but we never got the commissioner before a judge. He bought the bank a new car to replace the one he dumped in the tank. As for the appaiser, Peel bought him a new, very expensive saddle and a beautiful pistol. I have said how dirty Galveston County politics were, but Montgomery County could show Galveston County a few tricks.

135

Company A, Early 1960s
Back: Me, Dub Clark, Mart Jones, Captain Eddie Oliver, Everett
Smith, Hollis Sillavan
Front: Bud Newberry, Sergeant Pete Rogers, Harvey Phillips,
Skippy Rundell, Clay Bednar *(Courtesy of Randy Sillivan)*

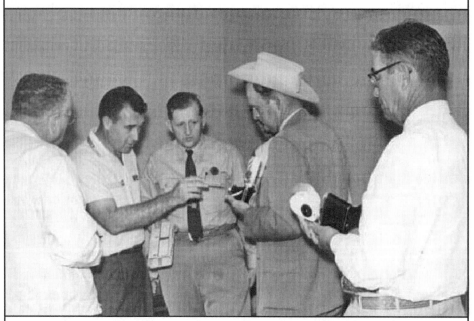

In Houston, receiving new cameras. Left to right: Unknown; future Ranger
Everett Smith (then a DPS photographer); future Ranger and always a
great friend, Skippy Rundell; Captain Eddie Oliver
(Courtesy of Randy Sillavan)

Divorce by Murder

On Monday, November 19, 1959, at 7:35 a.m., forty-eight-year-old Wilma Selby arrived at her home on 4703 Deveon in the fashionable Houston suburb of Afton Oaks. Entering her house through the back door, she walked through the kitchen and the den. Just as she entered the hallway, a man suddenly stepped out and pointed a pistol straight at her. Two shots rang out in rapid succession, striking Wilma in the center of her chest. The bullets landed less than a quarter-inch apart. She fell dead under a framed scroll bearing these words:

> Bless this home, O Lord, we pray,
> And make it safe by night and day.

Before this case came to its conclusion, it took more twists and turns than a snake. Houston citizens and newspapers put overwhelming pressure on the police to bring the killer to justice. Private citizens even put up a reward. In the end, we were successful. By we, I mean all the local police officers. The Houston Police Department's investigation was headed by Captain Weldon Waycott. He did not hesitate calling in Sherriff Buster Kern's Harris County Sheriff Department and the Rangers.

This was a strange case from the beginning. Joseph Selby, a fifty-one-year-old certified public accountant, had arrived home shortly after his wife that fatal evening. According to Selby, when he had seen his wife lying on the hallway floor, he bent over and called her name. Getting no response, he had rushed to his next-door neighbor, G. E. Turbeville, crying that someone ". . . had killed Momma, but they meant to kill me."

Selby and the Turbevilles had rushed over and found Wilma still lying in the hallway. Mr. Turbeville later stated that he had first thought she had fainted. After that, Selby called his son John, who lived only a short distance away. John then called an ambulance and the family physician, Doctor George Gatoura. He said that his mother was hurt (he didn't know she had been shot), and that the doctor was needed immediately. It was over an hour before Doctor Gatoura had arrived, and it was only then that young Selby called the homicide office.

Detectives C. M. Leonard and J. O. Brannon arrived at the Selby home and began their investigation. They were soon joined by two other Houston detectives, B. S. Baker and Neal Todd. Little did Baker and Todd realize that this murder case would almost take over their lives for the next several months. After the case was solved, one of the detectives told me that Joseph Selby's performance during their questioning that night was deserving of an Academy Award. They said you would have had to see it to believe it. He cried and wailed and moaned and could not be consoled.

But I'm getting ahead of myself: that was still in the future. For now, many questions and clues immediately faced the officers. The main mystery was why they hadn't been called earlier. John Selby had said that he thought the ambulance company would call the police after he had called them. I don't know why he thought this. When the ambulance company had been called, no mention was made of death or possible foul play, and there seemed to be no need for the police.

Even though the bullets had not passed completely through Wilma's body, it was obvious that she had been shot at very close range. Yet the weapon had been fired far enough away to leave no powder burns. Later, the autopsy would show that the bullets' tracks were almost identical. This was only possible if the shots had struck in extremely rapid succession.

Still at the crime scene, further investigation revealed that the house had not been forcibly entered. Either the killer or killers were already in the house when Wilma entered or—and this was very unlikely—the killer followed her in. The possibility of the house not being locked didn't cause any extra concern or surprise. Today, it is unthinkable that anyone would go off and leave the house unlocked, but it was common practice in the 1950s and 1960s.

At first, it was naturally assumed that Wilma had come into the house unexpectedly and surprised the intruder. The trespasser had then panicked,

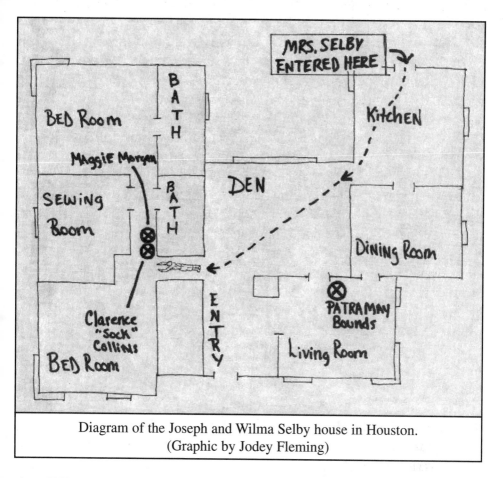

Diagram of the Joseph and Wilma Selby house in Houston.
(Graphic by Jodey Fleming)

shot Wilma, and then fled the scene. But that theory was weak. Almost seven hundred dollars was found in Mrs. Selby's purse. In her bedroom, less than ten feet away, was her undisturbed jewelry box that contained several thousands of dollars in valuable gems. Right beside her body was a mink coat that she had just picked up from storage. In fact, nothing in the house had been disturbed, and Wilma had not been assaulted. Outside the home, footprints were found near a window, and a garden hose was cut into several pieces. Neither of these clues led anywhere.

As is customary with this type of crime, a family member is always a prime suspect. The husband Joseph was no exception, but he wasn't a strong suspect. He was a certified public accountant, fairly well-to-do financially, and wouldn't gain much with his wife's death. He voluntarily went with detectives Brannon and Leonard to their office. For seven hours, he was questioned by Houston Homicide Detective Weldon Waycott, Dis-

139

trict Attorney Dan Walton, and members of both men's staffs. During the whole time, Selby was extremely cooperative and had an answer for everything. In time, we would see that he had too many pat answers.

Selby was asked what he meant when he rushed into the Tuberville home saying that they had killed Momma, but they meant to kill him. He answered that a man had been calling Wilma, claiming that he (Joseph) had been running around with his wife and that he was going to kill him. Joseph thought that the killer had been waiting for him and killed his wife by mistake. This didn't hold water either. Wilma Selby had turned the lights on as she went through the house. She had been shot at close range—so close that the shooter could not possibly have mistaken her for her husband. No, the killer knew he was shooting a woman.

But Selby did have a rock-solid alibi. He said that earlier in the afternoon, his wife had called and said she was downtown. They had arranged to meet outside his office at the 711 Main Building in downtown Houston after he got off work. They had met at six o'clock and had gone to the Colonial Club on San Jacinto Street for drinks and sandwiches. He said they talked about their nine-day-old granddaughter. After leaving the Colonial Club in Mrs. Selby's car, they had driven to the Rice Hotel garage where his car was parked.

Continuing with his story, Selby said that he had told his wife that he needed to stop at the Highland Village Pharmacy to buy some deodorant, shaving lotion, and cigarettes; he would meet her at home later. The pharmict verified that Selby had indeed stopped to buy supplies. The clerks at the pharmacy remembered him well. He had drunk a cup of coffee and made a big deal out of paying for his purchase by check so he would have to show a positive identification. He wanted everyone to remember seeing him in the store.

There the case sat for weeks. Nothing seemed to be happening, and all the Houston papers were demanding results. As they say, looks can be deceiving. From all accounts, the Selbys had been a happily married couple, and the press and the public were in total sympathy for the poor, widowed Joseph Selby.

Sheriff Buster Kerns had as good a detective as I've ever seen: Johnny "Red" Williams. Red had informants all over Harris County, and it wasn't long before he started hearing about a man who had been trying for months to hire someone to kill his wife. Red was told he needed to talk to a black woman named Patra May Bounds. That wasn't a strange name to Red. He and Patra May went way back.

Patra May was no trouble to find. She worked in a black "massage parlor," called the Medico Clinic, in South Houston. She was picked up and brought to the homicide office. Of course, she denied any knowledge of the murder. The more Red questioned Patra May, the more she kept lying through her teeth. But Red was a tough, persistant interrogator who had never learned to back off, and she eventually broke down and told us the whole sorry story.

Joseph Selby had been coming to the Medico Clinic, where Patra May had worked for a year and a half. As he was leaving after one of his visits, he said that he needed to get rid of someone. Did she know anyone who could do it? She told him that she didn't, but she would look around.

A few weeks later, he was back at the clinic. This time he didn't want a treatment; he only wanted to talk. He asked if Patra May had been able to find anyone to kill someone for him. Again, she said no. However, a couple of days later she ran into a Maggie Morgan. Maggie didn't have a job, and when Patra May told her about Selby's request, Maggie told her to send Selby to her.

The next day, Patra May had called Selby and given him Maggie's phone number. A few days later, Selby came to the Medico Clinic and gave Patra May an envelope containing sixteen hundred dollars. He told her to give Maggie seven hundred and fifty dollars and keep the rest until further notice. Maggie came by Patra May's that night and collected the money. Selby again called Patra May and told her to give Maggie another two hundred and fifty dollars From this point until a day or two before the crime, Patra May claimed that she saw neither Maggie or Selby. Then on the day of the murder, she was forced to go along to the Selby home with Maggie and this huge man whose name she claimed not to know.

We finally had a name: Maggie Morgan. We went before a judge and got an arrest warrant for her. With warrant in hand, Red and I headed straight for Maggie's house.

We didn't want to give Maggie any chance to run, so when we got to her house, we didn't bother to knock. With a murder warrant, we were under no obligation to knock and we didn't. The inside of her house was a real experience. Maggie was a fortune-teller and a voodoo queen of some sort. She had candles of every color under the rainbow burning all over the place. Later at her trial, I guess she had a conversion. She showed up with a Bible in one hand and a crucifix around her neck.

Her house was a two-story job and when we entered, Maggie was coming down the stairs. We arrested her on the spot and went right on up the stairs, searching the house for anyone else. Sleeping in one of the beds was a huge mountain of a man, Clarence "Socks" Collins. I don't know if he was having a sweet dream or not, but he was getting ready to have a real bad one. We arrested him, and then hauled both of them downtown to the sheriff's office. Even though Maggie would say several times that Collins was her son, he wasn't. He was a friend of her son Perry.

Under questioning, old Maggie was as tough as boot leather and resisted all our questions, but Red and I kept at her. We told her that Patra May Bounds had already rolled over on her, but still Maggie wouldn't break. She never did.

Even in the grimmest situations, you'll sometimes find humor. I'll never forget that Maggie had this big hat sitting on top of her massive head of hair. The more Maggie resisted questioning, the more aggravated Red became. Suddenly, he reached over and grabbed for Maggie's hat. He not only got the hat, but he also got her hair! She had on a wig. Old Maggie was as bald as an eagle. Red looked at me with a look of utter astonishment on his face that perfectly matched mine. He looked back down at Maggie, threw the hat and wig down, and said, "Forget it!" There were also a few other choice unprintable adjectives. Then he stormed out the door.

Maggie was no longer just an uncooperative suspect: she was a mad suspect. I watched as Red went out the door. When I looked back at Maggie, she was trying to stare a hole through me. Never blinking an eye, she reached into her purse (it had been thoroughly searched) and pulled out a small black bottle. Opening it, she took a pinch of black powder and sprinkled it on my boots, chanting some voodoo nonsense. It took all the patience I could muster to just sit there and let her mess up my carefully polished boots (I worked hard to keep my boots well polished). But when she finished her chanting, I let her have it.

"Don't throw your voodoo crap all over my boots!"

She rolled her eyes around and said, "Young man, you will never live to see Christmas."

Well, I hate to to break the news to her, but I have seen more than forty Christmases since then, and the powder still hasn't worked. Someday, I'm bound to not live to see another Christmas. So, I guess you could say that sooner or later, she'll be right.

There was another humorous sidebar to this story. There was a barber shop close to headquarters, and every two weeks I would get a haircut and get my boots shined. The shoeshine man was working away on my boots, and I asked him if the voodoo powder on my boots would cause him any trouble. He jumped back as if my boots were filled with rattlesnakes and refused to finish polishing them. I left the barber shop with one boot shined and one not.

Clarence "Socks" Collins didn't have the same backbone as Maggie. To be as big as he was (he weighed more than three hundred pounds), he was spineless. With little or no prodding, he admitted to killing Wilma Selby. In fact, he laughed about it. He thought the whole thing was funny.

Listening to the details of the murder was anything but funny.

It had been nearly six o'clock that night when Maggie had picked up Collins and then Patra May Bounds. They cruised around while Maggie went over the details of the murder. Selby had furnished her a key to his house so they wouldn't have to break in. Their victim, Wilma Selby, should be home at about 7:30 p.m. Once inside the house, they were not to turn on any lights and were to keep quiet. It was possible that the Selby's son John might come by, but they were not to worry about it. If he did come by and saw no lights on, he would keep going. After driving by the house, the three had parked two houses down the street. As they exited the car, Maggie handed Collins a .22-caliber pistol.

Inside the Selby home, Maggie, armed only with a flashlight, had quickly positioned Collins and Patra May Bounds. She told Patra to stand in the living room and watch for Mrs. Selby's arrival. Maggie joined Collins around the corner at the end of the hallway and told him to wait until Mrs. Selby turned the light on. He was to then simply step into the hallway and shoot her.

As the three had waited, the Selby's son John pulled into the driveway. As the elder Selby had said, when John saw no lights on in the house, he backed out and went on his way without ever leaving his car.

Shortly, the conspirators had heard another car pull into the drive. No one said a word. Moments later, they heard the back door open and saw the kitchen light come on. Mrs. Selby entered the den and flipped on that light. Collins said he could hear Mrs. Selby walking toward the hall-way. When he saw her shadow, he stepped out. Mrs. Selby had a package of some kind in her arms.[53] Before she had a chance to comprehend any danger, Collins shot her twice, as quickly as he could pull the trigger. He said she had dropped like a rock.

Collins, followed closely by Maggie and Patra May, stepped over the body and headed for the car. Maggie had left the car's engine running, and Collins climbed into the backseat and lay down so no one could see him. Maggie drove to the bus station, where Collins got out of the car. He claimed that she never paid him a penny of the money she had promised him.

When Collins was asked what he did with the murder weapon, all he would say was, "I eat it."

"Say what?"

"I eat it."

That went on and on, and all he would ever say was "I eat it."

We really needed Collins to identify the murder weapon. The lab people had examined the bullets that killed Mrs. Selby and told us that the land-and-grooves[54] on the bullets were not precise enough for them to swear any specific gun was the murder weapon. At best, all they could do was be reasonably certain. That would never be admitted in court, so we had to have Collins positively identify the weapon.

About this time, we received a call from a foreman at the Sheffield Steel Company. He said that he had seen Willie Morgan, Maggie's husband, hide a pistol in his locker. We just knew we were ready to put the final wrapping on this case. Wrong.

I had believed Willie Morgan when he insisted that he knew nothing of the murder and had only taken the pistol because his wife had made him. You could tell he was just an old, hard-working man who was terrified of his wife. Meanwhile, Maggie was still denying any knowledge of the murder and all Collins would say was "I eat it."

Once we recovered the gun (a German made .22-caliber Rohm Zephyr), the ballistic boys went to work on it to positively identify it as the murder weapon. In the words of the lab people, the killer got "the luckiest

---

[53] This was a mink stole she had picked up from storage earlier that day.

[54] Every weapon leaves a distinct marking on a bullet as it travels down the barrel of the gun. This is called land-and-grooves.

break a killer ever got." The weapon had originally been manufactured as a starter gun that only fired blanks. It had been converted to a working pistol when a real barrel was exhanged for the fake. The only problem was that the barrel was not an exact .22-caliber barrel. It was slightly larger—larger enough that each shot did not have the exact lands-and-grooves. Even after firing more than one thousand rounds through the pistol, the lab people said they overwhelmingly believed that it was the murder weapon but could not swear with total certainty that it was. When Collins and later Selby admitted to the murder, the positive identification of the weapon turned out to be not so important. Such is the frustration of police work.

When Joseph Selby was arrested and his involvement became public, it created an even bigger sensation than his wife's murder. Remember, this was 1960 and race relations were quite different from today. When it was revealed that Selby was a regular visitor to black houses of prostitution, all the sympathy that the public had felt for him evaporated. The public was shocked and outraged. And the outrage grew as more facts came out.

It seems that Selby had a special fondness for twenty-one-year-old Willie May Stuart. Willie May operated a massage parlor, Sue's Baths, at 2905 Milam in Houston. Selby had been seeing Willie May regularly for two years. She was light-skinned and frequently crossed between the white and black worlds. Selby had often taken her to well-known restaurants in the Houston area—even to the Colonial Club, the same one where he had met Wilma on the day he ordered her murder. He had given her thousands of dollars in cash, signed notes for her at a local bank, bought her diamonds, and even signed a note for her to buy a Cadillac convertible.

With their confessions, it seemed a pretty open-and-shut case against Selby and Collins. But then the lawyers got involved. Maggie Morgan never admitted to anything, and Patra May Bounds turned state's evidence and testified against the other three.

Maggie Morgan was tried first, convicted, and received the death penalty. Then it was Selby's turn. By now, his case had generated so much publicity that it would have been nearly impossible to conduct an unbaised trial in Houston. It was not surprising when his attorneys asked for and received a change of venue to Austin.

The trial was a three-ring circus from the start. It lasted for several weeks but in the end, it didn't help Selby. He was sentenced to life in prison. Likewise, Clarence "Socks" Collins received a life sentence. Patra May Bounds was given a reduced sentence since she had turned state's evidence. Collins' and Selby's life sentences were life-saving verdicts for Maggie Morgan. Since her co-killers had received life-imprisonment terms, her death sentence was also reduced to life imprisonment.

This was a particularly satisfying case because a vicious crime was solved, and it was solved through the cooperative work of the Houston Police Department, the Harris County Sheriff's Office, and the Texas Rangers. Captain Weldon Walcott of the Houston Police Department's Homicide Division summed it up best in a press release:

> I would like to impress that this was no one-department deal in finally solving the crime. It took the equal work of the District Attorney's Office, Sheriff Kern and his office, the Police Department and the Rangers.

The Sam Houston Museum Burglary

Mart Jones was a Ranger from the old school. He may have been a bit old-fashioned, but he was overloaded with common sense. He instinctively knew people and how to figure out what they were likely to do under any set of circumstances. I had an opportunity to work a case with Mart that could have had serious repercussions throughout Texas.

On Saturday, June 27, 1959, the Sam Houston Museum and the nearby Sam Houston home in Huntsville were burglarized. Among the thirty-one guns stolen were rare muzzle loaders, cap and ball pistols, derringers, and flintlocks. There were also three swords, two knives, several tomahawks, powderhorns, and peace pipes that had belonged to General Houston's son Temple. Five of the guns had belonged to Sam Houston. Among these were two dueling pistols that had been given to him by the citizens of Cincinnati, Ohio; an 1862 Colt revolver with Houston's name engraved on the barrel; and his prized shotgun, "Meat in the Pot." Because of the general's accuracy with that weapon, whenever the locals had heard the roar of that old shotgun, they would say, "There'll be meat in the pot today." Also stolen was the documentary proof of the collection's authenticity. Obviously, the thieves knew what they were after. Ironically, they missed a sword that had belonged to one-time Mexican general and president, Santa Lopez de Santa Anna.

Entry into the museum had been obtained by prying open a basement door. Houston's home, which stood a few hundred feet away, had been gained by breaking a window. Inside the museum, the thieves had broken open only one display case before finding a lock box in the basement that contained the keys to the museum's display cases. After prying open the lock box they had simply gone around the museum, opening up the display cases and gathering up their loot. In the words of the museum director, Grace Longino, the thieves "could name their own price." I really doubted this. The material was too well-known and would be almost impossible to fence. A fence only wants things he can unload quickly at a huge profit. These objects were way too hot to handle.

Huntsville Chief of Police Elmer Nichols and Walker County Sheriff Floyd Farris put every effort into the recovery. They were certain that the thieves had moved outside their areas of jurisdiction, so they contacted their Ranger, Mart Jones. None of us doubted that if this case wasn't solved double fast, the outrage of the people of Texas would be unbelievable. Mart knew that, and so did Captain Oliver. Mart requested help, so Captain Oliver sent me to Huntsville to assist with the investigation.

When I arrived in Huntsville, I went directly to the museum and joined Mart. He was talking to Grace Longino. She was related in some way to General Houston and she was not taking the loss of the general's guns calmly. By the time I arrived, Mart had her calmed down.

Mrs. Longino had had the presence of mind to contact an elderly man[55] from Dallas who happened to be a tinkerer and a gunsmith. He had been coming there for years, fixing old weapons that the museum acquired. He had a very small lathe and some miniature tools he used to work on the old pieces. He may have been up in years, but he still possessed an unbelievable memory.

The artifacts had been displayed in the main lobby of the museum and housed in glass-topped showcases. The old man went from case to case and named every piece that had been in each one. Since the thieves had entered the museum office and taken all the inventory cards to the guns, his precise details were critical to our investigation. Using his description of the contents of each case, we made a list of the missing items. Once the list was completed, we made several hundred copies and mailed them to every gun dealer in north Texas, western Louisiana, southern Arkansas, and southern Oklahoma.

The flyers paid off several days later. Two antique dealers in Dallas had been approached by two young men wanting to sell some old guns. One of the dealers had become suspicious of their actions and had written down the license-plate number of the men's car. He immediately contacted Cap-

---

[55] I can't remember this man's name.

148

tain Jay Banks, the commander of Texas Ranger Company B in Dallas. Jay ran the license number and found it registered to Virgil Fielden, Jr., 22, of Mesquite,[56] Texas. Jay called Fielden's father, who turned out to be a minister, at his home. Fielden said the last he had heard of his son was that he was going to his aunt's home in Dallas. The elder Fielden called his sister, and she said that Virgil and a friend, Henry Thome, 18, of Mesa, Arizona, were headed to Daingerfield, Texas, to visit Virgil's grandmother.

The next day, Wednesday, July 1, Sheriff A. E. Howell of Morris County arrested the boys without incident. They admitted that they had stolen the guns and told the sheriff that the artifacts were in two different places. They also described where they could be found.

Red Arnold, the Ranger in Mount Pleasant, called Mart and told him that

Red Arnold
(Picture courtesy of the Texas Ranger Hall of Fame and Museum)

he had the boys in custody. I headed out immediately for Daingerfield, stopping in Huntsville only long enough to pick up Mart and Sheriff Farris. We arrived in Daingerfield late that night.

I was looking forward to working with Red Arnold again. He was already a legend in the Rangers. During my career, I was priviledged to work with Red four times. He was truly one of the great Rangers of my era and I am proud to have known him.

Red had already talked to the boys, and they were anxious to tell us what we wanted to know. That was a good thing because we had driven too far—right at three hundred miles—to put up with any games from these youngsters. They told us exactly what they had taken and where it was stashed. Their descriptions matched our list of stolen property.

Fielden and Thome said that they had visited the museum late Saturday, June 27, and decided it would be an easy place to loot. At four o'clock

---

[56] Mesquite is a suburb of Dallas.

the next morning, they hit. Using a screwdriver, they pried open one of the doors and stumbled onto the lock box containing the keys to the display cases. They had carried the booty in their car for several days and intended to sell all the stolen property. When they discovered that their loot was too hot to fence, they decided they had better hide their plunder until they could find a buyer. They hid the property on the banks of the Sulphur River near Commerce. They had chosen that spot because both had attended East Texas State College in Commerce and knew the area well. And yes, they would be happy to lead us to the hiding places.

We left Daingerfield and headed north in Red's car, stopping only when we reached the Sulphur River. The boys said the loot was "down there," pointing to some brush near the bank of the river. Red pulled over to the side of the road and said if the boys were telling the truth and the guns were "down there," pointing down the hill to the river bottom, he wasn't going to drive the car off the pavement. It had been raining for days, and he said that as muddy as it was, it would be awhile before we could get the car out of there if we drove down. Of course, it would have to quit raining to dry out, but the weather forecast didn't look promising.

We stuck our pants into our boot tops and started walking down the hill, with Fielden and Thome leading the way. We finally reached the bottom, where we came to a fence that bordered a field. Following the boys, we continued along the fence until we came to a gap in the wire. Passing through the gap, we walked to a cluster of button willow trees in the corner of the field. One of the boys pointed into the thicket and said, "The stuff's in there."

Red said, "You put it in there, you bring it out."

They went into the bushes. After a few minutes, they stumbled out, saying that all of it was too heavy to carry.

"How'd you get it in there if it's so heavy?" I asked.

They said that it had taken several trips. They had spread out a tarp in the thicket, placed the stolen items on it, and then covered them up. We followed the boys into the bushes and picked up all we could carry.

I have to admit I felt a bit overwhelmed to have in my hand both of Sam Houston's personal pistols that had been given to him by Samuel Colt. Colt had had the butts of the pistols inscribed: "General Sam Houston from Samuel Colt." I also picked up a couple of the long guns and stuck some of the tomahawks in my belt. The others in our group did the same. Once we had made the tarp light enough for the boys to carry, we started back up the hill. It had been much easier going down than it was going back up. We would take two steps forward and slide back in the mud, but we finally made it to the top. I have often wondered what a stranger would have thought if he had come up on us carrying all those old firearms and tomahawks with mud up to our knees and our belts stuffed full of weapons of all descriptions.

We arrived back in Daingerfield late at night and went directly to nearby Greenville, where one of the boys had taken his share of the weapons. We drove out in the country where he had hidden his guns under a stump. After loading the stolen property in the trunk of my car, we headed back to Huntsville, arriving at the museum at nine o'clock the next morning. We unloaded the property on the loading dock as Mrs. Longino counted each piece. We had recovered everything that had been taken from the museum. It was a good thing we recovered all of it when we did; they were already starting to rust.

Our job completed, we went to Mart's house and went to bed. It had been a long two days and we were totally exhausted. Dutch, Mart's wife, fixed us breakfast before we passed out. I slept until nearly noon and then went back to Houston.

Virgil Fielden Jr., and Henry Thome were each given a three-year suspended sentence by District Court Judge, Max Rogers.

We're Not Here to Embarrass Anyone

One of the strangest incidents I was ever involved with happened in May 1963. It was during a wildcat strike[57] at the Shell Refinery on the La Porte Highway,[58] just east of Houston at Pasadena. We received a call from nearby Deer Park's chief of police, B. J. Bickerstaff, asking for our assistance. I had known Chief Bickerstaff since my days in Baytown as a Highway Patrolman when he was the resident deputy sheriff. Captain Oliver sent Sergeant Pete Rogers and me to the strike area to keep a lid on a potentially explosive situation.

I hate strikes, and I don't know of a single Ranger who would disagree with that statement. I will talk about another strike later in this book, but I want to say categorically that Texas Rangers have no business working strikes. It puts us in a lose-lose situation. No matter what decision we make, one side or the other is going to claim we were biased for the other side. But like them or not, we were told to go to La Porte. So we went.

When Pete and I arrived at the refinery, we found the four-lane highway completely blocked by a hundred to a hundred and fifty cars and pickups. All the vehicles had their hoods raised and their motors off. The owners claimed they were "broke down." The press estimated that more than one thousand additional vehicles were stacked up behind the "broke down" ones. Needless to say, the people unable to get to work because of the strikers were not a bit happy.

Pete had an outside speaker mounted on the grill of his car. He had attached it to his two-way radio. By simply flipping a switch, he didn't have to be in his car to hear incoming messages. As soon as we pulled up,

---

[57]Unauthorized by the union.
[58]Highway 225 Freeway.

he flipped the speaker on. He called the DPS office in Houston and told them to go to the wrecker section in the yellow pages and "start at the *A*'s and keep sending wreckers until I tell you to stop." Of course the strikers heard this, and a few decided their civil disobedience didn't go all the way to the impound yard. They moved their cars before the tow trucks could snatch them.

When the first wrecker arrived, we flat out got the strikers' undivided attention. We had the wrecker driver back up to a car. Before he could hook up, the owner came running up, claiming we couldn't tow his car. Wrong! Watch us! We were more than willing to give him and all the other roadblockers a chance to move their vehicles. We didn't want to cause anyone any trouble, but one way or

Captain Pete Rogers, my long-time friend, a fellow Ranger in Houston, and my boss in Amarillo while I was with Comapny C.
(Courtesy of The Texas Ranger Hall of Fame and Museum: Waco, Texas)

another, we were going to open the highway. So they had a choice: they could either drive their vehicles off the highway right-of-way, or they could have the cars towed. It was up to them. They all needed to understand one thing very clearly: we had already told the wrecker driver that once he hooked onto a car, he was to keep it until he got every single penny of his money. And we would back the wrecker driver to the hilt. Did anyone have any questions? I don't guess this guy did; he got in his car and drove away.

That also resolved it with a few of the other strikers: they took their cars and left. But most stayed put, leaving plenty of cars for the tow trucks to haul off. In short order, enough cars had either been towed or moved so that the backed-up traffic could, by driving down the center lane, weave its way through the cars still on the highway.

Pete and I headed for the demonstrators. As we approached the middle of the remaining vehicles, a Volkswagen came tearing out of the refinery, heading toward Houston. Two strikers were walking in the center of the highway just in front of us, but had not seen us. As the driver of the Volkswagen came abreast of the walkers, one of the strikers pulled a short chain about sixteen inches long out of his shirt. He had welded a handle onto it and he swung it into the windshield of the Volkswagen. The windshield shattered into the car, but the driver wisely kept going. Stopping in the middle of the screaming, mad strikers would not have been too smart on his part. Both men were laughing when they finally saw us, not ten feet from them. They ran for what they hoped would be the safety of a nearby ditch, where a couple hundred of their buddies were making all the noise.

Pete cut one of them off and I caught the other as he rounded the front of the car. I put him up on the fender of Pete's car and searched him. Nothing. Not even a pocket knife. Pete had the man with the chain. I told the man I had that he could get on the shoulder with his buddies and do all the mouthing he wanted, but he better stay off the roadway. As for the man with the chain, R.W. Errington, we hauled him before Justice of the Peace Bud West in La Porte. Judge West freed Errington on his own recognizance.

Once we finished with Errington, Pete and I returned to the strike area. The wreckers were still working full blast, and the more cars they towed, the madder the strikers got. We could hear someone trying to stir them up with some very angry rhetoric. This mob—and that was what it had turned into—was big enough that if we didn't do something to defuse it really fast, things were probably going to get very ugly.

Standing on a large, wooden cable spool was the man we had earlier told to stay off the right-of-way. He was waving a clenched fist in the air, urging the men to riot. "Let's take this thing over! We outnumber them a hundred to one! We can run this anyway we want to!" He had them going pretty good and was working them into a frenzy. The more agitated the mob became, the more dangerous the situation was. A riot was right around the corner unless we stopped this nonsense right now.

Pete looked at me and said, "I think he sinned. Don't you?"

"Real bad."

Before wading into the mob, we pulled off our hats and put them in the car. We eased our way through the crowd, heading for the speaker. When we got close enough to the striker, I yanked him off his stump and started for the car before anyone knew what was going on. I had the seat of his pants in one hand and his shirt collar in the other. By now, the mob realized what was going on and they started trying to form a circle around us to stop us. But anyone who got in our way . . . well, let's just say that Pete got them out of our way. All the while, the yelling was so loud you couldn't hear a thing. But we were not going to be stopped. When the striker and I made it to the car, Pete had the back door open, waiting for us. I bent the old boy over, put my knee in his seat, and pushed him into the backseat. By then, Pete had the car moving. I slammed the back door, grabbed the handle of the front door, flung it open, and jumped in.

All of a sudden, we had a new man in the car with us. Sugar would have melted in his mouth. Everything was, "Yes, sir. No, sir. I was only joking. I'm terribly sorry." There was one apology after another for causing us so much trouble. As soon as we were well away from the mob, we stopped to question the man. It turns out he was Bruce Tuck, a city councilman of nearby Deer Park. We asked him why in the world he was trying to stir these men up the way he was.

"I belong to the union and that's my job."

We told him, "We're not here to embarrass anyone. You know that if we file on you, your job as a city commissioner is finished, don't you?"

"Yes sir. I realize that."

"If we take you to your car, will you promise to go on home and leave these people alone?"

"Yes sir, I sure will. I'm very sorry for what I did."

To be on the safe side, we followed him to the driveway of his house.

About two weeks later, two federal marshals came to the Ranger office and served Pete and me with a stack of papers that would have choked a horse. Bruce Tuck, the "oh, I'm so sorry, I was only joking" councilman, had sued each of us for seventy-five thousand dollars for false arrest, defamation of character, and a couple of other charges I can't recall.

The same Eddie Dykes who had saved Skippy Rundell and me from charges of tearing up the Silver Moon on Galveston Island answered the summons for us. The only difference was that when he had taken care of Skippy and me, I never met him. This time I got to meet Mr. Eddie Dykes personally. He was definitely a good man to have on your side. City Committeeman Tuck didn't give in until the evening before we were to appear in federal court. I guess he and his lawyer finally realized that we were not going to back down. Late that afternoon, the clerk of the court called and told us the case had been dismissed. Needless to say, Pete and I were greatly relieved.

A Special Breed of Men

As I said earlier, I had the privilege of working with Red Arnold on four cases in my career: the Kilgore slant-hole business, the terrible Lone Star Steel strike, the theft at the Sam Houston Museum, and one situation during the Galveston gambling days. The only good things about these cases were that I not only got to work with Red, but I also met and worked with almost every Ranger in the state.

In the early 1960s, I did several short stints during what was sometimes called the slant-hole business. It all happened in Kilgore at the giant East Texas Oil Field. It was discovered that some crooked oil-drilling companies were buying up abandoned or low-producing oil wells from the major oil companies in order to rework them. Their theory was that since their overhead was so low, they could make a profit from the small output of the wells. The only problem was that these poor-producing wells started mysteriously gushing like the mother lode. What the small drilling companies were doing was running their drills down into the original holes, attaching a whip stock, and then slanting toward a nearby rich lease in order to steal the oil.

This was no small operation. There were hundreds of these slant-holes all over the field, and that covered a lot of territory. Until oil was discovered in the Middle East, the East Texas Oil Field was the largest oil field in the world. It is over ten miles wide and more than forty miles long.

This problem was Company B's baby, and Rangers Jim Ray and Glenn Elliott were basically running the show. They had their hands full. Not only were they battling the men doing the slant-hole drilling, but with millions of dollars involved, they were also dealing with some of the wealthiest and most powerful men in East Texas. These men stood to make thousands and possibly millions of dollars, and they did not want the Rang-

Two great men and the finest of Texas Rangers
Jim Ray (left) and Glenn Elliott (right)
(Pictures courtesy of Jim Ray and Glenn Elliott, respectively)

ers or anyone else standing in their way. They used every means at their disposal to combat the Rangers. They threatened to physically harm some of the railroad commissioners who would do the actual inspecting. They were smart enough to never try physical threats on the Rangers—they weren't that stupid. They did try the political influence game, but that didn't work either. Some tried to involve Governor Price Daniel, but the slant-hole potato had gotten too hot. He wouldn't or couldn't help them.

The problem was too much for two men, even men of the stature of Jim and Glenn. In fact, it was too much for even one whole company of Texas Rangers to handle alone. At one time or another, I guess just about every Ranger in the state was in Kilgore. I went to Kilgore twice, two weeks each time, during this dance. It was then that I first met Red Arnold, Jim Ray, and Glenn Elliott. Three better Texas Rangers never lived than those men.

During my time in Kilgore, I was paired mainly with Hollis Sillavan. Our job had a two-fold purpose. One was to sit on the oil wells and not allow anyone to drop anything down into them. Those old slant-holers were dropping anything they could down those wells to prevent the railroad commis-sion people from determining the direction of the well. When I say anything, I mean anything: rocks, concrete, two-by-fours, tree limbs, and anything else they could get down the hole. The second reason we were there was for the protection of the railroad commission people. This was a dangerous game with big dollars involved. Most of the inspectors feared for not only their safety, but also for their lives. Our main job was to make sure nothing happened to the inspectors. I'm happy to say we accomplished that job.

I understand that even though numerous indictments were handed down, no one was ever sent to prison over this. I do know that the list of people indicted by the grand jury read like a social register of Gregg and Rusk

Counties. Money talks.

While working the gambling cases in Galveston, Red and I found ourselves caught in the middle of a

Hollis Sillavan was a wonderful man and was already a Ranger when I joined Company A in 1957.

small hurricane. There was heavy rain in the forecast that afternoon, but at the time the storm had not yet been graded a hurricane. We went about our business of checking out the local joints. By about four o'clock, the weather was starting to get serious. We had just turned onto Post Office Street, and it was like someone had turned the faucet on full blast. The water started getting deeper and deeper, and ahead of us, we could see parked cars with only the roofs sticking out of the water. We turned on the radio to get a weather forecast, but all we found was static. We decided that the better part of valor was to retreat to the Buccaneer Hotel and hunker down until the storm passed. Red turned down 23rd, a four-lane street that had an esplanade running down its center. Since the walkway was the highest point, Red drove on it until we reached the seawall. He turned there and headed toward our hotel. By now, the rain was coming down so hard that it was almost impossible to see the end of the car's hood. Red was an excellent driver, however, and we made it to the hotel.

In the lobby, the desk clerk said we were in for a real blow. The storm was headed straight for Galveston and the winds had increased to hurricane force. Hurricanes were something that Galveston definitely took seriously. In September of 1900, Galveston had suffered a great tragedy when somewhere between six and eight thousand people were killed by a hurricane.

There was nothing we could do, so we went up to our room and watched the fireworks from there. We could tell by the sparks flying through the rain that high-line wires were breaking. By morning, the storm had blown by and we could get out of the hotel.

When he had parked the night before, Red had found a place close to the building. That was a lucky chance, we thought. When Red went to get in the car the next morning, he opened the driver's side door and water gushed out. The Buccaneer Hotel's roof was red Spanish tile. The wind had been so hard that about half of the roof tiles had blown off. One of the tiles had come straight down through the roof of Red's car and water had poured into it all night.

Red's week of duty was finished and he was scheduled to go home to Mount Pleasant. A wet seat wasn't going to stop him. He put on his raincoat, cranked up his car, and headed north.

The last time I worked with Red was during the Lone Star Steel strike in 1968-1969. Of all the strikes I had the misfortune to work as a Texas Ranger, this was the granddaddy. Bombs, beatings, shootings, murders—all of these happened during what a Dallas newspaper called "A Strike Gone Mad." Like the slant-hole business, this was also Company B's baby, since the plant was in its area. Also like those two cases, at one time or another I guess every Ranger in the state was there at least once, and most were there several times. Only two Rangers, Glenn Elliott and Bob Mitchell, were there from beginning to end. Bob told me that he and Glenn checked into a motel in nearby Daingerfield and didn't check out for seven months and three days. They didn't rotate in and out like we did in Galveston: they were there the whole time.

From my own experience in Galveston, my hat is off to Bob and Glenn. I know how hard it is to be gone from home for such a long time, even with home only about fifty miles away. But such is the life of a Texas Ranger.

Sick or Not

One case above all stands out in my mind durring my years in Houston: the attempted burglary of the Tube-Lite Sign Company at 5606 Stuebner-Airline Road. Tube-Lite was not far from Ranger headquarters, which at that time was on the North Freeway in the northern part of the city.

It started early in the evening of Wednesday, May 24, 1962. I was at home, nursing an ulcerated stomach. A steady diet of all work and no play had taken its toll on me, and I was in real pain when the phone rang. It was Don Moffet, a detective from the Houston Police Department's burglary division. He said, "We've got a tip on a burglary that's coming down near the Ranger office at the neon sign company. That place is full of cutting torches and they're going in to steal a torch. Once they've got it, they plan on burning a safe somewhere. Tony Colca and I are going down there to wait on them. Can you meet us?"

You bet I could. One of the main ways a Ranger is or is not respected by his peers is whether he will come when called. It's seldom that a Ranger will get a call for assistance if there isn't a genuine need. All you have to do is say no a few times and suddenly you won't be getting any calls at all from the departments you are supposed to be assisting. Then you have to explain to your captain why no one's calling you. I am extraordinarily proud of the fact that in all my years as a Texas Ranger, I was never questioned by my captain or anyone else for not getting calls to assist officers in my area.

So sick or not, I was going on this case, too. By the time I got dressed and drove to headquarters, the last vestiges of light were gone. It was pitch dark, and Detectives Tony Colca and Don Moffet were waiting on me. After a quick briefing, we loaded into my car and drove to the Tube-Lite Sign Company to wait on the burglars. We didn't have any idea when the burglaries would hit or in which door of the 62' x 70' building they would try to gain entrance. All we knew for sure was that they were coming. At least, that's what one of Moffet's informants had told him. We arrived at Tube-Lite at about 7:30 p.m. As we walked toward the warehouse, Moffet asked Colca for some shotgun shells. Colca said he thought Moffet had brought the shells. They asked if I had any ammo. All I had were the five 00 buck-shot shells in my 12-gauge Remington automatic: four in the magazine and one in the barrel. I ejected three shells and gave Moffet two and Colca one, keeping two for myself. Moffet was carrying a .38-caliber snubnose, Colca a .45-caliber automatic, and I had my Colt .38 Super.

Colca and Moffet had contacted the owner of Tube-Lite Sign Company, Woody Marsh, and told him what was getting ready to come down. Marsh met us in the parking lot and let us into the building. He lived in one end of the building, and we told him to go to his apartment, turn the lights off, and under no circumstances answer a phone. If the burglars followed normal procedure, they would call to verify that no one was there. If the phone was answered, they would simply walk away. So it was important that he not answer any calls.

Once inside the building, it was black as coal. We were afraid to turn on a light in case the burglars happened to show up at that moment. We positioned ourselves along one wall, under a row of windows, in such a way that we would not be in each others line of fire if shooting started. Then we settled down to wait. At about 8:45, we heard a noise that sounded like someone was tearing the whole north end of the building off. The burglars had pried a huge twenty-five-foot door off its bottom track and pinned it back enough to crawl through. Seconds later, I saw a small pocket light come on, and I could tell that the thieves were moving toward us.

They were only about ten feet from us when Don Moffet stood up and yelled in a loud, clear voice, "Hold it right there!"

A streak of fire and a loud roar from a pistol were the answers. My first thought was, "I've been here before." Suddenly, I was back in Europe, and eleven months of combat experience took over: "When fired on, open up with everything you have." And that is exactly what I did. All three of us started blazing away. I popped two rounds through my shotgun (remember, that's all the shells I had), threw it down on the bench in front of me, and drew my .38 Super. It was darker than the inside of a cow in there, and all I could do was fire at the muzzle flashes. I did that until my pistol was empty.

As in most gunfights, it was over as quickly as it had started. Suddenly, everything was deathly quiet. We started looking for the light switch. Finding a battery of switches on the wall, Colca began flipping them on. Moffet and I stood watch in case either of the thieves was hiding and still had some fight left.

We need not have worried. In the middle of the floor, one thief was dead with a chest full of buckshot and the whole left side of his head gone. The other thief was gone, but there was a trail of blood leading back to the door. We crawled through the small opening the thieves had made to enter the building and looked the outside over pretty well. We could find no one.

Police Inspector Woody Stepenson and two or three other detectives came in right after the shooting stopped. They had heard about our opera- tion and were only a couple of blocks away when the shooting started. That didn't bother me, but what did was the news media that showed up with them. Why they let them in on this is still beyond me.

Searching the area, we couldn't find a gun. From the hulls, it was clear that the dead burglar had been using a .38 Super. Since I shot the same gun, the first question I was asked was how could they know that all these shells hadn't come from my gun? With no weapon on the dead guy, I knew where this was going.

But there was no problem. I said, "Just look at the hulls. The shooter's are brass; mine are chrome. Totally different brands." That settled that.

Of course, it was impossible to tell who had fired the fatal shot. The thief on the floor had been hit in the neck, chest, abdomen, and head. He had caught a couple of full loads of 00 buckshot in the chest. Either Colca or I had hit him just above the left ear. The size of the wound ruled out Moffet and his .38, but either Colca's .45 or my .38 Super could have done that kind of damage. Since the bullet had passed all the way through his head, it was impossible to tell which one of us had fired the fatal shot. One thing is for sure, we were both trying to.

We started investigating the scene and realized it was a miracle that none of us had been hit. There was a window behind us that was shot out and holes in the wall behind where we had been stationed. There was a truck beside us, and it also had bullet holes in it. The shooter, who we believed had gotten away, must have gotten excited. As close as we were, there is no

162

other way he could have possibly missed us. Excited or not, he had kept his head enough to get out. We could tell from the blood trail that he had gotten down on his hands and knees and crawled out of the building.

Pointing to the dead man, Moffet said, "I think I recognize him. He's Clarence Bourg, an old-time safe burglar, and he lives at the Northline Mo-tor Hotel over on Airline Drive. His old lady is a sister to Gene Paul Norris."[59]

Clarence Anthony Bourg, 50, had a police record as long as your arm. His list of crimes went all the way back to 1940. One of his places of residence had been Leavenworth Penitentiary. Upon further investigation, we learned that besides his full-time job of stealing, he had also been working as a meat cutter in a local grocery store.

We brought in three police dogs, hoping they could lead us to Bourg's partner, John Forrest Lowe, but we had no luck. We also checked all the local hospitals, again with negative results. Well, we knew where to go. Once we finished at the warehouse, we drove over to the Northline Motor Hotel. We secured Bourg's room number from the clerk and headed for the room. We didn't bother to knock. For all we knew, Lowe was waiting on the other side of the door with his pistol. We kicked open the door.

The only person there was Bourg's girlfriend, and she claimed not to know where Lowe was. We were not going to argue with her. For her own safety and to know exactly where we she would be, we had her picked up and put in jail. We then settled into the darkened room for our second wait of the night. About 1:15 a.m., there was a faint knock at the door. Moffet and I positioned ourselves so that we would not be in a crossfire, while Colca got behind the door and reached across to open it.

When the door opened, Lowe came staggering in. He was shot up pretty good and was very weak from loss of blood. He offered no resistance, but denied that he had been in a shootout with us. He claimed that some-one—he didn't know who—had picked him up as he walked down the street, robbed him, and then shot him.

There was one big problem with his story: armed robbers don't usually use shotguns. Lowe's back and legs were full of buckshot. He had so

---

[59] If there has ever been a more prolific killer in Texas than Gene Paul Norris, I don't know who it would be. He wanted to be known as the worst killer in Texas history and he probably was. It is believed that he killed more than fifty people. Usually, he killed for hire. His murderous ways were brought to a bullet-riddled end in 1957 when Captain Jay Banks from Dallas killed Norris and his partner, Carl Humphries.

much lead in him that lead poisoning was a definite possibility. We told him the buckshot would have to come out. He didn't like the idea of being cut on and said that he would just live with the buckshot. I told him that you don't live with as much lead in your body as he had. Whether he wanted to or not, we sent him to the hospital. We kept him in hospital custody until he healed up enough to stand trial. This was his third or fourth conviction, and it took the jury less than an hour to sentence him to life imprisonment as a habitual criminal.

Sadomasochistic

While I was stationed in Houston, I worked three other cases that stand out in my mind because they were so gruesome.

I was still fairly new in law enforcement, and I was looking for all the experience I could find. The Harris County Sheriff's Department was more than willing to help me get that experience and called whenever they could. Once they called and said they had a double killing. Would I like to go to the crime scene?

I worked some weird cases as a Ranger, but none weirder than this one. It involved sadomasochism,[60] S & M for short. A young couple had been married only a short time when the girl's mother noticed bruises on her daughter's arms and legs. Once she had even seen a cigarette burn on her arm. The girl always had excuses: she had fallen down or had dropped a cigarette. The list went on and on. As it turned out, the girl was the masochist and the boy was the sadist.

How in the world these two ever found each other is a mystery, but they did. I suppose each time they practiced S & M on each other, they became more and more intense with their sickness. One day they decided on the ultimate high.

In all my years in law enforcement, I rarely saw a bloodier mess. The girl was nude and hanging by a wire clothes hanger in a doorway just inside the house. She had been burned, sliced, and punctured. As a final act

---

[60] According to the *Harcourt Dictionary*: a tendency to derive pleasure from inflicting or receiving pain or humiliation.

of sadism, her stomach had been slashed from one side to the other. Her husband was lying on the floor with a single .38-caliber bullet through his head.

The girl's mother said that at first, she and her husband had loved the boy and were proud their daughter had found a good man. When they started seeing the bruises and cigarette burns, however, they became deeply concerned. With her daughter refusing to complain, there was nothing the mother felt she could do.

And there was nothing we could do. Since both people were dead, there was no one to file charges against. The case was closed.

The Torso Murder Case

I was in Houston six years. One of the most baffling cases I worked occurred in 1962. The Houston media called it "The Torso Murder." I hate to say it, but contrary to the movies and TV, we don't solve all of our cases. This was one of them.

Two men, whose names I have forgotten, stopped at a bridge on Highway 59 near Sheppard, Texas, to go fishing. Before starting, they noticed two cardboard boxes sitting nearby at the water's edge and went to investigate. To put it mildly, the men were stunned when they discovered that the contents of the boxes contained a dismembered torso. The lower part of the torso was in one box, and the upper part was in the other. Dirty, oily clothes had been stuffed around the body parts in each box. The two men contacted the San Jacinto County Sheriff's Department, and they contacted me.

What we found was grizzly. Scattered over a large area near the water were the intestines. When we investigated the boxes, the arms of the torso had been removed at the shoulder, the legs at the hips, and the head had also been severed. The killer had also cut out the victim's heart. We never did find any of the missing body parts. I don't know if the murderer carried them with him, threw them away, or gave them to a dog. We never found out anything.

When we completed our crime-scene investigation, the local justice of the peace ordered the body taken to Houston for an autopsy. The autopsy revealed the remains to be that of a woman about forty-five years of age. She had given birth to at least one child, probably two. The pathologist estimated the woman to have been approximately five feet, eight inches tall and had weighed about one hundred seventy pounds. She had a scar running horizontally across her abdomen from an earlier appendix operation.[61] It was estimated that she had been dead seven to ten days. Unfortunately, due to the absence of a head, fingers, and other normal identifying parts, we could not put a name with her.

We checked the missing persons file with the Houston Police Department and the Harris County Sheriff's Office. Again, nothing. We didn't have a clue as to the identity of this lady. We put as good a description as we could on fliers and posted them throughout the area. We immediately started getting calls. We found people that had been missing for years, many who didn't want to be found.

We received a call from a woman who said her neighbor was moving and was digging in his back yard. We drove to his house and found him with a box the size of an Army footlocker. He was very cooperative. His said that his dog had died some time ago, and he had buried him. He was moving out of state, and he couldn't bear the thought of leaving his dog behind. He had dug up the dog's remains so he could take them with him. He opened the box and showed us the proof.

All this happened while I was rotating in and out of Galveston. For the next four years, we continued to run every lead we received. We had a meeting with officers from five states that had reported similar cases. In fact, we found them scattered all over the country, but we were never able to solve our mystery. The woman's remains were buried in a pauper's grave in a San Jacinto County cemetery.

---

[61]The pathologist told me that pre-1949 appendix operations were made with a vertical incision.

Swimming in the Bayou

One of the last cases I worked in Houston was with Buck Echols of the Texas Southwestern Cattle Raisers Association. A band of cattle rustlers were operating just north of Houston in Montgomery County. And no, rustling did not go out with the Old West. Truth be known, there's probably more rustling today than at any time in history.

I had an informant that I had worked with many times over the years. He was very well-connected with this kind of crime. He told me the name of a man in northeast Houston who was selling meat out of his deep freeze. Following his lead, I went to the suspect's house. The suspect was there, and I identified myself and asked for permission to look in his deep freeze. I don't know if he thought frozen meat couldn't be identified or if the jig was up, but he agreed to the search. I couldn't believe what I found. There were chunks of meat wrapped in everything from newspapers to tinfoil to plain brown paper. It was easy to tell that a professional butcher had not cut these up. They were in hunks of every size and shape imaginable. Grass, hair, pieces of skin, and other things I never did figure out were mixed in.

When I asked him where he had gotten the meat, he said it had come from two men in the area. He claimed not to know their names, but he knew where we could find them. All he knew was that every once in a while, they would show up with some meat to sell and he would buy it. We didn't arrest this old boy right then. When you've been in this business awhile, you develop a sixth sense that is seldom wrong as to who will run and who won't.

He wasn't the type to run. Anyway, we didn't want to spook the men who were selling him the meat.

He didn't have to give us their names. These old boys were well-known in the area, and it didn't take long to find them. We arrested them and carried them to the jail in Conroe. They both admitted they were part of a much larger rustling ring. Being an old cowboy, as I listened to them describe their method, my blood began to boil. It was pretty simple. They had an old 16-gauge shotgun with even older shells that sometimes functioned correctly and sometimes didn't. I got madder and madder as I listened to them describe how they sometimes had to shoot some of the cows two, three, even four times before they got them down.

They said that after the cow was finally dead, they would skin it and cut up the meat. Then they would wrap the meat in whatever was handy and take it to their outlet in Houston. Their outlet was the same man who had told us where to find these guys. After they finished this, they would load the hides up and dump them in one of the ditches or bayous that dotted the area around Conroe.

These two guys comprised just one of several groups who were butchering cattle in and around Conroe. We questioned them for two days and nights before they started naming names and telling places. We ended up with nine men in Houston, Conroe, and several other surrounding areas that we charged with cattle theft and put in jail. This included the buyer. We were right; he hadn't run.

Now, all we needed to wrap this thing up were a few hides with brands on them so that we could tie them directly to the cow theft. The rustlers told us that one of the places they were dumping the carcasses and hides was in a bayou between Conroe and Houston. We loaded up and headed that way. We traveled down Highway 75 until we came to an old oil-top road, and we drove down it until we came to the bayou. You would not believe the smell when we stepped out of the cars. The whole area was black with flies.

We made the thieves go down into the water with orders to find us a hide with a brand. You wouldn't believe the cries of anguish!

"You ain't going to make us get in that dirty water!"

Buck's reply was straight to the point: "You put the hides in there; you're going get them out."

After a couple of minutes, I noticed one of the thieves was missing. I looked around and saw him standing close to Sheriff Buck Echols, peeking over the edge of the bridge. I punched Buck and pointed. Buck was not happy when he saw that guy standing there. He grabbed him by the scruff of the neck and shoved him in the bayou. When he hit the water, the others started yelling that he couldn't swim. Buck yelled back, "I don't want him to swim; I want him to find a hide."

You better believe we got a branded hide—real quick.

Send Him to Me

As soon as we put the rustlers in jail, I went home. I was one sick puppy. I walked in the door, hit the couch, and put an ice pack on my stomach. My ulcers were screaming. I couldn't sleep, and I told Lena to call Sergeant Rogers and get the telephone number of Dr. Michael DeBakey. I had suffered enough: I was going to call him Monday morning.

Earlier tests had revealed that I had two ulcers: one in the lining of my stomach and one in the lower part of my intestines. When Lena and I moved to Houston in 1967, I had weighed 215 pounds; six years later, I weighed 180. I looked like death warmed over and I was hurting all the time. Ulcers in Company A, especially in Houston, were a common problem. We lived on cigarettes and coffee with an occasional sandwich thrown in. Before he died, Captain Klevenhagen had half his stomach removed. Captain Eddie Oliver and Sergeant Pete Rogers were veterans of the same operation. It looked like I was next on Dr. Debakey's list.

This was in 1963. Lena and I had talked about moving out of Houston several times. So instead of calling Dr. DeBakey, I went to the office Monday morning and talked to Captain Oliver. He said he didn't know of a vacancy anywhere. I had gotten word from Captain Bob Crowder of Dallas' Company B and Captain Clint Peoples of Waco's Company F that if I ever wanted out of Houston, just let them know. I didn't want any part of Dallas. I would not have been gaining much by simply trading one big city for another, so I had Captain Oliver call Captain Peoples in Waco.

Captain Peoples told Captain Oliver: "Load him up and send him to me. I'll find a place for him." I wound up in the Hill Country of Kerrville. As we loaded our household onto a moving van and left the city limits of Houston, I stopped and looked back one last time. Then I said goodbye, got in my car, and never looked back.

I had spent some of the happiest and saddest years of my life in Houston, but I had had enough. I left some mighty good friends there, some living and some dead. The living I have visited whenever I could since I transferred; the dead will be in my heart forever. Now (2001), I am the only surviving Ranger of Company A's class of 1957-1958. Even though he came into the Rangers after me, I always considered Skippy Rundell one of the originals. Even Skippy is gone now. I said the eulogy for him at the annual Texas Ranger Reunion at Waco in 1999. May God rest his soul.

The cases that I have just presented to you were mixed in with our regular duties of going to Galveston about once a week to raid some old gambling house or find and arrest someone for ourselves or some other company. Whenever we arrested someone for another company, it seemed that they always wanted to meet us at the Houston city limits. No one wanted to come into downtown Houston. I think that the only reason I was appointed a Texas Ranger is because I was already in Houston and knew the city fairly well. Even then, the population was nearing a million people. I understand it is over two million now.

Chapter V

Kerville-Amarillo
1963-1969

A Bird Out of His Cage

I started a new duty station in Kerrville on September 1, 1963. To say the least, it was quite a shock to my system. Both as a Highway Patrolman and as a Texas Ranger, I had worked out of the headquarters office in Houston. There, we were expected to be in the office at a certain time, quit at a certain time, dress a certain way, and follow a multitude of other rules. In my first few months in Kerrville, I was like a bird out of his cage. I was two hundred miles from my captain, Clint Peoples, in Waco. I had five counties to roam where there were more deer, wild turkey, and wild hogs to hunt than ten men could shoot. Every creek was filled with clear running water and every stream was full of fish of every description. I thought I had found a true heaven on earth. Of course there was a workload, but nothing compared to what I had left behind in Houston.

As much as I love to hunt and fish, I had been sent to Kerrville to do a job. Besides, it took an amazingly short time until the hunting and fishing began to get boring. I was just too accustomed to a heavy workload. I'll be the first to admit that I didn't want the backbreaking schedule I had in Houston, but I did want more action. One thing about being a Texas Ranger: if you want to work, there's plenty of it out there. I don't care if you are in Loving County, the most remote part of Texas, I promise you there are plenty of crooks and outlaws to keep you busy. If you don't want to work, you can be stationed in Houston, Dallas, or San Antonio and not find anything to do.

I quickly got into a routine. To be perfectly honest, with the experience I had gained in Houston, the cases I worked were not that difficult, with a few exceptions. It took me a while to adjust to Kerrville. It was an entirely different world from what I was used to. I couldn't get over the laid-back attitude of the area.

The first thing I had done when I arrived in Kerrville was introduce myself to the sheriff of Kerr County, Vernon Moore. One day I was in Sheriff Moore's office and I noticed, lying on his desk, an arrest warrant on a crook I had known in Houston. I also happened to know that he was the foreman on a ranch close to Arcola and would be easy to find. I asked the sheriff what the warrant was for, and he said the man had stolen some cattle from the Rocky Ford Ranch. I told Sheriff Moore that I knew right where to find him. I quickly added, "Let's go get him."

If I live to be a hundred, I'll never forget old Sheriff Moore leaning back in his chair and saying, "Nah, he'll come back through here one of these days and we'll get him then."

I couldn't believe it. True, Arcola was a couple of hundred miles away. But so what? In Houston, we would have been on our way in a heartbeat, whether it was three in the afternoon or three in the morning. That was the way we did things in Houston, but not in Kerrville.

I do not mean to imply that Sheriff Moore was lazy. He wasn't. The area and the sheriff just operated at a much, much slower pace. But there was a very positive side to the slower pace: it was just what the doctor ordered for my ulcers. In about two months, my stomach stopped bothering me and I threw away all my pills and antacid medicine. I was healthy again.

It was a good thing I got healthy, because the pace was going to pick up. Vernon Moore did not run for reelection and Leon Maples was elected to office.

To say that Leon worked at a faster tempo than Vernon would be the understatement of the century. During his campaign, Leon had taken a map of Kerr County and marked it off into blocks. Then he started going door-to-door, contacting everyone in every block. After contacting each household, he would take a crayon, color that house on the map, and then move on to the next block and repeat the procedure. I think Leon contacted just about voter in the county personally, and it paid off. He was elected and he made the citizens of Kerr County a fine sheriff.

Looking back almost forty years, I can't recall the first case I worked in Kerr County. I know I hadn't been there long when it came to me through the grapevine that I had been paid one of the best compliments a law officer can ever get. Word came out of Austin and went like this: "The thieves in that area had better move out of Kerr County. The law has arrived."

Charlie Miller

Captain Charlie Miller
(Courtesy of The Texas Ranger Hall of Fame and Museum: Waco, Texas)

I had only been in Kerr County a few days when I received a call from Charlie Miller, the Ranger in nearby Mason. This was THE Charlie Miller, a legend among the Texas Rangers even in his own time. Charlie is one of only thirty men in the three-century history of Texas Rang- ers to be elected to the Texas Ranger Hall of Fame. He was calling me, Ed Gooding, to meet him for coffee. I couldn't have been more honored if the governor of the state of Texas was calling.

Earlier, I said that I worked with every Ranger in Texas except Charlie Miller and Hardy Purvis, Jr., during our three-and-a-half year operation against the Galveston gamblers. I had heard a story as to why Charlie wasn't there, but with each telling, it always varied a little. One day Charlie told me the real story.

Charlie had been working in Galveston on detached assignment as a bodyguard for the Internal Revenue Service. This was during the 1930s, and the IRS had just had success putting Al Capone away for income tax evasion, and they were trying the same thing with the Galveston gamblers. As in Chicago, IRS men were accountants, not peace officers, and they were not allowed to carry guns. Thus, Charlie entered to work as a bodyguard for the IRS men.

The IRS had made a case against one of the more prominent gamblers in the area. With Charlie along to make sure the job got done, they arrested the gambler and took him to the jail. When they walked in the door, Charlie saw the chief of detectives sitting behind his desk and said, "We need to put this fellow in your jail."

Charlie said he didn't know if the detective was on the gambler's payroll or not, but he wasn't going along with putting the gambler in his jail: "No, you ain't going to put him in my jail."

This didn't set well with Charlie, and he was not one to sit on protocol. He reached across the detective's desk and got the cell keys. Charlie said he just looked at the glaring chief and said, "Well, if you won't put him in there, I will." And he did! After he locked him up, instead of giving the keys back to the detective, he put them in his pocket and walked out the door.

The detective apparently had an extra set of keys because before they got to the car, Charlie saw the gambler come out a side door and head for the downtown area. Charlie was in a charitable mood and decided to let it ride. He knew where to find the gambler—and the so-called chief of detectives.

The next day, Charlie and the IRS agent were walking along the seawall, looking at trinkets in some of the little curio stands that lined the beachfront. Charlie was lagging a few steps behind, glancing at something. He suddenly heard a shot. Looking up, he saw the IRS auditor lying on the ground with what turned out to be a bullet in his groin. Standing over him was the detective chief from the night before.

"There, smart guy. So you thought you could put a friend of mine in my jail?"

Charlie always carried his pistol, a 1911 Colt 45 semi-automatic, not in a holster, but stuck down in the front of his pants. Don't let that fool you. He could draw and fire in the blink of an eye. And he did. He hit the chief just above the nose and squarely between the eyes before he could move a muscle. Needless to say, Galveston's chief of detectives was dead before he hit the ground.

After getting the IRS auditor to a doctor, Charlie called Colonel Homer Garrison in Austin and told him what had happened. The next morning, the chief of police called Charlie and told him he needed to come to the police station; they needed to talk. Entering the chief's office, Charlie

179

saw several officers standing around the room. They had a warrant for his arrest for murdering their chief of detectives and they were going to put him in jail.

Charlie looked at the police chief and said, "There's two things wrong with what you just said. First, you don't have enough men here to put me in your jail and second, you don't have nearly enough men to take my pistol away from me. One of you has already died messing with me. You don't want to go for more."

The situation was reaching flashpoint when a Catholic priest who was familiar with the personality of Charlie Miller came in the back door. In a glance, he sized up the situation and said, "Just cool it boys; back off. Mr. Miller, you go on and get out of here. If we need you, we'll get in touch with you." Charlie walked out of the door. As per his earlier instructions from Colonel Garrison, he kept right on going until he was off Galveston Island.

The auditor didn't die. After telling his story, Charlie had the full backing not only of the federal government, but also the state of Texas. Above all, he had the approval of Colonel Homer Garrison. Believe me, Colonel Garrison was a force to be reckoned with in Texas. Charlie had nothing to worry about from a legal standpoint, but he wouldn't have been welcome in Galveston by the local police department when we were working the gamblers.

Dumb Lucky

Kerrville may be smaller and more laid-back than Houston, but they still know how to kill one another there. In my seven years of service in Kerrville, I had only three murders. I regret to say that my batting average for them was not very good.

The first murder case I had centered around a domestic argument between a man and his wife, with the woman ending up dead. I hate to say it, but this case was botched up from the start by just about everyone involved.

This murder happened right after the Earl Warren Supreme Court had ruled on the Miranda case. At the time, most of us thought the high court had pulled nearly all our teeth. After its ruling, you had to "Mirandaize" anyone when you arrested them. You had to read the suspect a list of all the "bad" things that could happen to him if he talked to you. About all this accomplished was to scare the suspect half out of his wits before we could even start to question him.

A woman had died by natural causes. At least that's how local Justice of the Peace Orr, who was also the county coroner, ruled in his inquiry. But the woman's daughter was having no part of that verdict. She said her mother and her stepfather argued endlessly, and she believed that he had murdered her mother. She kept after Judge Orr to have an autopsy performed, and finally her persistence paid off. The judge ordered the body exhumed and shipped to San Antonio for an autopsy.

I was in the county attorney's office when I first learned that a possible murder had been committed. The district attorney, Robert Barton,[62]

---

[62] Judge Barton later would retire as Kerr County's District Judge.

181

told me he had just received an autopsy report that left several things un-answered, and that I might want to look into it. Judge Orr was a retired military adjutant general and had only worked military law cases. He had little expe-rience with civilian matters and didn't feel completely comfort-able as to the best direction to take. I could understand that. We're all in the same country, but civilian and military law proceedings are as different as daylight and dark.

I read in the autopsy report that the victim had unexplained bruises on her throat and that her hyoid bone[63] was broken. The report offered no opinion whether this was the cause of death or not. With such an unclear report, Judge Orr refused to reverse his earlier ruling. But I wasn't ready to let it go. I talked some more to the DA about the case. He carefully re-viewed the complete file and advised me to proceed with a murder inves-tigation. We would try to clear up the autopsy report later.

When the victim's husband learned that an autopsy was going to be performed, he went to a local doctor. We learned later that he admitted to the doctor that he had killed his wife. He told him that this had been his second marriage and was a huge mistake from the first. He was much older than his wife and she continuously made fun of his lack of sexual prowess. It was humiliating to him, and one night as they lay in bed, she started laugh-ing at him. That was it. He claimed that something snapped and in a rage, he strangled her to death with his bare hands. He asked the doctor to certify that he needed a psychiatric examination and to get him admitted to the Kerrville State Hospital. The doctor agreed that he indeed needed evaluation and had him admitted.

The husband was from San Antonio, so that's where I headed to get all the background information I could find. As soon as I arrived, I contacted Zeno "Zero" Smith, the local Ranger, and asked for his help. We contacted the suspect's first wife and she said she had no doubt that her ex-husband was capable of killing. She said that he had nearly choked her to death on more than one occasion.

After finishing in San Antonio, I returned to Kerrville and immedi-ately contacted the district attorney. After listening to my report, DA Barton advised me that we needed to have the suspect see a state-appointed psy-chiatrist for further evaluation. He suggested I take him to San Antonio and get the psychiatrist that the Bexar County Sheriff's Office used.

---

[63] A small bone in the throat.

I contacted the doctor in San Antonio and set up an appointment. When the suspect and I arrived at the psychiatrist's office, he was suddenly not available. I began to smell a mouse. We had an appointment and the doctor doesn't show up? It appeared I had gotten ahold of a suspect who had some powerful political connections.

The receptionist directed me to the nearby state hospital. After getting the suspect admitted, I was told it would take about a month to reach any conclusions, which they would forward to me. Instead of keeping him in San Antonio, however, they loaded him up and took him back to the state hospital in Kerrville. While in the hospital, he confessed to his two doctors that he had killed his former wife. Since the doctors were state employees—working for the state and not the suspect—no doctor-client relationship existed. Whatever he told the doctors, they could testify to.

Several local businessmen, public officials, and I loved bluegrass music and we would meet at various homes and "jam" about once a week. We were at the district attorney's house one night about a week after returning from San Antonio when he received a call from the state hospital. Our suspect wanted to talk to us. The DA and I dropped everything and took off.

We were ushered into a visitation room, and there sat the suspect with his first wife. Looking at me, she said he wanted to tell me something. Before we allowed him to say a word, we issued him his Miranda warning. He said he understood his rights, but he wanted to talk anyway. He laid it all out. His wife had been drinking heavily and they were doing what they usually did—arguing—when she physically attacked him. He fought back, and the next thing he knew, he had choked her down. He didn't mean to kill her: it just happened.

We got all this down on paper and the suspect signed it. Since he was under the care of a doctor, we didn't take him into custody but left him at the hospital. We also got a statement from the doctor in charge of the hospital that the suspect had come in under his own free will, was not in custody, and could have walked out any time he wanted to.

We filed murder charges and the case was set for trial. The suspect's lawyer requested a preliminary hearing before the trial date, and it was granted. The purpose of a preliminary hearing is to determine if there is enough evidence to present the case to a grand jury. With the suspect's written confession, the hearing should have just been a formality. We went through his statement admitting the murder and also his statement to the doctors. After nearly a full day in court, the judge called a recess. When court resumed, the roof fell in. The judge ruled that even though the suspect had made the request to talk to us that night and had agreed to his Miranda rights, since he was in the state hospital, he was actually in our custody and had been given a statutory warning by a magistrate. Since his mental capacity was in question, an attorney should have been present when he made his statements. Continuing along the same line, the judge overruled the doctor's testimony, therefore also making the suspect's statement to him inadmissible. Our case was deader than his murdered wife.

District Attorney Robert Barton was aghast, I was stunned, and the suspect was free.

Barton and I must have talked this case over a dozen times in the ensuing years, and we never could figure out why the judge had ruled the way he did. The district attorney had presented precedents from similar cases where a man had been in voluntary custody and statements had been taken and admitted as evidence. But the judge is the judge, and his ruling is final in all matters of law. The state cannot appeal to a higher court in Texas: only the defendant can appeal if he is found guilty.

I have often wondered if this guy was this smart and hoodwinked us, or if he was just plain old dumb lucky.

The Tivy Mountain Killer

The second murder case in Kerrville happened in 1967 and was exceedingly baffling. One morning a man was walking his dog near Tivy Mountain, a prominent hill near Kerrville, when he saw what looked to him like a body in a ravine. As fast as he could, he rushed home and called the police. The sheriff's office called me, asking for my assistance.

When the sheriff and I arrived at the murder site, we found the body of a female. She had been rolled down an embankment beside the road and had lodged, face down, in a brush pile. All she had on was a red pajama top. There was what appeared to be a deep scar running diagonally across her face. However, once the funeral home finished preparing the body, this turned out to be something different: it was an indentation where she had been lying on a limb in the brush pile. She had been strangled to death with a stocking. We assumed her killer had to have been a very large man, because she was a big woman. If you went by size, she was big enough that she could have taken care of herself. We believed an autopsy would prove us correct in that she had been raped.

None of the deputies, ambulance workers, or anyone from the funeral home had any idea who our Jane Doe was. Once she had been transported to a local funeral home, we issued news releases asking anyone who knew of a missing woman to please come by the funeral home to assist in making a possible identification. The response was good, and several people were able to tell us that the woman was Claudia Mason, a nurse at the local veterans' hospital in Kerrville.

We secured Ms. Mason's address and immediately went to her home. At her house, we found the bottom part of her pajamas, but little else. There was no evidence of forced entry, but that wasn't strange. In those days, people in Kerrville never locked a door or worried about intruders. We questioned everybody in the neighborhood but drew a blank. We contacted members of the Mason family, but they were not a particularly close family and none had seen Claudia in several years. No one could shed any light on her posses-sions or who her friends and acquaintances might have been. After about a month, we ran out our string and put the case on the back burner.

In 1972 (I had transferred to Amarillo by then), I got a call from Henry Ligon, who had replaced me in Kerrville. Henry said he had cleared the Claudia Mason murder. He had had a case which was almost identical. A girl had been abducted and found on a country road outside of Kerrville. Like my case, all she had on was her pajama top. But there was one huge difference in our cases: Henry's victim had been in ter-rible shape, but she was alive and she knew her assailant—James Woodward.

It had taken a while for the victim, Susie Turner, to recover her voice. When she did, she easily identified the man who had kidnapped, raped, and attempted to kill her by strangling her with a piece of seatbelt. She had been incredibly lucky. She had passed out, and the man thought she was dead. Otherwise, he would have made sure she was.

It had turned out that Woodward was a neighbor of Claudia Mason and just a teenager. He was a prominent student at Tivy High School and also one heck of a good football player. When my wife Lena heard his name, she said she knew his mother and father: they traded at the store where she worked. Lena said they were good people and this would just kill them. They were always bragging on him and were extraordinarily proud of him. Woodward's father was always talking about his son's football abilities.

Henry asked if I wanted to attend the trial. I wanted to, but by the time the trial started, I had transferred to Temple and was up to my ears in half a dozen murder cases. There was no way I could get loose to go. Henry kept me up to date. James Woodward's pattern was to assault his neighbors. His last victim had also been a neighbor. She lived just across the street from the Woodwards.

For the attempted murder of Susie Turner, Woodward was sentenced to fifty years. For the murder of Claudia Mason, he was sentenced to thirty years. Both were to run concurrently.

Smell

I guarantee that you will never find a law enforcement officer that does not loathe domestic problems. I don't care how they end up; we lose. At best, the couple gets together and blames us for interferring. At worst, somebody ends up dead.

Shirley Ruth Bierswell was missing, and her husband John was suspected of foul play. I talked with Hugo Klaner, sheriff of Gillespie County, and he related the known facts he had at this point. The Bexar Sheriff's Office in San Antonio had received a call from a lady who said that Shirley Ruth Bierswell had left a small baby with her while she went shopping. That had been a week before, and Shirley Ruth had not returned for the child. They had contacted the infant's father, John Bierswell, and he went to San Antonio and retrieved his son.

I questioned Bierswell later. He said that about a week after he had returned from San Antonio with his son, he was at work at his father's butane company when he saw Shirley Ruth and a man drive by, going north on Highway 290. He followed them. When they stopped, he confronted his wife wanting to know why she had left their son in San Antonio and where she had been for a week. A fight ensued between Bierswell and his wife's boyfriend, and the sheriff was called to separate the men.

The sheriff had run a check on the boyfriend and found that he was wanted in San Antonio on some outstanding traffic warrants. He locked him up until officers from San Antonio could come get him. There was no charge the sheriff could file on Shirley Ruth, so he released her. The last time any-

187

one saw Shirley Ruth Bierswell was when she and her husbandhad left the jail.

The Bierswells lived in Fredericksburg, and I made several trips to that beautiful little city to talk with John. He claimed that after leaving the jail, he and Shirley Ruth had had a tremendous fight. He had dropped his wife out on the highway at a rest stop and had not seen her since.

I put out a missing person all-points bulletin on Shirly Ruth and continued questioning Bierswell. He still denied he had harmed his wife in any manner. I knew that Bierswell had done something with his wife, but knowing and proving are two different things. About a week later, I again went to Fredericksburg to question Bierswell. I was told that he had left word with his mother and other members of his family that he had taken a job with an oil company and had gone to South America to work. I knew they were lying, but again I couldn't prove it. I was stuck with no suspect and an uncleared murder case.

Shirley Ruth's father, a Mr. Shipman, lived in Ingram, Texas, just outside Kerrville. I had talked with him on several occasions regarding his missing daughter. He suspected Bierswell had done something to her and urged me to keep trying. I didn't need urging. My batting average had not been up to par in Kerrville since moving from Houston, and the absolute last thing in the world I wanted was another unsolved murder.

Mr. Shipman showed me his daughter's hunting rifle and the knife she used to skin deer. He told me he had taught her to hunt and she was good at it. Shirley Ruth was a little wild but had respect for other people. Mr. Shipman couldn't see how she would let anyone get the better of her in a fight, even though Bierswell was much larger than she was.

Without breaks, no murder case—or any case for that matter—would ever be solved. Mine came about three weeks after Bierswell had supposedly gone to South America. I got word that his father had died and the family would be having the funeral in Harper, Texas. I attended the funeral and saw Bierswell there with his brother-in-law and several other family members.

I waited until after the funeral and talked with some in attendance. They said John had been in West Texas with his sister and brother-in-law, working on an oil rig. He had only missed South America by a few thousand miles.

I waited until the family had gathered after the funeral. I approached them and asked to speak with John Bierswell. His mother came to the door and verbally lit into me like a tiger. She called me everything but a gentleman. Finally, Bierswell came to the door with his brother-in-law, and we walked out in the yard.

All the while, Bierswell's mother was still raising cane, so he and I got in my car. Bierswell wanted his brother-in-law with him, so he went along with us as we drove away from the house. I talked for about an hour with Bierswell without success. He wouldn't admit to anything. He asked if there was any reason he couldn't return to West Texas with his brother-in-law.

I looked him straight in the eye and told him I knew he had harmed his wife in some way. I put my finger on his chest and told him he could go anywhere he wished, but he had better remember one thing: I was a Texas Ranger and I was going to find his wife some day. When I did, he would be walking down some street, feel someone tap him on the shoulder, and it would be me. He could bet the bank that I was not going to give up until I exhausted every effort to nail him. Then I took him and his brother-in-law back to his mother's house and I left.

The next day, Gillespie County Deputy Sheriff Lawrence Buror called me and said John Bierswell was in his office and wanted to talk to me. I immediately left for Fredericksburg. Beirswell admitted I was right. He and Shirley Ruth had had a fight at home and it had turned physical. He had knocked her down and she had hit her head on the baseboard of the wall. At first he thought she was just knocked out, but when he saw blood running out on the carpet, he knew it was much worse. Shirley Ruth was dead. He picked her body up, carried her out in the backyard, and buried her in a chicken coop. The coop had a Spanish tile floor, which he removed. He dug a hole and put his wife in it.

Several officers joined me at the chicken coop, and we quickly found the spot where Bierswell had buried his wife. The officers began to dig, but soon a God-awful stench came from the hole. We had found Shirley Ruth. Suddenly, I was alone in the makeshift grave. Trust me, a decomposed body has a smell like no other on the face of the earth. I have been around more than my share of bodies like this, and I have learned a secret for handling the gut-wrenching smell. You take a cigar and cut it in half so that the end of the cigar is near your nose. Then you light it and put it between your teeth, in the middle of your mouth. That kills any smell you can imagine.

It wasn't long before we uncovered the body, along with several pieces of clothing, a .22-caliber rifle, and an old blanket. I called the justice of the peace. After his inquest, he ordered an autopsy. I let the ambulance crew remove the body and load it in the ambulance. I followed them to San Antonio.

I was determined to make sure this case went right. I had had two murder cases: one lost in a preliminary hearing and the other unsolved. I was 0-2.

The autopsy revealed that Shirley Ruth had died of a massive hemorrhage to the frontal lobe of her brain. This is common with a heavy blow to the back of the head. There was a four-inch gash in the back of her head. All this supported Bierswell's story that he had knocked his wife down and her head hit the baseboard of the wall.

The body was in such an advanced state of deterioration that it was impossible to determine if she had been shot. Why Bierswell buried the .22 rifle with the body, we never determined and he never answered. Maybe he did shoot her. I don't know, but he was smart not to admit it. If he had, that would have taken preference over the accidental death from her head hitting the wall when he knocked her down.

I filed murder charges on Bierswell and he was denied bond. While awaiting trial, the district attorney and I had an occasion to be in Fredericksburg one day. When we walked into the sheriff's office, there sat Bierswell at a domino table, playing dominoes with a deputy sheriff. The district attorney and I just looked at one another. After a stunned few moments, we walked back a few paces and the DA said to me in a low voice, "Am I seeing things? Wasn't that Bierswell sitting there playing dominoes with that deputy?"

"Yes."

Bierswell was a local boy who had known the deputy most, if not all, of his life. The deputy trusted Bierswell.

Bierswell was convicted of murdering his wife and received a twelve-year sentence. As I said, he was a local boy.

The Trail Drive

Charlie Schreiner III (he was commonly known as Charlie III), owner of the YO Ranch just outside Kerrville, became a very good friend of mine, as he was of all Rangers. He was a real Ranger buff and an avid gun collector. Actually, he was a collector of anything pertaining to the Texas Rangers. His grandfather, the first Charlie Schreiner, had founded the mighty YO Ranch, was a Texas Ranger, fought Indians and outlaws, and was the driving force behind Schreiner College in Kerrville. He was a true legend of American and Texas Western history of the 1800s.

The love of Texas and the West runs deep in the old man's grandson. In 1966, Charlie helped organize the Texas Longhorn Cattle Raisers Association. Like his grandfather before him, Charlie wasn't content to just help start the ball rolling and then sit back and collect the praise. Charlie was a doer. He wanted people to know about the Longhorn Association and he needed money to operate. Charlie came up with a wonderful publicity scheme.

Charlie organized a trail drive of one hundred longhorn steers from San Antonio to Dodge City, Kansas. He would follow the same path his grandfather had followed a hundred years before—the Western Trail. It went up from San Antonio to Abilene, Texas; then to Vernon, Texas at the old Doan's Crossing of the Red River; from there to Altus, Oklahoma; and finally terminated in Dodge City, Kansas. Anyone who wanted to tag along could, but not for free. Every horse and rider was charged fifty dollars; a wagon and driver, one hundred dollars. The cowboys and security people worked and rode for free.

Charlie put together a herd. In my spare time, I worked with his

191

ranch hands getting the steers not only used to each other, but also to the automobile traffic, people noise, and other various hazards we would run into on the trail. Some of the steers were as wild as deer and had never been put in a herd. It took some doing to get them settled down.

Charlie had several Mexican *vacqueros* (cowboys) working on green cards,[64] and they were good. Charlie had a set of portable-steel cattle pens built. Each section was built in a curve so that when all were attached, they formed a circle. The Purina Company wanted in on the publicity and fur-nished a truck loaded with feed, hay, range pellets, and other necessities for the horses and steers. Altogether we had ten trucks, one truck for each ten head of steers. We also had another truck load of horses from the YO Ranch and an additional closed-in truck and trailer for our tack.[65]

Since the main purpose of the drive was for people to see the rare longhorn cattle with horns that sometimes spanned ten to twelve feet, we had to be extra careful not to let any be broken off. As Charlie liked to say, "They are not worth much without the horns."

My commanding officer, Captain Clint Peoples, had become intrigued with the drive, and he assigned me to act as security. My area would span as far as the Red River, which forms the Texas-Oklahoma border, but that was as far as I could go on state time. I also couldn't take my state car into Oklahoma. But I had come this far, and I didn't want to stop with the end in sight. I took a week's vacation time, crawled on the back of a horse, and helped push the herd on to Dodge City, Kansas.

My Texas Ranger badge wasn't big enough to cover Oklahoma and Kansas. Few knew that, though, and just like today, a Texas Ranger draws a lot of attention. (I wish I had that proverbial dollar for the times I've been told, "I just wanted to meet a real Ranger.") To help identify everyone and what part of the drive they were involved with, Charlie had various colored ribbons made up that resembled a Texas Ranger badge.

We hauled all the steers to San Antonio and settled them in before starting the drive. Some lay down, while others were standing around peacefully chewing their cud. All was a picture of serenity, we thought. The next morning we lined up, and when Charlie yelled, "Move 'em out!" absolute, total bedlam broke loose. The ranch hands were supposed to handle the herd

---

[64]Official cards signifying legal immigrant workers.

[65] Saddles, bridles, blankets, ropes, and other gear that we didn't want to get wet.

192

and the wannabe cowboys were supposed to just tag along. Well, the wannabes had watched too much television, and they started running up behind the cattle, popping whips and yelling at the top of their lungs. Billy Beard was in front, trying to hold back the steers. Charlie, Ace Reed, and a senator whose name I can't remember were ahead of him. Before we could get control the mob, steers were breaking around the leaders, jumping over fences, and scattering all over the country. Dudley White, a Ranger from Midland, was also working security. He ran into the herd of wannabes, grabbed the bridle of one of the men, and jerked his horse down. That got everybody's attention, and we finally got control of the herd before anyone was hurt.

By the time we had re-gathered the herd, it was late in the day. We only drove the herd a few miles out of San Antonio and then penned them for the night. They didn't much care for the pens to start with, but by the time the drive ended, those old steers were so used to them that they just walked in whenever they saw the gate open.

The next day, we loaded the steers on trucks and carried them to the LBJ Ranch near Fredericksburg. At the ranch, we unloaded them and put on a short drive; then we penned them up and fed them. Because of an incident just out of San Antonio in which some teens had thrown fire-crackers in the pens and almost caused a stampede, we posted several men around the pens to keep spectators at a distance.

Then we all enjoyed a fish fry, courtesy of the perfect host, President Lyndon Baines Johnson. After the good eating, we again loaded the steers on the trailers and drove to Abilene to an area known as Old Abilene Town. We spent the night there, and the next morning we put on a drive around Old Abilene Town; then we headed for our next stop, Vernon, Texas. We traveled in a convoy, with me in front and Ranger White in the rear. We set a pace that the big trucks could maintain without bouncing the steers around too much.

In Vernon, we camped in the Old Fair Grounds very near the Red River. This area is known as Doan's Crossing. At the crossing, there is a monument with an inscription stating that in the mid-1800s, nine million head of longhorn steers had been put across the river at this location on the Western Trail, headed for the railheads in Kansas. The brands of each of the herds were engraved on the monument. One them was the Lazy S brand, Charlie Schreiner's origianl brand. We were indeed retracing Charlie's grandfather's tracks.

By the time we reached the Red River, the steers had become so accustomed to us that they gave us very little trouble. That allowed more time to watch the cattle as a spectator, and I learned a lot about longhorns on that drive. Each steer has his place in the herd and he will fight to keep it. There is a lead steer,[66] usually a young, strong animal that takes the lead every morning when you move out. The herd moves in the form of an hour glass. The younger, stronger steers bunch up in front, while the middle slims down to almost single file. Then there is a smaller group at the rear called the drags, which consists of the older, weaker steers.

Billy Beard was the cow boss in charge of the cowboys, and every morning when we were ready to move out, he would position himself at the head of the herd. He would start a low call that I can't begin to describe, and then slowly move off. The old steers followed behind him like he was the Pied Piper. Longhorns are a smart breed of cattle and they learn fast, but they learn things their own way. If you try to change or deviate them, you will have a jumbled-up mess on your hands.

When we crossed the Red River at Altus, Oklahoma, a local cowboy guided us around the many quicksand areas in the river. Once safely across, we penned the steers in Altus' rodeo grounds. The next day, we made the final leg of the drive when we convoyed all the way across Oklahoma and arrived in Dodge City. At Dodge, we put on our final show. We drove the herd down Front Street, stopped in the Long Branch Saloon, and had a drink (soda pop) with Miss Kitty (Amanda Blake) and Doc (Milburn Stone) from the cast of the hit television show, *Gunsmoke*. Unfortunately, neither Matt (James Arness), Chester (Dennis Weaver), nor Festus (Ken Curtis) were there.

We penned the steers in the old stockyards and locked the gates. Dodge City threw us a city-wide party that night. Boy, do they know how to party! Just like a hundred years before, the next morning we scattered with each man for himself and went back to Texas. The drive was over.

The purpose of this drive was to raise money for the Texas Longhorn Raisers Association, but I think it wound up costing Charlie more than it made. I have no idea of the actual expense to Charlie Schreiner, but I have heard him say it was costly.

---

[66] A steer is a male bull that has been castrated.

"The See-More Kid"

All too soon, my week's vacation was over and it was time to get off the horse (play) and back into the car (work). That work centered around a four-month-long manhunt in Kerr, Bandera, Medina, and Real Counties looking for a character named Charles "The See-More Kid" Brogdon. He was half-Indian on his mother's side and half-Irish on his father's side and considered fully bad news.

My predecessor in Kerrville, Hardy Purvis, Jr. (Little Purvis),[67] had chased Brogdon for nine months without results. But Little Purvis finally got a break—literally—when Brogdon fell off a bluff he was walking along, badly spraining his ankle. Barely able to walk, he had hobbled into nearby Rock Springs. After buying some liniment to put on his ankle, he checked into a sleazy motel. The owner recognized him and notified Sheriff Tom Henderson of Edwards County, who in turn notified Little Purvis in Kerrville. Purvis went immediately to Rock Springs and arrested Brogdon without incident.

It had been a long chase, but it was finally over. Brogdon had toyed with the officers chasing him, especially Little Purvis. He would leave notes in the various deer camps he looted, telling Little Purvis how close he had gotten to him. Another one of his favorite tricks, one that really aggravated his pursuers and sometimes confused their bloodhounds, was to climb over fences at four-way intersections and then leave false trails down three of them. He would do this by walking down the fence line several yards, double-back to the fence post, and do it again in another direction. All this time, he would be crossing back and forth over the fence. By doing this, he would leave his scent on both sides of all four fences and in four different

---

[67]Little Purvis was the son of the great Ranger Captain Hardy Purvis, Sr., of Houston's Company A. It was when Captain Purvis retired, thus creating an opening, that I was able to become a Texas Ranger.

directions. He knew that all four fences would have to be cut to let the dogs through so they could follow the scent.

To rub salt in the wound, there were these notes signed "The See-More Kid: I see more and do less than any thief in history." It wasn't long before "The See-More Kid" was well on his way to becoming something of a local hero. Purvis and the other local law enforcement officers didn't give up, but try as they might, Brogdon always seemed to elude them.

But then Brogdon fell off that ridge. He was caught and sentenced to ten years' imprisonment. He was paroled after a local rancher offered him a job if he was released to him. Brogdon was a good cowboy and worked off his parole with no problems. After completing his time, he left the country and traveled to Wyoming, where he again worked on a ranch. It was while he was in Wyoming that I transferred to Kerrville, but the stories of "The See-More Kid" still abounded throughout the area.

I was still new in the area when I got a call that a deer camp had been burglarized. Kerr County has a reputation as a great deer-hunting county, and it is. Some of the wealthiest hunters from all over the country sometimes lease an entire ranch and build elaborate deer camps to satisfy their every whim while on their "hunt." It was not unusual for these "cabins" to be equiped with heaters, air conditioners, bunks, televisions, swimming pools, deep freezes full of steaks, and beer and whiskey stacked on the shelves. They really roughed it.

These camps were pure honey to Brogdon. He would go from one camp to the other, feast on the food, and get drunk on the whiskey. But he never stayed in the cabin. With his rifle as his only companion, he would take a blanket, go up on the side of a hill, and bed down for the night—one night only. He never spent two nights at the same site. In no time, he was really hitting a lot of camps and was causing all of us in law enforcement a great deal of embarrassment. It was *deja vu* all over again. Just like ten years before, he couldn't be caught.

Whenever a report came in that a deer camp had been hit, I would jump in my car and drive to the site as fast as I could. What a waste of the state of Texas' gasoline that was. All right, I hitched up my horse trailer and switched to a horse. Well, at least I wasn't burning up that much gas, because I still came up with the same results—nothing. One day, I was in Bandera talking with Sheriff Bryan Miller trying to figure out some way to catch Brogdon before some of the local citizenry erected a statue to "The See-More Kid" on the courthouse lawn. We were becoming the laughing stock of the area and, not surprisingly, this was not sitting well with me or any of the other local officers.

As we jaw-boned, I told Sheriff Miller that for years, officers had tried to catch Brogdan by riding up on him. To my way of thinking, the only way we would ever catch him was to follow his example: the shoe leather express. The sheriff agreed and we devised what we considered a simple but effective plan to trap "The See-More Kid."

It was only a few days later that we got a call from a rancher in far western Kerr County. He had been at his camp, preparing for the coming deer season. Entering his cabin, he found half a bottle of coke and a cigarette still smoking in an ashtray. Like everyone in the area, he had heard of "The See-More Kid" and knew Brogdan had to be nearby. He kept his head, acted as if he had seen nothing out of he ordinary, and continued checking the camp. Once he finished, he got in his truck and drove to his house, where he called me. I immediately called Sheriff Miller and we made our plans accordingly.

Early that night, Ranger Jouquin Jackson (whose area Brogdon had also been hitting), Sheriff Miller, two of the sheriff's deputies and I drove to within about a mile of the camp and started walking as quietly as possible. Nearing the site, one of the deputies and I took up a position to cover the front of the cabin while Jouquin went around the hill and positioned himself on a bluff overlooking the rear of the camp house.

Our plan was simple. At daybreak, Sheriff Miller would go back to the vehicle and then come roaring up to the cabin as fast as the terrain would allow him to drive. Everything went exactly according to plan except for one little hitch—no "See-More Kid."

A few weeks later, on March 27, 1967, we got another call that a cabin in the same area had been burglarized. From the description of the scene, it was obvious that Brogdon had struck again. We decided to use the same tactics we used on the previous raid. Again we drove to within a couple of miles of the deer camp and started walking. On the way, Sheriff Miller said there was another deer camp off to our right and we might as well check it out.

It was still dark as we quietly approached that camp. I went around to the back of the cabin and shined a flashlight through a small window. There stood Charles Brogdon with a .30-caliber carbine, aiming at the men in front of the cabin. I yelled and he whirled around toward me. I ducked before he could bring the sights of his rifle on me. Since there was no back door, there was no need for me to stay behind the cabin: I worked my way back to the front. Brogdon threatening us with a rifle came as a surprise. He had never been known to carry a weapon except to shoot game and had never threatened anybody. But there he was, aiming at the officers in front of the house. I called out to him asking what was the matter with him. He knew we wouldn't shoot him unless he gave us no choice. He didn't answer.

We talked among ourselves for quite a while, trying to figure out the best plan to force Brogdon out without a shooting. Coming up with nothing better, I looked at Jouquin and said, "We'll never get a chance to die any younger." He didn't disagree with me. We walked up on the porch and kicked in the door. Our lights circled the room, but Brogdon was nowhere to be seen. Leaning against a wall was a mattress, and I aimed my shotgun at it and told Brogdon to come out with his hands empty. He threw out the carbine, stepped out from behind the mattress, and fell on his stomach with his hands stretched out.

The first thing I asked him was why he had pointed his rifle at us. Didn't he know that most of the county considered him a hero? If we had shot him, we would have been the ones who would have had to leave the area. He said that the day we had tried to catch him at the other deer camp by walking up on it, he had already left the cabin for the night and gone up the hillside to bed down. He wrapped up in a piece of carpet, lying just a few yards down the hill from where the deputy and I had stopped and looked down on the cabin. He awakened about daylight and turned the corner of the carpet back to get up. The first thing he saw was the white shirt I was wearing. He just covered his head back up and lay still until we left. While he was lying there, he heard the officer who was with me say that he would like to catch him in an open field so that he could get him in the sights of his rifle. That was what had scared him. He thought we were going to shoot him on sight. He added that he was getting old and couldn't take the cold any more; otherwise, we would not have caught him in a cabin.

We took him to Kerrville, arraigned him, and charged him with two counts of burglary. That was just the beginning. Before we finished, we cleared almost a hundred burglaries in Bandera, Real, and Kerr Counties—all lake houses and deer camps.

He told us how he had been successful for so many years. He had walked almost everywhere he went and wouldn't go into a town or follow a road if he could help it. He felt a road was just an open space he had to cross. He just didn't believe in following roads.

At one of the deer camps, he had stolen a 30-06 rifle that we needed to recover. He said he would take me to the rifle if I wouldn't use handcuffs on him; they made him nervous. Brogdan was about 6'2" and was just a bean pole. I agreed not to handcuff him, but told him in no uncertain terms that if he tried to run, I would shoot him dead. The handcuffs may have made him nervous, but it didn't begin to compare to how nervous I was walking behind him. I knew if that long, tall, drink of water bolted, he would be gone in three strides and there was no way I could run him down. But we both knew I meant it when I told him: I would shoot him if he ran.

As we walked, Brogdon told me about some of his past. He said he had been in prison once and he also had the sentence that he had served on parole. After serving his parole, he had gone to Wyoming to work on a ranch. One night he broke his own rule and went to town, got drunk, and ended up in jail. But it wasn't much of a jail, and he and two other men broke out and started walking. The other two got to complaining that their feet hurt and said that they wanted to steal a car. He had stopped and told them, "You two point in the direction you're going, because I am going the other way. All you two are going to do is get caught."

Going the opposite direction of his companions, he had caught a freight train and ridden it back to Texas. The deeper into Texas he got, the better he felt. Riding in from the west, it wasn't long before he saw the beautiful Texas Hill Country he had roamed for so long. When the train slowed down, he jumped off and headed for those hills. That was when he had started his second burglary spree in the Hill Country around Kerrville.

We walked down a deep, cedar-choked draw. At the bottom, Brogdon walked straight to a cedar tree and pointed up to a rifle, hanging on a limb by its shoulder strap. He said to be careful because it was loaded. He had wiped the rifle down with some sort of grease, and the bolt worked just fine. The scope had been ruined by rain, but otherwise it was in perfect working order.

I turned Charles "The See-More Kid" Brogdon over to the Bandera County Sheriff's Office. After they finished with him, Real County got him. I don't know exactly how many cases they cleared, but it was several score. In the end, Brogdon was tried as a habitual criminal and sentenced to life imprisonment. I hated to see the old boy get such a hard lick. He had never hurt anyone. But *que sera, sera.*

The Fugitive

The Kerrville State Recreation Area had become overgrown with brush and weeds, so arrangements had been made with the state prison system to send over about a hundred convicts to clean it up. The prison set up a camp on the west side of the Guadalope River and brought in a field kitchen with cooks. Several tents were set up to be used for a mess hall, barracks, and quarters for the guards.

I got a call one morning that one of the convicts was missing. I drove over to the camp and talked with the captain of the guards. As far as any guard, let alone a captain, is concerned there is nothing in the world worse than an escapee on their record. We questioned the convicts, but got nowhere with them. Not surprisingly, none of them had seen anything, heard anything, or knew anything. The escape was, they said, as much of a total surprise to them as it was to us. Why, never in their wildest dreams would they have ever suspected our escapee was capable of planning and carrying out such a bold scheme. Yeah, sure.

I walked down to the river and started searching along the riverbank. I hadn't gone far when I found a small cabin with some clothes and food inside. Also in the cabin were a pair of white pants, a shirt, and a pair of brogue shoes[68] the convict had been wearing when he escaped. Dressed in civilian clothes, it seemed reasonable that the convict had crossed the river, which he could have easily forded, and was on the move, probably trying to catch a ride with someone. I went back, got my car, and crossed to the other

---

[68] I was told that brogue shoes originated in Ireland. They were made of a rough, untanned leather. I never wore any,but they sure didn't look too comfortable. I didn't blame him for getting rid of them.

side of the river. I drove along the bank as close to the cabin on the opposite side as I could get. Leaving the car, I started walking again. Looking closely along the water's edge, I found a fresh footprint in the mud where the convict had come out of the water. I followed his footprints up the bank to Highway 16. He was still on foot, and his tracks showed he was heading in the direction of Fredericksburg.

I was joined by Sheriff Cale Ligon of Llano County, and together we stayed on the escapee's track as he headed toward Fredericksburg. Our man had gone into the woods about one hundred yards from Highway 16, but it still appeared he was making a beeline for Fredericksburg. The sheriff and I put about fifty yards between us and continued tracking. We crossed a sandy, dry, creek bed and there were footprints in the sand. We were making good progress until it got dark. Just as it was getting too dark to be able to track, we came up on a house and asked the lady if she had seen anyone walking in the vicinity earlier in the day. Yes, she had seen a man walking a short ways from her house only a few minutes earlier, heading in the direction of Fredericksburg.

By now it was pitch dark, and we had posted guards farther down the road than the escapee could have possibly walked. We were confident he was not going to get out of our web, so we decided to get a little rest while we could. During the night the bloodhounds from Huntsville arrived, but before they could pick up the convict's scent, we got about an inch of rain. Meanwhile, someone in Fredericksburg had found suspicious footprints crossing a man's yard. These footprints were the same ones I had found earlier on the bank of the Guadaloupe.

Several Highway Patrol units were in the vicinity, and a License and Weight patrolman by the name of Starr was also helping us, working Highway 290 West of Fredericksburg. All of a sudden, Starr called, saying that be had seen what he thought was our subject just cross the highway about five miles from Fredericksburg. Everybody left their current locations and headed for the sighting. We brought the dogs and horses, cut the fence, and let the dogs start working west from where our suspect had been seen. As I watched Starr, he started backing up. All of a sudden, he pulled his pistol and yelled, "Come out of there!"

After hopping the fence, our escapee had huddled up against a big old cedar tree. Seeing us, he took off running as hard as he could go, with the bloodhounds right on his heels. They caught him about fifty yards from the fence and took him down. As soon as he could get to him, the dog handler (we called him the dog sergeant) pulled the dogs off him. The bloodhounds had torn his clothes pretty badly and maybe took a little hide here and there. Needless to say, the dog sergeant had no trouble apprehending the escapee and bringing him to us at the fence. I guess the escapee figured anything was better than the dogs. We carried him to Kerrville, filed charges of felony escape and theft of property, and made him a guest of the Kerr County Jail.

The district attorney at that time was Bob Barton, whom I had worked with before. He had never seen a man that had been captured with dogs. He asked about the man's clothing, and I told him truthfully that the escapee had been running in the brush and briars all day and all night, and the briars had torn his clothes. I added that the dogs had caught him before the guards could. Our fugitive was tried and had ten years added to his sentence for felony escape. The theft-of-clothes charge was dismissed.

I used to really enjoy tracking and I was a pretty good at it when I was younger, but I'm so old and beat up now, I doubt if I could see a track in deep mud.

Amarillo

Ranger Henry Ligon was from Kerrville and kept a home there, even though he was stationed in Austin. He knew that I had no permanent attachment to Kerrville and one day I would retire or move on. Joe Davis, a Highway Patrolman in Houston, had just made Ranger and was scheduled to be posted in Amarillo. There was only one problem: Joe didn't want to go to Amarillo and was considering turning down his Ranger commission rather than move to the Panhandle. Even though I liked Kerrville and had made many friends in the community during the seven years I had been there, I didn't have any personal connections in the area. Lena and I talked it over and decided Amarillo might be a nice place to be stationed. We didn't know much about the Panhandle but from what little we knew, Amarillo seemed like a nice place. I knew it was clean, and other Rangers from that area said the folks were friendly and made good neighbors. I went to Captain Clint Peoples and told him I didn't mind transferring to Amarillo. By my doing that, Henry Ligon could finally come to Kerrville, and Joe Davis could go to Austin. Captain Peoples agreed and was happy about that. He didn't like the idea of losing Joe Davis before he ever got started. Joe didn't disappoint anyone in all the years he was a Ranger. He would eventually end up in Kerrville after Henry retired. When Joe finally hung up his gunbelt, he had made one mighty fine Texas Ranger.

So on October 1, 1969, I assumed my new duty station in Amarillo.

Looking back, I wish I hadn't been so quick to have volunteered for that transfer. I had been to Amarillo in the summer once with Sheriff Leon Maples to pick up a prisoner. This time, I knew I had made a bad mistake by the time I got to Plainview. It wasn't summer: it was autumn and it was already as cold as winter. I hadn't been in anything this cold since Europe in 1944-45. You haven't felt cold until you experience a Texas Panhandle winter. It is said, and I believe it, that there isn't a thing between the Texas Panhandle and the North Pole but a few strands of barbed wire. The Panhandle is so flat you can see all the way into next week.

Everything that could go wrong went wrong. To start with, when Lena and I got to Amarillo, we had to wait three days for our furniture to arrive. I don't know what happened to the moving van—got lost, I guess. Then came the biggie. On the night of the third day, I was sitting on the couch watching TV when I felt a sharp pain in my chest. The longer I sat there, the worse it got. The stress had finally caught up to me: I was having a major heart attack. At the time, I only knew one person in Amarillo, Ranger M. D. "Kelly" Rogers. I called him and told him I thought I was having a heart attack and asked where the nearest hospital was. I had hardly hung up before Kelly was at our apartment and drove me to High Plains Baptist Hospital. I'll say this for Amarillo: High Plains is a great hospital. Not only did they save my life, but they also put up with me until the end of November. I'm afraid I didn't make a very good patient.

I absolutely convinced myself that I was on my deathbed. Back in 1969, it was a common belief that if you had a heart attack, you died. I believed that. too. I knew I didn't want to saddle Lena with a lot of excess baggage after I died, so lying there in that hospital bed, I arranged to sell a lifetime of possessions. I have regretted letting all that go ever since. I sold a huge collection of Indian arrowheads, my bird gun, a deer rifle, and a guitar and amplifier—all for next to nothing. I figured it was better for Lena to have a few dollars in cold, hard cash than have to worry with moving all that stuff back to the Hill Country and then still have to get rid of it for pennies on the dollar.

I went back to the doctor in December. When I told him what I had done with my personal collections, he said that he had obviously misdiagnosed my condition. He said he didn't know how he could have made such a terrible mistake confusing my heart attack for a brain attack, because if I thought I was going to die, I obviously had to be crazier than a loon. Well, I was relieved that I wasn't going to die, but I almost had another heart attack thinking of all my things that I had basically given away. But that was water under the bridge, and I couldn't worry about that anymore. I had to move on and live as productive a life as I could. The doctor put me on a strict regimen of walking a mile a day and told me I had better quit smoking or that diagnosis of a fatal heart attack would be correct. So I quit smoking, started walking, and pulled through the heart attack with only minimum damage. I guess the doctor was right. Unfortunately, to date I have had three more heart attacks, but none like that first one. I'm still kicking.

After we decided I wasn't going to die, Lena and I bought a home and settled in for the winter. By January, the doctor allowed me to go back to work full-time. The very night before I was to return to work, it came a blizzard. It snowed fourteen inches during the night. The next morning when I started out of my front door to get my paper, I couldn't get the door open. I opened the inside door and then when I tried to open the storm door, I flattened my nose against the glass. Snow was piled almost to the top. I went to the back door and it was the same thing.

This was a fine how-do-you-do! My first day back to work and I couldn't even get out of my house! I had been cooped up long enough and one way or another, I was going to work. I finally found a kitchen window that was higher than the snowdrift, and I crawled out of it and went around to the front of the house. The Texas Panhandle has very low humidity, and the snow was so dry the wind had piled it all the way to the top of the door. Out in the yard, however, you could see the grass sticking through. I looked over to the curb, and my car was just a hump. I tried to rake some of the snow away, but it had just enough moisture in it that it was frozen solid. I figured there was nothing I could do but go back in the house, call Kelly, and report my predicament. But I was determined that I was not going to climb through a window to get into my own

I made some great friends in the two years I was in Amarillo, none better than Ranger Kelly Rogers.
(Courtesy of Texas Ranger Hall of Fame and Museum: Waco, Texas)

house. After what seemed hours and hours, but was only a few minutes, I managed to rake enough snow away from the front door so that we could use it. This was definitely not a smart thing to do. One of the main things a heart attack victim is told is not to expose himself to long periods of intense cold, and here I had been shoveling snow.

Anyway, once I got back in the house, I called Kelly and asked him what he did on days like this. He just laughed. He said to just show

Company C – 1971
Back: Leo Hickman, Clay Bedner, Jim Singleton, Jesse Priest, Bill
Baten, Homer Meton, Billy Peterson
Front: Frank Horgen, Kelly Rogers, Captain Pete Rogers, Sergeant
Selwyn Denson, Me, Bryon Currin
(Courtesy of Texas Ranger Hall of Fame & Museum in Waco, Texas)

"digging out state equipment"on my report. Our headquearters in Austin realized how much it snowed in Amarillo and that when it did, you couldn't go anywhere even if you dug out.

That was enough for me. I started looking south. If I had ever had any second thoughts about the error in my ways by transferring to Amarillo, I didn't have any now. There were sixty-two Rangers by that time, and vacancies were almost nonexistent. My territory ran from the New Mexico border on the west to the Oklahoma line on the east and consisted of six counties: Deaf Smith, Oldham, Randall, Donley, Armstrong, and Hall. This covered a lot of area, but very few people. And fewer people means fewer problems.

There may have been just a few people, but some of those few caused big problems. I hadn't worked many gambling operations since my days in Galveston, but an intelligence agent by the name of Dan Self and I got onto a bookie operating out of a local motel. We decided to pay him a little visit.

When we arrived at the motel, the owner was reluctant to give us a key to the bookie's room. I explained to him that if he gave us the key, there would be no problems or expense for him. If he didn't, Dan and I would have no choice but to kick the door in. Then he would have the expense and aggravation of having to replace the door and frame. I guess he saw the logic to our argument because he gave us the room key.

When we opened the door, the bookie was sitting at a table and had a telephone held up to each ear. I really wished I had a camera: the look on that bookie's face was priceless. He was doing such an outstanding business, we didn't want to just stop it dead in its tracks. After talking with him a few minutes, we told him to just go sit down in a chair in the corner, be a good bookie, and keep quiet.

The phone kept ringing, and Self and I kept answering. Usually, as soon as the caller heard a strange voice, he would hang up—but not everyone. Those who didn't usually wanted to know what the spread and the odds were on this game or that game. For example, let's say that the Texas Longhorns were playing the lowly Rice Owls and the spread was Texas and twenty. That means as far as the betters are concerned, even before the game starts the score is Rice-20, Texas-0. Dan and I had some of these betters believing they had died and gone to heaven with the spreads we were giving, like Rice favored by 20. We were doing this with every call and every game; it didn't matter which one. You could hear a deep intake of breath on the other end of the line, followed quickly by a quick laying of bet after bet.

Of course, we wanted these people to win their bets so that they would come around looking to collect. Then we could arrest them. I had a lot of fun with this case. I got to do all the playing, and since it was Dan Self's case, he got to do all the work: file charges, write reports, go to court, and do all the follow-up.

A few months after the bookie case, I was elected to the board of directors of Cal Farley's Boys Home in northeastern Oldham County. It had one of the finest setups I have ever seen for the detention of youthful offenders. The reform school was located on the banks of the Canadian

River and occasionally one of the boys, usually a new one, would make a break. Where in the world did he think he was going? There were miles and miles of prairie, with no towns or houses You can understand when little or no ruckus was caused when one or two boys made a run for it. Invariably, in a few days they were caught—cold, hungry, exhausted, and more than ready to get back into the warmth of their beds.

Kelly and I were attending a board meeting at the home one day. When the meeting was over, we came out and noticed a huge thunderhead building in the southern sky. We didn't think anything about it because thunderstorms are as common as dirt in the Texas Panhandle. We headed back to Amarillo, but before we got home, we were summoned by Captain Pete Rogers[69] to come to Lubbock[70] and bring clothes for a few days. Lubbock had been hit by a tornado and had received severe damage. I was there along with other Rangers and Highway Patrolmen for about a week, patrolling the area against looters and trying to be of help.

Lubbock was completely devastated from Red Raider Stadium northwest to the airport, a distance of about seven miles. The destruction was almost a mile wide and was total. An insurance building, High Plains Life, was damaged so badly that after examination, it was deemed unsafe and was never occupied again.

I was making the rounds one morning and saw a group of people standing beside the road. Some were crying and others were talking. I stopped and asked what the trouble was. They were Mexican-Americans but could not speak English. Being born and raised in South Texas, I could speak a little Spanish. I got a real workout trying to talk to them.

They said that one of the children's ponies had been tied on a stake rope near the house, and all that was left was the iron stake on the ground. Horse and rope were both gone. I told them I would put the word out about their pony and do my best to help recover it.

I made a round through the devastated area and finally wound up back on the road where the pony was missing. I came up on the same group of people again, but this time everybody was excited and happy. It seemed

---

[69] This is the same Pete Rogers I had worked with on the vehicle blockade at the Shell Refinery in La Porte several years before.

[70] Lubbock is the headquarters of Company C, which I was now a part of.

the pony had come back to the house from who knows where. The rope was gone and so was most of the pony's hair and skin, but no one seemed to mind. I'll never forget the look of joy on that little boy's face to have his pony back. Loving horses the way I do, I could easily understand his feelings.

Amarillo was an entirely different environment from any I had ever worked. It was colder than Siberia, but the people were friendly and, on the whole, the most law-abiding community you would ever want to be in. But as I said, Amarillo did have a few crooks. It is in the middle of feedlot country. A feedlot is just a pen where you stack cattle in so tight, they can't do anything but eat and get fat.

One of these feedlots was between Amarillo and Dumas, in Moore County. It had a capacity of 50,000 head of cattle and stayed full most of the time. The blizzard of 1970 blew snow in great banks up against and over the fences and froze solid. The cattle simply walked over the fences and out of the pens. As cattle will do when they have an opportunity, they scattered and drifted with the wind. Much to my surprise, this didn't seem to overly concern the cattle owners. After the weather cleared, the ranchers and their cowboys mounted up and gathered up the wandering beeves in an old-fashioned roundup.

Each feed lot put its individual brand on the cattle but made no identification as to which rancher the animals belonged to. Usually, this didn't cause any problem between the ranchers because they knew the feedlot would straighten out everything to everyone's satisfaction. One day, I received a call from Captain Rogers to go to one of the assembly areas south of Dumas to assist the Texas and Southwestern Cattle Raisers Association. This was one of those times where things had not been worked out to everyone's satisfaction.

When I arrived at the feedlot, two ranchers were going at it with fists and boots over who owned which cow. I managed to get them separated and calmed down a little bit, but only a little bit. They both wanted to have another go at it. I looked at the brands and they were similar, but some of them were blurred. I borrowed a horse from one of the Cattle Raisers' cowboys. Along with the ranchers and cowboys, we took turns separating the cattle and then separating the men.

Raising cattle was the lifeblood of these ranchers, but that wasn't the biggest problem that day. The ranchers had been on their feet in the biting cold for days with little to eat and practically no sleep. They were simply cold, tired, hungry, and out of patience. In this state of mind, tempers were understandably just below the surface and would erupt at any moment. We got a big break when an enterprising soul brought some mesquite stumps and built a huge fire. At least now we could all warm up once in a while, and that helped calm the tempers as much as anything. We worked three days, mainly keeping the peace and separating fighters. Eventually, we got all 50,000 head separated. True, some of the ranchers were not satisfied with the final count we made. However, it stood. The cattle were all driven back to the feed lots in separate groups or hauled by some of the ranchers. The cattle had lost an average of 200 pounds each during the storm while they were drifting around without food or water. As for me, I went home and sat by the fire for a full day before I finally got thawed out.

I worked one bank robbery in the two years I was in Amarillo. It occurred in Canyon, just south of the city. Bank robbery is a federal crime, and I was not in the mood or inclined to take the case away from the FBI. Kelly Rogers and I were in nearby Vega when word came over the radio of the robbery and the news that the subjects were headed north on Interstate 27. Kelly and I headed south on Highway 385 to County Road 1062. Going south, the roadway was clear. However, when we hit 1062, an east-to-west road, we hit a snowbank. The north-south roads were swept clean by the wind, but the east-west road was banked full, fence to fence. Luckily, we got behind a big semi, and the driver plowed a trail for us all the way.

We continued east on a country road. As we passed an abandoned farm house, I spotted a car sitting beside the house, fitting the description we had been given. We were in no mood to put up with any funny business from these would-be tough guys. When Kelly and I got out of the car, we charged the house like Eliot Ness charging one of Al Capone's speakeasies. I guess Ness and his Untouchables had better luck than us: the house was empty. I felt the car's hood and it was still warm. We were on County Road 217. I got on the radio and called to one of the officers that I knew was near the last place the robbers' car had been seen, the intersection of Interstate 27 and County Road 217. Several cars arrived, and in one of them was an FBI agent with two passengers The agent requested that we have the car towed to Canyon and stored in a dry place until it could be dusted for prints. We did, and that ended my involvement in the bank robbery. We left the rest up to the FBI.

I was in Amarillo only two years, and I spent most of that time either recovering from a heart attack or trying to stay warm. There are only two seasons in the Panhandle: July-August and winter. Sure, we had some warm weather during the summer. It would get up to a sizzling 85 or 90, but even then you could wear a suit with a coat and tie and be comfortable. I don't think I ever got warm the whole time I was there.

I said earlier that I didn't care what part of Texas you're in, if you want to work, there's work to be had. Amarillo was no exception, but there were different kinds of work. I enjoyed working homicides, robberies, and other serious felonies. I don't know how it is today, but in the 1960s, the Panhandle of Texas just didn't have that many felonies that required my help. When someone did commit a serious crime, more often than not the sheriff knew who had done it and would take care of it in his own time. In fact, I don't remember any of the sheriff's department even having a criminal investigation division. They just didn't have enough serious crime to justify one. I would drive from county to county to visit with the sheriffs or deputies. Likely as not, the only person at the sheriff's office would be a clerk or dispatcher. Everyone else was busy serving civil papers of one kind or another. All of that was getting ready to change for me—drastically.

A vacancy had finally came up in Belton, Bell County, when Trenton Horton retired. I called Butch Albers, captain of Company F and told him I would sure like to fill that vacancy. He answered with the sweetest words I've ever heard, "I would love for you to have that station."

I had a working agreement with Captain Rogers in Lubbock that if I ever got an opening I wanted to apply for, I could go ahead and request that station. That doesn't sound like much to a civilian, but in the Ranger service, that was a big deal. It was standard procedure to tell your captain first that you wanted to transfer and then make the application. I had known Captain Albers when he was a Highway Patrol sergeant in Houston. He had made Ranger, been assigned to Canyon, and knew the Panhandle and what I was up against. On May 1, 1971, Lena and I packed our belongings and moved to Belton—and blessed warm weather.

Chapter VI

Belton-Temple
1971-1983

Hanoi Jane

On May 1, 1971, I assumed my new, and last, duty station. It encompassed the counties of Bell, Lampasas, and Milam. I settled in Belton, but later Captain Bob Mitchell moved my office to nearby Temple. This station was a lazy man's nightmare and a workaholic's dream. I was there until I retired in 1982: ten and a half years, and I never did get caught up. Trenton Horton had been the Ranger in Belton for a long time, and my work was more than cut out for me to try and fill just a little bit of Trenton's boots.

Killeen is in Bell County and is one of the prettiest places in Texas, but it is also the home of Fort Hood Army Base. That in itself spelled trouble. Around any military base, especially one as large as Fort Hood, the crime rate was high. The soldiers got money on payday, and that brought in the hookers, gamblers, thieves, killers, and every other kind of lowlife you can imagine. As if that weren't enough, I had the great misfortune to land there right at the height of the Vietnam War. To my disgust, the anti-war protesters were not confined to the East and West coasts: we had more than our share in Texas.

Lester Gunn was the sheriff of Bell County when I arrived. A finer, more honest man never lived. I don't care if you are an old, grizzled veteran with many years of Ranger service under you belt, when you start at a new duty station, you are a rookie as far as the local officers are concerned. They could care less what you did yesterday or someplace else; you have to prove yourself to them. I was lucky. Lester Gunn took me under his wing and treated me almost like a son. I can never repay him for his kindness.

Lester called me one day and asked if I would mind assisting his men in managing an anti-war protest in Killeen. Rangers do not normally get

214

Near Fort Hood during an Anti-War Protest
That's me, on the right, with my arms crossed.
(Picture courtesy of James Roper of the Bell County Sheriff's Office)

involved with protesters unless they commit a serious felony, but there was no way I was going to say no to Lester Gunn.

I had seen many anti-Vietnam protests on television and a few minor demonstrators here and there in person, and nothing seemed extraordinary about this protest when I arrived in Killeen. The streets were full of bearded, long-haired hippies. The only thing dirtier than their bodies was their language. And brave? They were so brave that I'd bet a month's meager Ranger pay that if they had faced an enemy soldier whose sole purpose in life was to kill them, they would have sung a different tune. It's real easy to be brave when you know you're not going to get hurt, let alone killed.

The protesters had their headquarters in Killeen at the corner of Avenue D and 2nd Street in a dive called the Oleo Strut. Don't ask me where they came up with that name. It was called a coffee house, and it was from there that these so-called peace-lovers started their march down the middle of the street, yelling obscenities of every description at the top of their lungs. I couldn't help thinking about all the buddies I had lost in Europe

215

during World War II. This was what we fought and died for? Ah, for the good old days in Houston and Galveston when I started as a Ranger. What I wouldn't have given for my trusty axe-handle! Unfortunately, the Rangers had become civilized and we couldn't do that any more. The only thing we could do was stand aside and watch.

The last two years, I had been in a deep freeze in Siberia, a.k.a. Amarillo, and hadn't thought much about the Vietnam War. Admittedly because of the weather, I didn't like living in Amarillo, but I'll say this for that city: it didn't have this sort of thing going on.

After the march was over, the peaceniks disappeared as if they had never existed. I guess they crawled back to the Oleo Strut. There had been a few arrests by the Killeen City Police, but considering the number of people who had been in the march, the arrests had not been very many. I guess the protesters knew they better not give us excuse to start arresting them.

A few days later, we received a call that the big queen protester herself, "Hanoi Jane" Fonda was coming to Fort Hood for a "peaceful" demonstration on May 16. This was the same Jane Fonda who posed for the communist press sitting on a North Vietnamese anti-aircraft gun in Hanoi and advocating shooting down American planes and killing American airmen. She was coming to Fort Hood to hand out leaflets protesting the war to the soldiers. Hanoi Jane and her kind claimed that the Army was violating the troops' First Amendment constitutional rights by not allowing this literature to be passed out on the base.

These First Amendment free-speech pamphlets called for the immediate withdrawal of all American troops from Southeast Asia; the avenging of the Kent State 5;[71] an end to the use of police, National Guard, or federal troops to suppress popular movements; and the freeing of the chairman of the Black Panthers, Bobby Seale. All were ridiculous, but the last was unbelievable. The Black Panthers were the equivolent of the Ku Klux Klan except they hated anyone white. Unbelievable.

I didn't have to be asked by anyone to assist on this; I definitely wanted a part of Hanoi Jane. I drove to Fort Hood's east gate at Rancier Avenue where Fonda was supposed to arrive. I parked and waited. We all heard her long before we saw her. About 11:15 a.m., she came roaring up to the gate with her complete entourage of several hundred, closely fol-

---

[71] Five Kent State University students were killed by Ohio National Guardsmen during a so-called peaceful anti-war demonstration.

lowed by the press and the television cameras. Of course if the cameras hadn't been there, Fonda wouldn't have been there either.

She had been pre-warned that she would not be allowed to pass out any leaflets on the base. Of course with the television camera whirling, she defied the order and started passing them out. Why shouldn't she? No one would do anything to her: she was a movie star, the daughter of film legend Henry Fonda, and the darling of the liberal press.

She jumped out of the car, making sure the television cameras got a good shot of her, and headed for the gate. She was met by post officials who told her again that she could not hand out pamphlets on the grounds of Fort Hood. She said she believed this to be a violation of her constitutional rights as guaranteed by the First Amendment and, she added, the only way anyone could stop her was to arrest her. Then she stepped forward and handed leaflets to two soldiers.

She was immediately taken into custody by the Military Police and driven to the provo marshal's office. In the provo's office, she was read a statement barring her from the base. Base officials emphasized that being Jane Fonda had nothing to do with her being banned. Anyone who attempted to hand out such literature at Fort Hood had been barred in the past and would be in the future. Twenty minutes later, she had sucked all the publicity she could out of this demonstration and was on her way back to another protest or, more than likely, to Hollywood.

The Bottom of the Barrel

To me, Fort Hood in the 1970s was one giant headache after another. During the Vietnam War years, it was nothing unusual for a judge to give a person convicted of a felony a choice of either going into the military or going to the penitentiary. Given that choice, most picked the military.

I think Fort Hood was getting more than its share of these criminals. That's where I came in. Many of these so-called soldiers made it clear that there was only one thing they hated worse than the military—Texas. As anyone who has been here in the summer can tell you, it gets hot in Texas, real hot. Take the heat, add to it the type of people we were getting, and it made for a bad situation.

Fort Hood was an open base, which meant that anyone could drive on or off the base at any time. There were some restricted areas, but on the whole, you could go anywhere you wanted. All soldiers had a Class A pass basically giving them the right to come and go as they pleased. That caused me a ton of problems.

All a soldier had to do was have someone stand in for him at roll call. For some reason, names weren't taken; they counted bodies. If there were supposed to be one hundred men on the roster and one hundred bodies were counted, then everyone was present and accounted for. The soldier could be miles away and the record would show him as being on the base.

Every payday, the troops would receive half their pay by check and the other half in cash. I guess officials hoped that they might not blow the check half, but there were countless hole-in-the-wall check-cashing shops all around the base. For many, the routine never varied. As soon as he got his money, the soldier would head for town. Many never made it. A "shark" is what the military called payday predators, and with good reason. Most of the soldiers had no way to get anywhere except by hitchhiking, and this is what the sharks counted on. They would pick up a hitchhiking soldier, drive him out into the boondocks, and kill him for his pay. The pattern was all too familiar and varied little from payday to payday. A call would come in that a body had been found by the side of a deserted country road, usually with a bullet through the head.

There was so much of this going on that it would have been physically impossible for one man to tackle all the cases by himself. I had to pick and choose which cases I worked. You can't have five or six murder cases at one time and do any of them justice. To make matters almost impossible, it was sometimes days or weeks before a soldier would even be reported as missing or AWOL. That goes back to counting bodies instead of names. I have no idea how many times I spoke to a platoon or company or sometimes even a whole regiment trying to warn the troops of the dangers of the sharks and hitchhiking. But it never seemed to make any difference. Few paydays went by without a dead body turning up somewhere.

Stunned

I went through a terrible war and I thought I knew how cheaply life could be counted in other places, but I never dreamed it could be held that cheap in the United States, let alone Texas.

Four soldiers from Fort Hood—Juan Gonzales, Pete Ramerez, Joe Fuentes, and Joseph Randolph—decided to cash in on some easy drug money with a quick trip to Mexico. Randolph had somehow conned the other three into believing that he was from the Rio Grande Valley and knew his way around the border area. He must have been convincing, because he had them believing he had a lot of drug connections in Mexico and could lead them to the best deals. He was lying through his teeth. He didn't know the first thing about the Mexican drug trade; he just wanted to join them for what he thought would be some fun in Mexico. Here he was claiming to have been from the Texas-Mexico border and to know his way around the drug tariff, but he didn't know even the first word of Spanish!

The men had barely started out before Gonzales and Ramerez started arguing about first one thing and then another. It's about three hundred miles from Fort Hood to the border towns of Del Rio, Texas, and Ciudad Acuna, Coahuila, Mexico, where they were headed. The closer they got to Mexico, the more heated the argument became. Near the deep South Texas community of Batesville, the situation came to a fatal conclusion.

Joe Fuentes was driving and Pete Ramerez was in the front passenger seat. Juan Gonzales was sitting in the backseat directly behind Ramerez, and Joseph Randolph was sitting behind Fuentes. Without warning, Gonzales suddenly produced a .38-caliber revolver, put it to the back of Ramerez's head, and pulled the trigger. Ramerez pitched forward, with most of his face gone.

Fuentes didn't bat an eye. He just pulled the car to the side of the road, opened the passenger door, and kicked Ramerez's body into a ditch. Then, just for good measure, Gonzales shot Ramerez again. The three men left still weren't finished. In their infinite wisdom, they decided that what they really should do was burn the body so that no one would ever be able to identify the remains or connect them with the crime. I don't suppose they had ever heard of dental records.

They drove into Batesville, purchased a gallon of gasoline, and brought it back to the crime scene. They drenched Ramerez's body with the gas and set him on fire. Once they had satisfied themselves that the body was burning, they drove off.

A Zavalla County game warden[72] happened to be driving by, saw the blaze, and stopped to investigate. He was greeted with the sight of Ramerez's body. True, it was in bad condition, but not burned to the point that identifi-cation would not be possible. Identification was only a matter of confirmation, and the murderers had forgotten to remove Ramerez's dog tags!

After we were contacted, we notified Fort Hood's Military Criminal Investigation Division as to what had been found. Even though all the actors[73] involved were military, the crime had not been committed on a military base, so that made the case civilian. I had a good working relationship with the Army, and I was told by Fort Hood's CID[74] office that they would provide all possible assistance.

A day or so later, that office called and said they had a man, Joseph Randolph, who was from Texas. He would only talk to a Texas Ranger. When I arrived, I talked to Randolph briefly and asked him to take a polygraph[75] test. I also told him to think it over carefully and warned him that if he were guilty, it would be to his advantage to not take the test. He said he wasn't worried; he hadn't had anything to do with the killing. He agreed to take the test, and I left to make the necessary arrangements.

It was about ten o'clock that same night when I got another call from the base, asking if I could return. Randolph wanted to talk to "that Ranger"

---

[72] I don't remember his name.

[73] The term "actor," when referring to a suspect, is used by most law-enforcement personnel, at least in Texas. I have asked many Rangers and others where this term came from, and no one seems to know.

[74] Criminal Investigation Division.

[75] Lie detector.

again. When I arrived, I found him again in the CID office, crying. He was not only eager to talk to me, but he was even more eager to deny being the shooter. He said he had been thinking about that polygraph test and what I had told him about not taking the test if he was guilty. He claimed that he was totally surprised when Gonzales had shot Ramerez, but he was afraid the polygraph would be wrong and would show him being guilty of the shooting.

Randolph then proceeded to describe the episode to me. He said he had realized that Gonzales and Fuentes would kill him just as quickly as they had Ramerez if he said anything, so he had just hunkered down in the backseat and kept his mouth shut. Safely away from Gonzales and Fuentes, however, he started talking about the murder.

I got his statement put in writing and had him sign it. I then told him that at this late hour, it wouldn't be smart to file charges on Gonzales and Fuentes that night: I didn't want to alarm Gonzales and Fuentes if Randolph suddenly disappeared. I told him to go on about his business as usual the next day while I secured the necessary warrants from Zavala County. I wanted him to keep quiet. Since the crime had not happened within any lawman's sight or hearing, we couldn't just go arrest the two suspects. We had to get warrants and I would need time to secure them. I told Randolph that by the afternoon at the latest, Gonzales and Fuentes would be in our custody.

I notified Ranger Joaquin Jackson (Batesville and Zavala County were in his area) that I had a confession on his homicide. I said that he needed to get some warrants and hightail it to Fort Hood double-quick.

Everything would have been fine, except Randolph couldn't keep his mouth shut. In the chow line that same morning, he told Juan Gonzales that he had better make himself scarce because the law was looking for him. Gonzales wasn't a complete dummy and needed no further encouragement to cut and run. He found Joe Fuentes and got him to drive him to Georgetown, where he caught a bus for Mexico.

With warrants for Joe Fuentes and Juan Gonzales in his pocket, Joaquin was just getting ready to leave for Killeen when I reached him and told him that his fugitives had fled. I was preparing myself for a manhunt when Joaquin drove into Killeen with Gonzales in his car! You could have knocked me over with a feather. Joaquin said that as he was going down Killeen's long Castroville Hill, he met a Greyhound bus coming up the rise. On nothing but a hunch, he turned around, flashed his badge, and ordered the bus driver to pull the bus to the side of the road.

Joaquin stepped into the bus and asked if a Juan Gonzales was on the bus. When Joaquin speaks, you listen. He is the perfect-looking Ranger: broad in the shoulders, narrow at the waist, and handsome. Not only is Joaquin big, but he's also got a voice that can be heard a mile away. I think he learned to whisper in a sawmill. Anyway, Gonzales wanted no part of that Ranger, and he made a run for the emergency exit door at the rear of the bus. He didn't make it. Joaquin's big, but he's also fast. As for Joe Fuentes, a local officer arrested him while he was returning from Georgetown. Both men were arraigned for murder and released to Joaquin for transport to Zavala County.

The trial was held in Crystal City, the county seat of Zavala County. It lasted three days. Gonzales received five years on probation. I couldn't believe it! Five years for as cold-blooded a murder as I ever heard of. Life, indeed, is sometimes cheap, even in Texas. As for Fuentes and Randolph, they didn't even get that much.

Animals

I've said throughout this book that I have looked at death, violent and otherwise, too many times for it to get to me very much. That's true, except for children. I never did get used to that, thank God.

In all my years as a Texas Ranger, I never had a case any more tragic than the one I had in November of 1976. It started for me on the side of County Road 39, an alternate highway between Killeen and Belton. An elderly couple had been to Killeen to buy groceries. As they turned to go in the gate to their house, the lady saw a bundle in a brown paper sack lying at the side of the driveway. When she and her husband opened the sack, they found the bloody remains of an infant baby boy.

I received a call from the Bell County Sheriff's Office asking my assistance. Arriving at the crime scene, I joined Bell County deputies in the investigation. At the request of the sheriff, I called the justice of the peace and asked him if he could join us and hold an inquest, which he did. After that, Deputies Bill Miller and Birt Wilkerson carried the child to Dallas for an autopsy. The results indicated the infant had died of massive head injuries.

We soon received information that a theft-of-services complaint had been filed at a local Killeen motel on two men and a woman for running out on their bill. We got this kind of information as a matter of routine, but what made this of particular interest was that an infant child had been with the three individuals. Of course we had no way of knowing if these were our suspects or not, but I felt like they were. I asked for an APB[76] to be put out

---

[76] All-Points Bulletin.

on the woman and the two men. A short time later, we received a call from the Austin Police Department that they had just arrested Betty Johnson for prostitution. As was everyone who was arrested or stopped after the APB went out, she had been asked about the motel bill. She had readily admitted that she, her baby boy, and two men--John Lineweber and William Johnson[77]--were the people the motel was looking for. She told the officers where she was to meet Lineweber and Johnson and the police gathered them up also. She then told a story that they said would freeze a red-hot stove.

Even though the Austin Police Department had already filled us in on her story, we had to question her. You have to let the suspect do the telling. Obviously, you can question but you can't put the answers in their mouths. If you do, a good defense attorney will shove it down your throat in a courtroom.

We asked Betty to tell us about Lineweber, Johnson, and her baby. She then related as unbelievable and sickening a story as I ever heard.

John Lineweber of Cleveland, Ohio, was the main actor in this mor-bid affair. He was in the military, stationed in Ohio, and had gone AWOL.[78] Before heading out, he had picked up a buddy, William Johnson. Johnson had brought along his prostitute meal ticket, Betty, and her infant son. They all headed south. They arrived in Killeen in November for no other purpose than to try to stay ahead of the military police.

During the trip to Texas, they had abused the infant terribly. The baby was hit, screamed at, neglected, and starved. Instead of nursing the baby, the so-called mother tried to feed him pieces of bologna and water. Clearly, this was not satisfying the child and he cried most of the trip. The crying got on Lineweber's nerves, and he told Betty that if she was going to stay with them, the baby had to go. She was terrified of being abandoned so far from home, but she needn't have worried: Lineweber and Johnson were living off her prostitution. But she did as she was told. Betty would later self-rightiously claim that she wanted the baby to have a good home and would only agree to let Lineweber and Johnson take the infant if they prom-ised they would leave him with someone who would take good care of him. Lineweber, she claimed, agreed that he would make sure and leave the child somewhere that he would never have to want for anything.

---

[77] No relation to Betty Johnson.
[78] Absent WithOut Leave.

After taking their meal ticket to the motel, Lineweber and Johnson had gotten rid of the infant boy, all right, but not at a good home. They were in a van, and while Johnson drove, Lineweber opened the rear door and held the infant by his heels, letting his head hit the pavement. It took only a few licks to kill him. Lineweber wrapped the baby in a blanket and stuffed him in a brown paper bag. Johnson pulled over to the side of the road and they tossed the body by the side of a driveway and kept going. Back at the motel in Killeen, they told Betty that they had left her son on the steps of a large ranch house and that he would have a good home.

Wanting to get away from the murder area before the body was discovered, they had loaded all their belongings in their van and headed for Austin. They needed money, and Lineweber and Johnson did what Johnson always did: they put Betty on the street, hooking.[79] But their luck had run out. The first person Betty approached was an undercover policeman, and she was arrested. Detectives had barely started questioning her when she unfolded the whole story. We were contacted, and we immediately went to Austin and brought Betty back to Bell County. When told what had happened to her son, she barely shed a tear.

Murder charges were filed on John Lineweber, William Johnson, and Betty Johnson. They were tried and found guilty. Lineweber received a life sentence. William Johnson and Betty Johnson turned state's evidence and received lesser sentences. Lineweber should have fried. He didn't show the least bit of remorse or any sympathy. Nor, for that matter, did the other two.

---

[79] Engaging in prostitution.

The Skeleton

Every investigator worth his salt wants to solve every crime that he is associated with. I promise you I was no exception. Regretfully, though, if you work long enough, you won't solve them all. Unfortunately, I was not an exception to that rule either. One of the most frustrating cases I ever had involved—what else? A murdered soldier from Fort Hood.

On March 12, 1979, Amy Teresa Morio of Killeen was riding her horse when she came upon the remains of what appeared to be a man. She called John Foster, who lived in a nearby house, and he in turn called the Bell County Sheriff's Office.

A little after one o'clock that afternoon, I arrived at the scene with my number-one running buddy, Bill Miller[80] of the Bell County CID Office. What we found wasn't a body, but a skeleton. There was no skin on the legs, arms, or head. What little flesh was left on the torso was drawn up and discolored so badly that we couldn't be sure if the body was that of a man or woman, white or black. About twenty feet away, we found human teeth and a body impression. Obviously, varmints had recently drug the body to its present location. The skeleton had on what appeared to be a white T-shirt with the words "Riverside Trojans" written on it, white work pants, white or light-blue tennis shoes, and athletic socks. The only other thing we found on the remains was a small chain around the neck with a key attached to it. The key was stamped with *34010-4* and directly under these numbers, *316*.

After Justice of the Peace Madge Turland held her inquest and pro-

---

[80] As of this writing (2001), Bill is the head of Bell County's CID Department. He is as fine an investigator as I have ever known.

nounced the body officially dead, she ordered the remains sent to the Southwest Forensic Institute's lab in Dallas for an autopsy.

Working on the assumption that the body was that of a soldier, we searched the surrounding area with a metal detector. We were trying to locate the body's dog tags for identification, but none were found. As was standard procedure in cases like this, I talked to everyone who lived in the area, hoping they might know something they were not even aware of. Nothing produced any positive results.

This case, as much as any as I ever worked, showed just how far people would go to "not get involved." The area where the body was found was in an open space covered with short grass; there wasn't any brush near it. There were numerous tire tracks coming from Love Lane to within a few feet of the body. There was even one set of car tracks that went all the way around the body. The corpse was only one hundred yards from the home of a man who worked at the Darnell Army Hospital. When asked if he hadn't smelled the decaying body, he replied that about two months earlier he had smelled something, but he was unable to determine exactly where it was coming from. He even told us that his dog had come home once, smelling so bad several baths didn't wash it off. The man said that he thought the dog had found a dead cow.

After leaving the crime scene, I contacted Fort Hood's CID officer, Agent Alexander, and asked if he could shed any light on the key we had found with the skeleton. He said the numbers *34010-4* and *316* indicated Building 34010, Wing 4, Room 316. He assured me he would check it out and get back to me as soon as he knew anything. It wasn't long before he called back and advised me that Dexter Johnson, 21, had been living in this room and had been listed as AWOL since October 3, 1978. I requested Agent Alexander to try and secure Johnson's dental records. They were soon delivered to us and a positive identification was made.

The next day, Bell County Deputy Birt Wilkerson went to Fort Hood to talk to people who were close to Johnson. One, John Turman, said that the last time he saw Dexter Johnson he was wearing white medic pants and a gray T-shirt with the words "Riverside Trojans" on it. He explained that Riverside High School in Chattanooga, Tennessee, was Johnson's alma mater.

Johnson had been a member of Company B, 15th Medical Battalion, 1st Calvary Division. We asked the commander, Captain Astriab, if he could shed any light on Johnson's disappearance. He couldn't directly, but he checked company records and provided us with the names of two men who had signed the guest book to visit Johnson on the night of his disappearance. The two men had been in the Army, but had since been discharged. One was from Portland, Oregon, and the other was from Henderson, Texas.

We checked telephone records in an attempt to find out if the either of the men were still in the area, but without success. I had my good friend and fellow Ranger in Longview, Glenn Elliott, check out the Henderson area and see if he could get a lead. Glenn confirmed that one of our suspects lived in Henderson and was currently working in Tyler.

That same morning, Deputy Steve Moore, who had accompanied the body to Dallas, was contacted by the Dallas Forensic Institute. They advised him that during the autopsy, they had discovered an identification card in the corpse's pants pocket identifying him as Dexter Johnson. Dr. DeMaio, the pathologist, informed Steve that very possibly the subject had been dead since the preceding October or November. Cold weather tends to dry out and mummify a body.

While Birt and I were at Fort Hood, we continued to interview Johnson's friends. Derrick Garrett said that the night Johnson had disappeared, he had ironed and laid out the fatigues[81] he would wear the next day. Johnson was a dandy when it came to clothes. He was a male model whenever there was a style show at Fort Hood. Continuing, Garrett said that another soldier, Carl Thomas, told him that he saw Johnson get into a car with two unknown men about the time he disappeared.

Further questioning revealed that Maddox Thompson had been in the room with Johnson the night before his disappearance. Two unknown men had entered the room and asked Johnson if he wanted to take a ride. Thompson confirmed that he had also seen Johnson with the two men the following night. He said that Johnson did not appear to dislike the military and never gave any indication that he ever considered deserting.

We continued with the investigation with few concrete leads that would lead to an arrest. On March 21, Dr. DeMaio advised us that he had been able to take the badly shrunken skin from the chest and wet it in some kind of solution for several days. The solution had given it some elasticity, so he was then able to stretch the skin so that he could work with it enough to count numerous stab wounds. There were over sixty ice-pick marks in the chest when he stopped counting.

---

[81] Army clothes.

This fit a definite pattern. According to what we were taught in crime school, a body with that many stabbings, cuts, and excess mutilations was usually an indication of a sex crime—more often than not, a homosexual murder.

Unfortunately, that was as far as we ever got. There was never any doubt in my mind that the men from Henderson, Texas, and Portland, Oregon, were the killers, but I couldn't prove it. I had to mark this homicide up as an unsolved murder.

Henry Lee Lucas

I worked so much around Fort Hood that I might be leaving the impression that my area of responsibility was only Bell County. Nothing could be further from the truth. My area originally consisted of Bell, Milam, and Lampasas Counties. Later, Williamson County was added. Trust me, they had more than their share of crime. It's just that Fort Hood caught most of the killers and the headlines.

Never has the United States had worse serial killers than Henry Lee Lucas and his sometimes partner, Ottis Toole. During his sadistic career, Lucas probably killed somewhere between one hundred fifty and three hundred people, mainly women. It was in 1979, near Georgetown, that I got a sample of his handiwork. It was the murder of a woman the press dubbed the "Orange Sock Lady."

Sheriff Jim Boutwell, a longtime friend and a former officer in the DPS, called the Rangers asking for assistance. The body of a female had been found beside Interstate 35, just north of Georgetown. Except for an orange sock on her left foot, she was completely nude. The only other conspicuous things about her body were the bruises around her neck. The autopsy confirmed that they were caused when she was strangled to death. That's all we had: a nude body with one orange sock and some bruises. It is extremely difficult to get a case off the ground with so little. Of course, we had no way of knowing it at the time, but we were witnessing the work of a serial killer.

Seldom having a motive and usually wandering all over the country, serial killers are extremely difficult to catch. This is the reason that men such as Lucas, Toole, and Ted Bundy are able to kill in such astronomical numbers. But sooner or later—unfortunately, usually later—they invariably slip up and we get them.

This case was not at all typical. Identification of the victim was go-ing to depend a lot on pure old-fashioned luck. I know you've seen television and movie detectives take a single hair, send it to a lab, and presto! They are able to provide a detailed life history of that person. Not only are they able to determine what the victim ate for breakfast, lunch, and dinner, but also where they went to school, what they ma-jored in, who their favorite singer was, and—well, you get the point. That's pure hogwash.

We put a description of the victim on the National Crime Informa-tion Center's computer in Washington, D.C. We ran composite pictures of her in the local newspapers in Georgetown, Temple, Austin, and all the surrounding areas, all without results.

It looked like we had hit a wall and that was going to be the end of it. But out of the blue, Henry Lee Lucas was apprehended on an unrelated case and he started confessing. He didn't confess to just one or two murders. By the time he was finished, he had admitted to more than six hundred murders all over the United States. Out of all those murders, however, the killing of the woman with the orange sock was the only conviction in which he re-ceived a death sentence.

As was typical with Lucas, he hadn't even bothered to learn the victim's name before he killed her. He had picked her up hitchhiking, had sex with her, strangled her, and threw her body out beside the road like she was a piece of trash. We never were able to identify her, and she is buried in a pauper's grave in Georgetown.

Henry Lee Lucas was what I called a "Johnny Confessor." Hundreds of the six hundred murders he originally claimed to have comitted were false. He loved the notoriety: the bigger the numbers, the more publicity he got. Numerous times it was proven that he was in another state working and drawing wages when a murder he confessed to had occurred. I think most people aquainted with Lucas and Toole would probably agree that the duo likely killed from one hundred to one hundred fifty innocent men and women.

However, there is not the slightest doubt in my mind that the "Or-ange Sock Lady Murder" was his. He told us things about the woman that only we knew: exactly where and how she was lying in the ditch and several other things that had not been made public.

He was as guilty as sin. To many people's total disgust, including mine, Lucas' death sentence was later commuted to life imprisonment. I am a Christian, but I have to say that when this man died, all I could think was, "Good riddance. Justice was too long in being served."

Speaking of being a Christian. . . . In 1984, Lucas claimed he had found God, been born again, and knew that when he died that he would go to heaven. Of course, I've never known anyone on death row who didn't find God.

The Eagle

Some officers go their whole careers without having a minor involved in a homicide. I had two almost back-to-back in Bell County. The body of a Mexican male had been found just outside Belton at a construction site. It was easy to tell that the body had been there awhile because it was infested with maggots. Depending on weather conditions—and it was hot—it takes about a week for maggots to mature to the state they were in on this body. It wasn't going to take an autopsy to tell what had killed this man. His head had been caved in with some kind of blunt instrument. From the looks of the wound, it had been a large, heavy instrument.

The law required an autopsy, however. During the procedure, a tattoo of a large Mexican eagle that reached from shoulder blade to shoulder blade was discovered across the victim's back. There was another tattoo bearing the face of Jesus on his chest. I showed the photos of the man's face and his tattoos to several Mexicans in Belton and Temple. The Spanish I had learned as a young man on ranches in South Texas came in handy since many of the potential witnesses could not speak English. I finally struck pay dirt on a construction site near Temple. A man recognized the pictures and said the victim's name was Alejandro Villeda. He said Villeda worked on a bridge overpass that was being constructed in Temple but he had not been seen since payday the previous Saturday.

Word spread like wildfire throughout the Mexican community that Villeda had been murdered. It was only a short time later that we received a letter, in Spanish, from a female claiming to have known Villeda well—well enough that he had spent the night with her on more than one occasion. On the evening he disappeared, Villeda had been at her apartment and she heard him ask two men, Alcario Sanchez and Chris Villarreal, who lived in the same apartment complex, for a ride to a dance in Temple. Sanchez was very dark-skinned and was nicknamed *El Negro* ("The Black").

From the three men's conversation, the woman thought that instead of going to Temple, the men had decided to go to San Antonio. Since she wasn't in the room with them, the woman couldn't be one hundred percent sure. However, she was sure of one thing: only Sanchez and Villarreal had returned later that night. She said she remembered that Sanchez and Villarreal had seemed very excited when they came back and had wasted no time in loading up their car and moving out. Listening closely from her window, she overheard them say something about San Antonio, but wasn't sure what they meant. We checked with the construction foreman who knew Sanchez and Villarreal, and he said the two had originally come from San Antonio and had given an address of an apartment complex there.

I hate to think what my life would have been like without Bill Miller, head of the Bell County Sheriff's Office Criminal Investigation Division. Bill is a one of a kind. Besides being a true friend, he is one of the greatest investigators I have ever known.

As happened often, I teamed up with Deputy Bill Miller of the Bell County Sheriff's Office CID Division. We drove to San Antonio and contacted Captain Jack Dean[82] of Company D, Texas Rangers. He assigned Ranger Al Cuellar to accompany us to the address we had. Captain Dean told us that the area of town we were going into was a government project area and we had better watch our backs real close. The previous week, sev-

---

[82]Captain Dean had been my sergeant in Waco before making captain and taking command of Company D in San Antonio.

eral city police officers had been trapped there by an angry mob. The San Antonio Police Department almost had to fight its way into the project to get their officers out, and the situation was still red hot.

Ranger Cuellar drove us to the projects and we quickly found where the two men lived. Cuellar knew the area well and had contacts in the projects that would talk to him. He learned that Sanchez and Villarreal usually didn't come home until after dark, so we waited. But they failed to show up. Cuellar told Bill and me to go on home. Sooner or later they would turn up and when they did, he would grab them. But he said he wouldn't bring them all the way to Belton; we would have to do something to earn a little of our keep. We should meet him at a midway point—say Georgetown—between Temple and San Antonio and take possession of the men. We definitely got the best end of that deal.

Not surprisingly, Cuellar knew what he was talking about. It was only a short time later that he called saying that he had one of the subjects and was ready to meet us. Bill and I met Cuellar at Georgetown and took possession of Alcario Sanchez.

Leaving Georgetown, Bill got in the back seat with Sanchez and began questioning him. By the time we arrived in Temple, Bill had a written confession. The next day, we took Sanchez out of jail and he directed us to the exact spot where the body of the victim had been found.

That night, Cuellar drove to the sheriff's office with Chris Villarreal in custody. I guess he wanted to see Bell County after all. We also got a written confession from Villarreal. He stated that he and Sanchez had gotten Villeda drunk, driven him to the site where the body was found, knocked him in the head with a piece of iron, taken his money, and fled to San Antonio.

Even though Alcario "*El Negro*" Sanchez was only sixteen-years old, he was certified to stand trial as an adult. Sanchez and Villarreal were indicted by a grand jury and both received life imprisonment for the murder of Alejandro Villeda.

Villeda's body was shipped back to Mexico for burial.

Mother

Only a few days after Alejandro Villeda's murder, I was knee-deep in another murder involving a juvenile. On the morning of January 30, 1979, I got a call from Bell County Chief Deputy Frank Strange asking my assistance on a double murder. About ten o'clock that Tuesday morning, two men from the U.S. Army Corps of Engineers had found the bodies of two females floating in Stillhouse Hollow Lake near the Cedar Knob Bridge. Both women had been shot in the head and back with a shotgun, which inflicted terrible wounds. Half of the head of one of the women had been blown completely away. From the dog tags around her neck, we were able to identify her as Sergeant Judith Hyatt.

After a short inquest, Justice of the Peace Madge Turland of Killeen declared both women officially dead and ordered the bodies sent to the Scott and White Hospital in Temple for autopsies. The autopsies revealed that one of the women (not Sergeant Hyatt) had drowned. The gunshot had not been fatal, but the shock of the projectiles to her head had knocked her unconscious. When she went down, she fell face down in the water.

Officials at Fort Hood gave us what information they had on Sergeant Hyatt. She was forty-years old and was a member of Headquarters Company, 13th Corps Support Command. From her file we learned that she lived at a mobile home park at 305 South Amy Lane in Harker Heights. We went there at once. One of the neighbors, a Mrs. Lee, told us that Hyatt lived with her fifteen-year-old daughter and another woman, Sheila Johnson.

Mrs. Lee, who worked nights, said that the night before the murder, her husband Nathan had allowed their two children to go to Hyatt's to play with the two children who were in Sheila Johnson's custody while their parents, who were also in the Army, where in Korea. At about eleven o'clock,

Mr. Lee had gone to get the children and put them to bed. He said nothing appeared wrong at the time. Mrs. Lee added that when she got home around midnight, she had seen an unknown pickup with a motorcycle in the back of it parked in front of Sergeant Hyatt's mobile home. She had thought nothing about it. But at about two o'clock in the morning, she heard yelling and what sounded like banging against the wall coming from the Hyatt trailer. Mrs. Lee said that there was nothing unusual about that: Hyatt and her teenage daughter went at it like this with regularity.

Thanking Mrs. Lee for her help, we went to other neighbors in the hope they could shed more light on the goings-on at Sergeant Hyatt's. We learned that the daughter was currently in the Shoal Creek Detention Center, a home for disturbed children in Austin on Shoal Creek Road. Completing our questioning at the mobile-home park, I headed for Austin to talk with the detention center's supervisor. I wasn't surprised when I was told that the teenager and her sixteen-year-old boyfriend had both run away. But the trip wasn't a waste. The boyfriend was from the South Texas town of Beeville, and the school records indicated that his father owned a ranch in the area. I made a copy of the record and contacted the ranch, but the boy's father wasn't there. However, I did learn from one of the ranch hands that the two teenagers we were looking for had been there for a short time a few days before, but had already departed.

We also knew that before being placed in the Shoal Creek Detention Center, Hyatt's daughter had attended Killeen High School. I contacted the high school and found a familiar story. The teenager was very rebellious and she and her mother didn't get along. But the situation went way beyond the normal parent-teenager conflict. The girl was so uncontrollable that Hyatt had placed her in a home for troubled children. Killeen High's principal told me the girl had been a straight-A student until about her thirteenth birthday. Then her grades started to drop. She had been to counseling several times and had told the counselor that her mother was gay and lived with a woman, Sheila Johnson, as her wife. The teen said that she just couldn't stand it.

The following day, February 1, we were notified by the DeWitt County Sheriff's Office[83] that they had picked up Judith Hyatt's daughter and her boyfriend driving Hyatt's car. We talked to DeWitt County Chief Deputy Lasaro Campos and he said he would hold the teenagers as runaways until we could get there to question them.

---

[83]Cuero is the county seat. DeWitt County is in South Texas.

Before we could procede very far, we had major obstacles to over-come: the boy was sixteen and the girl was fifteen. They would have to be certified as adults before we could charge them with murder. This wasn't so easy. There was no doubt of their guilt—they readily admitted it—but their lawyers knew that the punishment would not be nearly as severe if they could keep the case in the juvenile courts. They put up a good fight, but on March 7, sixteen-year-old Stanley David Boysen was certified to stand trial as an adult. The following day, Judith Hyatt's daughter, fifteen-year-old Zina Lynn Denker, was also certified to stand trial as an adult. They were arraigned before Justice of the Peace Floyd Campbell of Belton, and each was charged with two counts of murder. Judge Campbell set a bond of $50,000 on each count.

Long before they were certified adults, we had found out the whole disgusting story. Zina had a strong hold on Boysen and she used that hold to her murderous advantage. In return for promised oral sexual favors, she had convinced Boysen to murder her mother and her lesbian lover.

In her statement, Zina said that the way her mother was living made her sick to her stomach. As far as she was concerned, her mother and Johnson were nothing but perverts and needed killing. I had to admit that what we found in the bedroom of the mobile home was, to say the least, disturbing. We found several items of pornography. One hanging on the wall was in the shape of the zodiac, with pictures of two women in every sexual position you could imagine. There were even photos of Hyatt and Johnson perform-ing homosexual acts on each other.

Zina said her mother had liked for her to watch as she and Johnson had sex. She said it made her sick. She had cursed her mother and physi-cally assaulted her several times trying to make her stop. When her mother refused to give up her lifestyle, Zina had threatened her. That was when she was sent to the home at Shoal Creek. But the school didn't soften her, it only hardened her hatred of her mother. She planned her revenge.

Zena knew that Boysen had access to a shotgun, and she had persauded him with promises already described to go to her mother's mobile home and force her and Johnson at gunpoint to Stillhouse Hollow Lake. Continuing her story, she said they had driven her mother and Johnson out to the lake and forced the women to wade out into the shallow part. Zina showed abso-lutely no remorse as she described her mother begging her not to hurt her or Johnson—a total waste of breath on the mother's part. Zina was almost bliss-ful as she told of screaming at Boysen to "Kill them. Kill both of them!"

As for Boysen, he admitted that he had made the two women wade out in the lake, just as his erstwhile girlfriend had said. But he claimed he told them he was going to shoot over their heads, so they should fall down in the water and play dead. For some strange reason that he could not understand, they refused. Sheila Johnson started to run and he shot her. She went down. He then shot Judith Hyatt and she, too, went down. With their mission completed, Boysen and Zina returned to their vehicle and drove off. And yes, Zina, according to Boysen, performed the promised oral sex as they drove away.

Neither Zina Denker or David Boysen showed the least bit of remorse for the killings. As far as Zina was concerned, her mother and Johnson needed killing, and they would not longer make her sick with their perverted acts. At their trials, Boysen was sentenced to twenty-five years in the state penitenerary and Denker to ten years.

The Boxcar Murders

I was just getting ready to leave for work one morning when I received a phone call and was told that the body of a male had been found in an empty boxcar on the yard of the MKT Railroad. The MKT was a railroad spur that ran from the Rockwool plant in Belton to Temple.

Fred Guffy, the owner of the MKT, and his helper L. B. Lewis were moving a string of cars when Guffy noticed a boxcar with an open door. Each time he put his train in motion, the door would slide one way and then the other. He told Lewis to go close the door and lock it down.

Lewis walked up to the car, looked inside, turned, and came running back. Guffy later said that Lewis' eyes were as big as saucers when he said that there was a dead body in the car and Guffy had better come and look for himself. Guffy did. He immediately notified the Temple Police Department. Chief Leonard Hancock of the Temple Police Department called me and asked if I could help. I left the house and drove to the railroad yard. At the scene, we realized the site was outside Temple's city limits, so we called Lester Gunn's Bell County Sheriff's Office to come.

Once inside the boxcar, we found not one, but two bodies of young men. Their hands had been bound behind their backs with pieces of parachute cord. Extra clothing and two sleeping bags were scattered all over the car. Both boys had been strangled to death. One of the boys was positioned on his knees with his chest in an upright fetal position. His pants were pulled down around his ankles and he had been sodomized. The other boy, who was in his bedroll, had also been sodomized. There was a jar of Vaseline on the floor with the lid still on. From the corner of the jar's lid, I was able to secure what appeared to be a large thumb print. Unfortunately, this print led nowhere. After completing our investigation of the crime scene, local Justice of the Peace Joe Harrison held his inquest and declared the boys legally dead. The bodies were then moved to Dallas for autopsies.

From their wallets, which where still at the crime scene, we identified the boys as James Patrick Carlisle, 14, and Patrick Ray O'Brien, also 14. Both were runaways from the Waco State Home For Boys[84] in Waco. We went to the parents of O'Brien. The stepfather said that he had had so much trouble with his stepson that he committed him to the facility in Waco. Of course, he denied any involvement in his stepson's death. We asked him to take a polygraph, but he refused. He said that he had been through so many angry times with his stepson, he was afraid the lie detector would show him guilty. The other boy, Carlisle, was also from a broken home. His stepfather said basically the same thing that O'Brien's stepfather had, and he also refused the polygraph.

The main railroad line through Temple was the Union Pacific Railroad. We requested that one of the UP investigators trace the boxcar back to its origin. In a short time, he was able to report that it had originated in Michigan and had been empty the entire trip. The Rockwool plant had needed an empty boxcar and this particular one, which had sat on a Waco siding the day before, was pushed off the main line onto the MKT spur.

We talked with the lady in charge of the Waco State Home For Boys. She said both boys had disappeared on the same day, but she had no idea where they gone. Knowing that the boxcar had sat for a day before being taken to Temple, the possibility that the boys had been assaulted by a hobo naturally crossed our minds. We questioned people in the hobo jungle just outside Temple without success. No one had seen either the boxcar or the boys, or so they claimed.

A month passed and we still had not been able to make any progress on the murders. Our break came when a carnival arrived in Temple and set up just west of the MKT Railroad yard. One of the carnival workers sent his young son, who was about thirteen-years old, to town to pick up supplies. As the young man crossed the rail yard, he was grabbed by a man and dragged into a boxcar. Thankfully, the man was drunk. Before he could assault the youth, he passed out. The young man had enough presence of mind to lie still until he was sure his assailant was indeed unconscious. Then he eased out and ran back to his father at the carnival.

---

[84] A reform school.

The father notified the Temple police and they went to the boxcar and arrested the man who was still passed out in his drunken stuper. He was carried to the Temple Police Station and he admitted assaulting the young boy from the carnival.

Once they finished their interrigation, one of the officers asked the man if he had anything else he wanted to tell them. He said no, not unless they wanted to talk about the two boys that he had strangled to death on the boxcar. The officers were definitely interested. He said that he had been to Michigan to visit his mother and was returning to the Veterans Hospital in Temple, where he had been living for several months. He had been riding a bus, but when he got to Bellmead,[85] he ran out of money. He jumped the empty boxcar, only to find it already occupied by Carlisle and O'Brien. He didn't mind sharing a boxcar with two nice young boys. Somewhere between Waco and Temple, which is about forty miles, he had assaulted one of the boys. The other boy, who had been asleep, woke up and tried to come to his friend's aid. For his efforts, he was choked to death with a cord and then his corpse was sodomized.

The confessed killer was transferred to the Bell County Jail in Belton, where I questioned him about the murders again. He said he was a psychiatric patient at the Veterans Hospital in Temple and admitted to the murders because, as he put it, "I'm crazy, and there is nothing you can do to me." He was right. He was crazy and we couldn't do a thing to him. He was examined at the Veterans Hospital in Temple, certified insane, and sent to Rusk State Hospital. He later died there.

---

[85] A suburb of Waco.

If the Colonel Calls

Rangers normally only work murders, robberies, and other high-profile crimes, but not always. I remember one time in particular when the attorney general's office sent two of its men to seize a pawnshop in Killeen for nonpayment of taxes. The AG's men entered the store, identified themselves, told why they were there, and started making a physical inventory of the property. The man on duty at the pawnshop called the owner of the shop and told him what was going on. He told him he had better get down there *pronto*.

In a matter of minutes, the owner came charging into the store, brandishing a pistol and demanding the men from the attorney general's office leave immediately. Discretion being the better part of valor, the AG men left. They returned to Austin and reported to Bob Bullock, the attorney general.

Needless to say, Bullock was not happy having his men treated that way, and he was not about to put up with it. He called Colonel Pat Spier and lodged a complaint in the strongest possible terms. I didn't know the future lieutenant governor that well, but I have several friends who did. They all say that one of the worst things that could ever happen to a person was to get on Bullock's bad list. As I said before, this was not a normal Ranger job. But whenever the upper brass wanted something done, and done right, they called the Rangers. So Colonel Spier called Captain Bob Mitchell with the order he gave in most situations: "Handle it."

Captain Mitchell contacted me and said he would meet me at my office. He said that we had a "little problem" at a Killeen pawnshop we needed to take care of. (You notice Captain Mitchell didn't say, "*You* go," He said, "I'll be over, and *we* will go.") When we arrived at the pawnshop, the owner was there and I didn't mince any words with him. I wanted to know if he had brandished a pistol at the two men from the attorney general's office a couple of days before. He said he had and would do it again if they came back.

I told him that was why we were visiting him. We were going to close his business right now, and if he still had his pistol, he had better leave it out of sight. If he chose to pull it, I told him, "The very best you can could hope for is a tie. Either way, you lose." He laid his hands on the counter and said he didn't want any trouble with the Rangers, and if it was all right with us, he would leave the store. We said it was fine with us and he left. We locked the store, and Captain Mitchell called Colonel Spier to say that the situation had been "handled." We never heard another word from the owner of the pawnshop.

I don't want to leave the impression that all the pawnshops were bad. They weren't. Most were legitimate operations run by honest, hard-working individuals, but like anything else, a few bad apples spoil the whole barrel. There were some pawnshops that would buy any kind of military hardware, from M-16 rifles to hand grenades, and sell it under the counter to anybody who had the cash to pay.

Adding to the problem were the soldiers we were getting at Fort Hood. They reminded me of that group of recruits from the Northeast I described earlier in this book. Far too many were not of the best character and were only there to keep from going to jail. They had one trick in particular they just loved. When on field maneuvers, they would "lose" or "report stolen" a rifle, backpack, ammo belt, or anything else they could turn into quick cash. Then as soon as they could get to Killeen or one of the other surrounding towns, they headed for the nearest pawnshop with their "lost" equipment. Regretfully, far too many pawnshops were more than willing to take the equipment off their hands.

Pawnshops were supposed to hold anything they received on pawn for ninety days before selling it. But whenever the unsavory shops bought something illegal, they naturally wanted to unload it as quickly as possible to get rid of the evidence. They didn't care who bought it, as long as they had the cash. Whenever a military hardware or civilian burglary occurred that included firearms, we headed straight for the pawnshops. We checked their records and, if need be, checked their inventories, too. The legitimate shops kept excellent records and never gave us any trouble. Not surprisingly, the shady shops kept poor records at best and, more than likely, no records at all.

They sure didn't want us checking their inventory. But their records were checked, like it or not. Sometimes we felt like we were beating our heads against a stone wall. The pawnshops must have had a powerful lobby in Austin, because of all the complaints that were made, no serious efforts were ever made to slow, let alone close, the illegal shops.

Company F: Mid-1970s
Left to right:
Jack Dean, Bob Prince, Henry Ligon, James Wright, Jim Ray, Dale Bryce, Wallace Spiller, Me, Troy Porterfield, Billy DeLoach, Bill Gunn,

---

The Wrong Girls

Rape cases usually turn out bad not only for the victim, but also for the lawman. Understandably, the victim doesn't want something as brutal and dehumanizing as being raped paraded before the whole world. All too often, the rapist gets away with his crime because his victim just keeps quiet or refuses to cooperate with law officers. However, I had an attempted rape case in Bell County that turned out well because the girls involved were not intimidated and refused to let this refugee from human decency escape justice.

Three girls[86] walked into the sheriff's office in Belton and lodged a complaint against a man who had attempted to rape them. They didn't know his name, but they gave an excellent physical description: one that was none to pretty. They described him as skinny; with long oily hair; dirty, yellow crooked teeth; and breath so bad it would have stopped a truck. According to them, he would be easy to find because he had to be the ugliest man on the face of the earth.

The local newspaper ran an article on the attempted rapes. An informant who worked in a clinic in Temple contacted Wayne Oldham, a deputy in the Bell County Sheriff's Office. The informant gave Wayne the name of a man who he thought met the description of our suspect: Jonathan Rivers. Wayne called me and asked for my assistance.

We ran a check on Rivers and found a mug shot of him in the DPS files in Austin. After securing a copy of the photograph, Wayne called the girls and asked if they would please come by and look at a picture lineup. When they arrived, we took them one at a time into a

---

[86] These girls were minors, so I am not using their names.

room and gave them six pictures. One was a picture of Jonathan Rivers and the other five were of men of similar physical characteristics and dress. With no hesitation, each one of the girls instantly picked out Rivers.

According to Rivers' rap sheet, he lived in Austin in a mobile home owned by his mother. Wayne and I headed for Austin and straight to the address. Just as we were turning into the driveway of the suspect's home, we met a car coming out. We stopped the car and asked the driver for identification. He was not our man. He said Jonathan Rivers was his younger brother and was at his mother's.

We went to the home, knocked on the door, and explained to Mrs. Rivers, who answered the door, why we were there and asked for permission to search her house. After a few choice, unprintable words, she declined our request. I then presented her with the search warrant we had obtained before coming to her house. She was none too happy as we began looking around.

If you have ever been in a single-wide mobile home, you know there are very few places to hide. Wayne and I searched thoroughly, but no Rivers was to be found. Double-checking ourselves, we went through the mobile home again, with the same results. I went outside and searched through some low brush. Still no Rivers. There was no underpinning, so I knew he wasn't under the house. Rivers' brother had said Rivers had been there minutes before, and there was no place to hide. This was turning into a real mystery.

Of course, Mrs. Rivers, being a mother, was protesting the innocence of her dear little boy to the high heavens. But she was carrying it a bit far with her filthy mouth. I hated to tell her, but she wasn't impressing Wayne and me. We had both been down that road many times before. The brother we met earlier had turned around and come back to his mother's house. After much effort, he was able to calm his mother down from a scream to a simple yell. Again, he told me that when he left the house just before we arrived, his brother had been sitting on the living room couch.

While the brother and I talked, Wayne continued to search. Suddenly I heard Wayne yell, "Come out of there!"

I ran to the back bedroom, entering just in time to see Wayne dragging Rivers by the neck, literally out of the wall. What we had missed earlier was a water heater compartment whose door was simply a panel that could be removed. Rivers had squeezed into the space between the water heater and the wall, and then pulled the panel closed behind him.

Rivers didn't bother denying his attempted rape of the three girls. He said that he had driven his older brother (not the one we had just met), who was in the Army, back to Fort Hood. After dropping him off, Rivers was heading back home when he came upon the girls. From here on, his story perfectly matched that of the girls.

On the night of the rape, the three girls had gone to the movies in Killeen and were driving home. A car came up beside them and forced them off the road. The driver of the car jumped out, ran up to the girls' car, and grabbed the driver before any of the stunned girls could react. He slid under the steering wheel and pushed the driver to the passenger side of the front seat. He then forced the other two into the backseat. Then he drove off.

The driver had said in her statement that the rapist stank so bad and was so ugly, she almost threw up just looking at him and thinking about what awaited her. She started crying and Rivers didn't like that, so he made the driver and one of the other girls in the backseat switch places. While she was in the backseat, the girl who now had to go to the front had spotted a longneck beer bottle in the floorboard.

Rivers meant to fondle the girl now in the front, and he ordered her to turn so that she was almost facing him. Doing as she was ordered, the girl turned toward Rivers. What he didn't know was that she could see the third girl (behind Rivers) with the beer bottle in her hand. Before Rivers could even think about fondling anyone, the girl swung with all her might and smashed him on the back of the head. Thankfully, Rivers had been so preoccupied with what he intended to do, he wasn't driving very fast. The force of the blow momentarily knocked Rivers unconscious, and he ran the car into a ditch. Even before the car stopped moving, all three girls opened their respective doors, jumped out of the car, and hit the ground running. They climbed through the fence and hid in some nearby brush.

After several minutes, Rivers regained consciousness. He started the car, backed out of the ditch, turned around, and headed slowly along the roadside. All the time, he was yelling at the top of his voice for the girls to come on out. He shouted that if they didn't, he would kill them when he found them. The girls just hunkered down and waited until he finally gave up and drove off.

Of course, the girls had no way of knowing whether Rivers was truly gone or not. Every time a car had come by, they were afraid their assailant was back. We've all heard the old saying: "A watched pot never boils." Those girls thought the sun was never going to rise, but of course, it finally did. As soon as there was enough daylight to see, they walked to a nearby house and told the startled man who answered the door what had happened to them. The man drove them to the police station, where they called their parents, who came immediately. The girls' parents were almost beside themselves with relief. They had been to every movie house, teen hangout, and house frantically looking for their daughters. As for the girls, they weren't in nearly as bad a shape as Rivers. That beer bottle had left him with a monster headache. The girls were no worse for wear except for one, who had a skinned knee and backside from where she had hit the gravel road when she jumped out of the car.

I transported Jonathan Rivers to the Bell County Jail, where he made bond; rather, his mother made bond for him. Each of the girls made as good a witness as I have seen on the stand. They were absolutely rock solid, and Rivers received a long prison sentence for attempted rape.

The girls were right about one other thing: Jonathan Rivers was the ugliest man I ever saw. Even after his lawyer dressed him up for his court appearance, he looked like he had been beaten half to death with an ugly stick.

Retirement

In my opinion, here is the greatest Texas Ranger captain of them all and my dearest friend—Bob Mitchell.

I worked for several Ranger captains during my tenure as a Texas Ranger. All were good. One, Johnny Klevenhagen, is a legend and is in the Texas Ranger Hall of Fame. But the best captain I ever worked for was Bob Mitchell. His philosophy was simple:

> You're a Texas Ranger now. By definition, that means you are the best of the best, and I expect you to act like it. Take care of your area and don't call me with ever little nick-picking thing that comes along. Just handle it. But if you do need me, I'll be right there.

And he was—every single time. Glenn Elliott was called a Ranger's Ranger. Well, Bob was a Captain's Captain. Look up a picture of an ideal Texas Ranger captain, and there you should find Bob Mitchell.

Co-author's note: While preparing this book, I was having dinner with Lieutenant Jim Miller of Company A in Houston. I told him that Ed thought Bob Mitchell could almost walk on water. Several years earlier, Captain Mitchell's men had commissioned a bronze statue made for each of them, proudly proclaiming themselves "Mitchell Rangers." Lieutenant Miller had served as a "MitchellRanger" when he was in Georgetown. His "Mitchell's Rangers" statue sits in a place of prominence in his office in Houston. One of the few pictures he has hanging on his office wall is one of Captain Bob Mitchell. In total earnestness, Lieutenant Miller looked at me and said, "He can."

By 1982, I knew it was time to hang 'em up. It had been a wonderful ride, but my time was behind me and I knew it. Captain Mitchell gave me a choice as to where I would have my retirement party: Fort Fisher at the Texas Ranger Hall of Fame and Museum in Waco or the Department of Public Safety's headquarters in Austin. I chose Fort Fisher. It was Company F's headquarters and I had been a member of that unit since transferring from Amarillo nearly twelve years before. As far as I was concerned, Fort Fisher was home.

Every member of Company F and several of my friends were there. They presented me with a plaque indicating August 31, 1982, as my official

retirement date. I had been given the privilege of joining the Texas Department of Public Safety on December 1, 1948, and I will always be grateful that the people of Texas allowed me to serve them for thirty-four years. It was a memorable time with many high spots and very few low spots. During those thirty-four years, I had more recognitions than any one man deserves. The greatest honor was to have served with people of the highest quality in both the Highway Patrol and the Texas Rangers.

That retirement party was one of the most wonderful things that ever happened to me. All too soon, however, the party was over and it was time to leave. I had turned in all of my equipment, including my car, and I needed a ride home. Captain Mitchell asked Joe Wiley to drive me to my home in Cleburne, Texas. Wiley would later become a captain and command both Company C in Lubbock and then Company F in Waco when Bob Mitchell retired. When we got to my house, I got out of the car, walked up to the door, and never looked back. I was a regular citizen again.

Joe Wiley
(Courtesy of The Texas Ranger Hall of Fame and Museum: Waco, Texas)

When Joe got back to Waco, he told Captain Mitchell he never wanted another assignment like that. He said that when I got out of his car and started to the house, he almost broke into tears. He said he thought to himself, "There goes a man who has spent most of his life in the service of the State of Texas. And now there he goes, stripped down to just his clothes, boots, and hat—no gun, no gun belt, and no Texas Ranger badge hanging proudly over his left breast." Joe may have been sad, but I was happy. I have never regretted my retirement for one minute.

All in all, I have had a very good retirement. I had started thinking about retiring in 1981, but decided to stay one more year to be absolutely sure I had my fill of the law enforcement business. I had seen too many men retire too early. They would go home only to start hanging around the local police or sheriff's office, getting in the way. I didn't want that, so I waited until 1982 to make sure. And I was sure; things

Company F 1970
Front: Sergeant Bob Mitchell, Captain Butch Albers, Sergeant Bud Newberry
Back: Bob Favor, Me, Dale Bryce, Joe Davis, Bob Connell, Wallace Spiller, Troy Porterfield, George Rotsch, Henry Ligon, Bill Gunn, Jim Ray (nephew of Chief Jim Ray), James Wright

had changed too much. The courts were now more concerned with the criminal's rights than with the rights of the victim, and I didn't like that one bit. I've just seen too much suffering caused by these animals to feel sorry for them. But mainly, I was just worn out. I had been through three heart attacks and it was time to quit. So no, I have never had any regrets.

I owe so many people so much for all they did for me during my career that I can't begin to name them all. But there is one person who rises above all others—my Lena. Just as much as I did, Lena completed thirty-four years with the Highway Patrol and the Texas Rangers. Twice, I seriously thought about quitting and going to work in the civilian world, but after talking it over with Lena, we decided to stay put. The money would have been much better, but Lena was much smarter than I

Good friends and fellow Rangers
Captain Kirby Dendy, Captain Bob Prince, Bob Connell, Me,
Glenn Elliott, Captain Bob Mitchell, Max Womack

and she knew I would never be happy being anything but a Texas Ranger.

After I retired, Lena had a serious stroke, and her health was bad during our last few years together. I lost her on February 20, 1995, to a massive heart attack. May God rest her soul. We had forty-four wonderful years together. It takes a special person to put up with the hours and days we were apart. I never doubted her loyalty to me, the Highway Patrol, and especially to the Texas Rangers. She was as much a Texas Ranger as I was.

I do want to take this opportunity to thank all my friends who have encouraged and helped me in writing this book. To all the Texas Rangers and Highway Patrolmen I have worked with and known over the years, I say, "Well done." Most of them have long since met their Maker. When I be-

Me with my successor, Johnny Aycock. No Ranger could ever hope to have a better man replace him than Johnny. Since the Department of Public Safety was formed in 1935, five Texas Rangers have been awarded the Medal of Valor for uncommon heroism. Johnny has two of them.

257

came a Texas Ranger on May 15, 1957, there were eight of us in Company A: Johnny Klevenhagen, Eddie Oliver, Pete Rogers, Mart Jones, Doc Holiday, Hollis Sillavan, Tully Seay, and me. I am the sole survivor.

I know the Highway Patrol and the Texas Rangers are in capable hands and will survive for another two hundred years. I am often asked to compare the modern Rangers to those of my era. Rest easy. Today's men are better than ever. On the grounds of the capitol in Austin, there is a statue of a Ranger with an inscription that describes them best: "There is no danger of surprise when the Rangers are between us and the enemy."

Citizens of Texas, the Rangers still stand between you and the forces of evil.

So I say, "Vaya con Dios."

Ed Gooding

Soldier, Texas Ranger

Index

Index

(pages with photos in BOLD)

263

265

O

O'Brien, Patrick Ray 242
Oldham, Wayne 247
Oleo Strut 215
Oliver, Eddie 100, 110, 118, 119,
    132, **133**, 135, **136**, 148, 172,
    258
Omaha Beach 19, 22, 25
"Orange Sock Lady" 231
Orgeron, Dusty Paul 121-127
Orgeron, Paul Harold 121- 127
Orr (Judge) 181

P

Panzer Tiger Tank 19, 36, 42
Panzerfaust 66
Paris (France) 41-42
Patton (movie) 54
Patton, George 38, 39, 41, 49, 50
    54, 55
Pawnshops 244
Pearl Harbor 12
Peel, J.T. 132
Peoples, Clint 172, 176, 192, 203
Peterson, Billy **206**
Philips, Harvey 110, **133, 136**
Pioneer Platoon 29
Plantation Club 84
Porterfield, Troy **246, 256**
Potts, (Sergeant) 43, 44
Priest, Jesse **206**
Prince, Bob **246, 257**
Prisoners, German 40
Protesters **215**
Purina Company 192
Purvis, Hardy 98, 99
Purvis, Hardy, Jr. 107, 178, 195

Q

Queen Elizabeth 18, 70
Queen Mary 18, 19
Queen of Battle 30

R

Ramerez, Pete 220
Randolph, Joseph 220
Ray, Jim 131, 156, **157, 246**
Ray, Jim (nephew of Jim Ray) **256**
Reed, Ace 193
Reed, George 108
Reimer, John **78**
Retirement certificate **254**
Rhine River 67
Rivers, Jonathan 247
Rivers, Mrs. 248
Riverside Trojans 227
Roberts, A.L.   89
Rockport Football Team 9
Rocky Ford Ranch 177
Rodeo 10
Rogers, M. D. "Kelly"
    204, **205**, **206**, 210
Rogers, Pete 106, 108, 110, 114,
    133, 135, **136**, **153**, 152-154,
    172, **206**, 208, 258
Rohr River 62, 64
Rose, Glen 84, 92, 100
Rotsch, Cecil 114, 115, 116
Rotsch, George **256**
Ruhr Valley 57
Rumca, Ansalem
    50, 51, 52, 67, 68
Rundell, Skippy 118, **119**, 132,
    133, 135, **136**, 173

S

Saar River 48
Sadomasochism 165
Sam Houston Museum 147, 156
San Antonio Police Department 235
San Jacinto County Sheriff's Department 167
San Patricio County 7
Sanchez, Alcario 235
Santa Lopez de Santa Anna 147
Sarreguemines (France) 49
Saving Private Ryan 24
Scarborough, James 127
Scholl, Ernie 84
Schreine, Charlie 191
Schreiner, Charlie III 191+
Schreiner College 191
Scott and White Hospital 237
Screwworm 78
Seale, Bobby 216
Seasickness 19
Seay, Tully 109, 110, 112, **133**
Secton 8 28
"The See-More Kid" 195
Selby house (map) **139**
Selby, John 138, 143
Selby, Joseph 137-145
Selby, Wilma 137-145
Self, Dan 207
Shell Refinery strike 152
Shipman (Mr.) 188
Shoal Creek Detention Center 238
Sillivan, Hollis 110, 112, 114, **133**, **136**, 157, **158**
Silver, Bob 122
Silver Moon Club 118, 119
Sinatra, Frank 111
Singleton, Jim **206**

Slant-holes 156
Smith, Everett **133, 136**
Smith, Zeno "Zero" 182
Snow (WWII) **53**
Snow (Amarillo) 205
Southwest Forensic Institute 227
Southwestern Cattle Raisers Association 209
Spakes, Howard 44
Spier, Pat 244
Spiller, Wallace **246, 256**
St. Lo (France) 25, **26**, 27, **37**, 42
Stepenson, Woody 104, 162
Stillhouse Hollow Lake 239
Stone, Milburn 194
Strange, Frank 237
Stuart, Willie May 145
Sue's Baths 145

T

Tanks 37, 39, 40, 42
Tatum, Maude 127
Tea 55
Temple Police Department 241
Texas Department of Public Safety 99, 100
Texas Livestock Sanitation Commission 5, 7
Texas Longhorn Cattle Raisers Association 191
Texas Ranger Hall of Fame and Museum 254
Texas Southwestern Cattle Raisers Association 169
Thomas, Carl 229
Thomas, Heston 84, 86
Thome, Henry 149, 151
Thompson, Maddox 229